THE SPHERE ILLUSTRATED

HISTORY OF BRITAIN

1789 – 1983

Derived from The Oxford Illustrated History of Britain

Edited by Kenneth O. Morgan

SPHERE BOOKS LIMITED

A Sphere Book

First published in Great Britain in 1984 as part of
The Oxford Illustrated History of Britain

First published in this paperback edtion in 1985
by Sphere Books
Reprinted 1991

ISBN 0 7221 6604 4

Printed and bound in Great Britain by
Collins Manufacturing, Glasgow

Sphere Books Ltd
A Division of
Macdonald & Co (Publishers) Ltd
Orbit House
1 New Fetter Lane
London EC4A 1AR

A member of Maxwell Macmillan Pergamon Publishing Corporation

CONTENTS

EDITOR'S FOREWORD
TO THE OXFORD EDITION

THE distinctiveness, even uniqueness, of the British as a people has long been taken for granted by foreign observers and native commentators alike. Visitors from overseas, from those omnipresent Venetian ambassadors in the late fifteenth century, through intellectuals like Voltaire or Tocqueville, to American journalists in the twentieth century, have all been convinced of the special quality of British society. This has equally been assumed by modern native chroniclers of the British scene, as opposed in their ideological outlooks as Sir Winston Churchill and George Orwell, patriots both. But the nature or essence of the Britishness of the British is far easier to proclaim than to define, let alone to explain. Very few attempts to encapsulate its quality have been more than marginally successful. One of the most celebrated, addressing itself to the English people alone and first published in 1926, came in G. M. Trevelyan's remarkable synoptic *History of England*. Trevelyan here focused on a number of themes which he believed to have marked out the separate experience of the English through the centuries—geographical severance from the European continent, with the consequent centrality of sea-power; a broad social fluidity in which the early demise of feudalism helped generate a new industrial and commercial enterprise; a flowing cultural continuity from the time of Chaucer and Wycliffe onwards; and above all—a theme especially dear to the heart of an old late-Victorian Liberal like Trevelyan—a long political and legal evolution expressed in the durability of parliamentary institutions and the rule of law. Secure in itself, a vibrant, outward-looking island had proceeded to colonize and civilize the world. None of Trevelyan's themes can be dismissed. Equally, none can be accepted uncritically in the more tormented, doubt-ridden age of the late twentieth century, with its well-founded suspicion of national and racial stereotypes. The problem of trying to come to grips with the essential reality of the British experience remains as pressing and as fascinating as ever.

The purpose of this book is to isolate and uncover the main elements in that experience throughout British history, from the earliest Roman period down to the later twentieth century. It is not concerned with the protean concept of 'national character', a difficult and perhaps unrewarding enterprise even when considering the English alone—and almost impossible when the distinct traditions of the Welsh, Scots, and Irish are included. It is rather intended to disentangle the main political, social, economic, religious, intellectual, and cultural features of these islands as they have revealed themselves to successive generations, and as trained scholars have tried to examine them. The illustrations provided in this book are offered not merely as physical embellishments, important though that may be, but as vital explanatory tools in demonstrating key points in the narrative. The question of a British 'national character', or the lack of it, will, therefore, be implicit rather than explicit. Readers will be left to draw their own conclusions, and to form their own personal visions. This is, inevitably, a multi-author volume, written by ten professional historians in close collaboration with one another. Such a collective approach is inescapable, since the days when one compendious mind such as Trevelyan's could have the capacity and the confidence to treat all aspects of British history with equal ease probably died with the Liberal intelligentsia some time after 1914. It is certainly neither practicable nor desirable, now that Renaissance men have vanished from the earth. Rather, each major phase in the history of Britain is examined here in depth by a specialist working in that field, but always directing his findings to the general reader. A basic premiss of this book is that it deals with the history of Great Britain, two partitioned, poly-cultural islands, and not merely with England alone. Indeed, the fact that the ten authors include three Welshmen and two Scots may help towards that end! Again, while the geographic and other distinctiveness of Britain from the European continent and the world beyond may constantly emerge, so too will the economic, intellectual, cultural, and religious links by which Britain and overseas nations helped shape each other's experience. The dynamic urge for exploration, colonization, and conquest from the Tudor period onwards, which led in time to the creation of the greatest empire the world had ever seen, also lent an outward-looking aspect to British historical development. Britain in this book remains the geographical island familiar to schoolchildren. But it is an island whose physical insularity was always qualified by a wider process of transmission from continental Europe, and later from North America, Africa, Asia, and Australasia, from the first arrival of the Roman legions onwards.

These chapters help to show how old clichés have dissolved in the searching light of modern research and scholarship. The 'anarchy' of the mid-twelfth century, the chaos of the Wars of the Roses, the inevitability of the Civil Wars, the serenity of Victorian England, familiar to readers of *1066 and All That*, tend to disappear like the autumn leaves at Vallombrosa. Again, the notion that British history, unlike that of less fortunate nations elsewhere, is uniquely marked by a kind of seamless, peaceful continuity emerges here as needing the most severe qualification. The history of the British people is a complex, sometimes violent or revolutionary one, full of disjunctions and abrupt changes of pace or of course. The idea of a tranquil, undisturbed evolutionary progress even for England, let alone the turbulent, fractured, schizophrenic history of the Celtic nations, comes out here as little more than a myth, fit for the refuse-heap of history, like romances of 'golden ages' over the centuries from Arthurian times onwards.

Roman Britain, as Peter Salway shows, was marked by constant, alternating phases of social upheaval and re-adjustment, long before the final retreat of the Romans in the early fifth century. John Blair describes the dynastic turbulence and the dramatic growth of urban life in the Anglo-Saxon period, until the final, violent end at Hastings. In the early Middle Ages, John Gillingham depicts a saga of conquest punctuated by frequent defeats on French and British soil, with an exploding society under such strain by the late thirteenth century that it is described here as being possibly on the verge of class war. Although that was avoided, in the later Middle Ages, as Ralph Griffiths writes, long wars in France were followed by aristocratic turmoil in Britain in the fifteenth century, accompanied by domestic recovery from plague and social revolt. The Tudor Age, as John Guy demonstrates, suffused in a golden glow in the patriotic effusions of later generations, was marked in fact by extreme pressure of population upon economic resources, by religious conflict, and the threat of foreign invasion. The resultant political and religious tensions inherited by the house of Stuart are analysed by John Morrill for a century in which—despite a marked decline in internal lawlessness—two civil wars, regicide, a republic, a restoration, and a revolution, followed each other in bewildering, breathless profusion. The apparent surface stability, prosperity, and cultural expansiveness of the Georgian age, as Paul Langford shows, gave way to an explosive tumult of industry, trade, and technology unprecedented in the history of the world, and also to the new revolutionary impulses surging in from the American colonies and from republican France. Somehow, the picture of Edward Gibbon, the urbane chronicler of the Rome of the Antonines and their successors, fleeing across Europe in the face of the Jacobin hordes in his beloved France, is symbolic. The early nineteenth century, as Christopher Harvie explains, did indeed manage to avoid the revolutionary malaria raging through other European states. But instead it brought massive dislocations in the social fabric and the notion of the legal community, and a seemingly unbridgeable class division that led Marx, fancifully, to see Britain as being in the forefront of the revolutionary apocalypse. The later nineteenth and early twentieth centuries, as outlined by H. C. G. Matthew, moved on rapidly from the bland self-assurance of the Great Exhibition, to the anxieties of the *fin de siècle* period, with its social tensions, imperialist neuroses, and sense of national vulnerability. The years since 1914, described by the present writer, saw two world wars, pulverizing economic pressures in the thirties and the seventies, and a forcible wrenching of Britain out of its place in the sun. The history of Britain, then, is not one of harmonious continuity, broadening from precedent to precedent, or from status to contract, as Victorian intellectuals would have it. It is a dramatic, colourful, often violent story of an ancient society and culture torn apart by the political, economic, and intellectual turmoil of human experience. Britain in many ways has been the cockpit of mankind.

And yet, a reading of these chapters may also leave the clear impression that, however elusive in definition, the sense of Britishness always survived in the post-Roman and post-Norman periods. Some elements of that consciousness, not necessarily closely related, can be clearly traced through the centuries. There were, variously, that Celtic Christian identity that survived the invasion of the Romans; the artistic flowering seen in the miniatures and sculpture of the late Anglo-Saxon era; the centralized governmental and ecclesiastical system created by the Normans and Angevins; the vivid sense of an English nationality emerging in the poetry, and perhaps even the architecture, of the fourteenth century. Even in the Tudor twilight, Shakespeare's plays testify to a growing sense of national cohesion—while the presence of that ubiquitous Elizabethan Welshman, John Dee, who invented the ambiguous viii

term 'British Empire', indicates some wider horizons, too. Equally, the intellectual values embodied in the revolution of 1688, Macaulay's famous 'preserving revolution', suggests a social and cultural continuity beneath the surface turbulence of high politics in the seventeenth century. The communal stability of much of the eighteenth and nineteenth centuries, together with their integrative developments in industry, transport, and communication, and perhaps even the democratic advances, political and social, of the present century, have reinforced this perceptible current of national awareness. At key moments in British history, society coalesced rather than divided. Class war, however defined, did not in fact take place in the later Middle Ages; while Marx's prophecies of violent revolutionary upheaval in the modern industrial period were, fortunately, not fulfilled. That Britain was able to assimilate the strains of its political revolution as early as the seventeenth century and of its industrial revolution as early as the eighteenth, in each case long before other European nations did so, testified to the rooted strength of its institutions and its culture. Consensus, no less than conflict, is a central part of our story.

In its many forms, this rooted patriotism, embracing the Welsh, Scots, and Ulstermen over the centuries—though, significantly, never the southern Irish—endured and remained unquenchable. The visible, recognized symbols of that patriotic sense still survive—Crown, Parliament, the processes of law, the legacy of empire, the urge for individuality and domestic privacy, the collective enthusiasm for recreation and mass sport. But what is equally striking, perhaps, is the patriotism of the dissenting critics also, with their alternative scenarios. The Levellers, Daniel Defoe, William Cobbett, William Morris, R. H. Tawney, George Orwell, all in their time emerged as passionate, libertarian opponents of the social inequalities and political imbalance of their day. Yet each of them emerged, also, as deeply committed to an almost religious sense of the civilized essence of their country and its people, their history and destiny. By setting this sense of national continuity against the recurrence of disruption and crisis through the centuries, the historian derives perhaps his ultimate justification in thrusting the British people face to face with their past and with the image of themselves. We hope that general readers will understand themselves, their society, neighbours, and an encompassing world with more clarity, subtlety, enthusiasm, and even affection, after reading this book.

KENNETH O. MORGAN

INTRODUCTION TO VOLUME 3

TOWARDS the end of the eighteenth century, Britain was swept up in a revolutionary experience without precedent in human history. It became the first industrial nation, with dramatic consequences for its culture, society and political fabric. Coal, iron and textiles formed the basis of a massive advance in manufacturing and productive capacity, backed up by a new transport infrastructure of canals, roads, and, most novel of all, railways. However, the impact of the other great revolutionary movement of the time, political radicalism from France following the events of 1789 and the wars that followed, was noticeably less profound. Britain was able to neutralize popular protest, at least in part, by remodelling its institutions, and extending the franchise to larger sections of the middle class in 1832. The continuous strains of the process of industrial change meant repeated challenges to the political and social order throughout the first half of the nineteenth century. Industrial progress was accompanied by a huge rise in the population, much of it concentrated in new manufacturing towns with intense problems of poverty, disease and social exploitation resulting. It also posed a series of problems for a traditional culture, not least for the Church and other religious bodies, and their associated educational and social institutions. But somehow—other than in Ireland which remained sunk in agricultural poverty, nursing bitter national grievances in consequence—Britain was able to make positive use of the opportunities that industrialization and urbanization brought. At home, the repeal of the Corn Laws, the expansion of communications, and the 'incorporation' of the early trade unions made for a growing political consensus. Abroad, the years of Palmerston seemed to herald an era of British authority, founded on commerce, naval power and diplomatic isolation from Europe. The great Exhibition of 1851 appeared to symbolize the crowning glory for a nation that felt, with some reason, that it ruled the waves and the world.

The dominant ethic of this industrial giant in the mid-Victorian era was liberalism. It was characterized by free trade and commercial enterprise, side by side with qualified civic and political reform. The franchise measure of 1867 and 1884, and the attendant political and social legislation of the Gladstone–Disraeli period, reaffirmed this commitment to toleration and gradual, but inexorable, change. Victorian Britain had to accommodate an enormously growing, increasingly urbanized (or suburbanized) population, with considerable gulfs dividing various strata of society. There was a large, vocal working class, increasingly organized into trade unions and with a mature culture of its own. There was also a many-sided middle class, reflecting the diverse facets of commerce, manufacturing and the professions. At the same time, land retained much of its old prestige, with mighty aristocratic estates continuing to flourish at the height of the industrial age. Late-nineteenth century Liberalism and Conservatism reflected all these elements, along with older themes such as the rivalry between the Church and nonconformity. From the 1880s, however, Victorian Britain was embroiled in a series of intractable problems. There was a marked sense of vulnerability; a chill was in the air. Politically, there was the irrepressible challenge of Irish nationalism which led to growing pressure for home rule. A crisis of empire showed itself, even as imperial rule reached its zenith. War with the South African Boers was a portent of colonial struggle to come. Economically, there was mounting evidence that an economy now reliant more and more on trade rather than manufacturing was facing pressure from foreign rivals. At home, there was the rise of socialism and other critiques, urging the state to intervene to redress social injustice and promote collectivist reform. Lloyd George's welfare programmes of the Edwardian period were far removed from the orthodoxies of the classical liberal state. Above all else, there were the threats from a turbulent world in Europe and beyond. In August, 1914, Britain's entry into world war cast the achievements of the liberal age into the melting-pot again.

The political and psychological impact of the Great War sank deep into the memory of the British people for decades to come. The war was not, in fact, without its positive side, especially in the social reform and mobility that it brought. It also marked a great advance for the Labour Party, at the expense of the Liberals. But the ravages of war upon human life and, less visibly, upon the economic fabric, were to throw Britain into a downward spiral of decline and struggle which marked its history from 1918 onwards. The post-war years were difficult, with massive unemployment in mining and other staple industries. The resultant social explosion took place in the general strike, a crisis which passed by in part because of the comparative prosperity of Britain outside the older industrial regions. There were renewed imperial strains, too, evidenced by the final concession of independence to southern Ireland in 1922, and rising tension in India and Egypt. In the thirties, matters became worse with the financial crash of 1931 and prolonged heavy unemployment. Foreign policy saw a series of retreats in the face of foreign dictatorships; in due course, appeasement led only to Britain and the commonwealth being engulfed in another war in 1939. In reality, the second world war was a time of some renewal and hope. Under Churchill, a revived sense of national unity showed itself in widespread social reform, and a positive commitment to planning a better post-war world. In some ways, the years after 1945 saw these hopes fulfilled, with the creation of the welfare state, and the continuance of full employment and popular affluence down to the 1970s. On the other side, though, were endemic economic decline; a steady retreat in the face of colonial nationalism in Africa and Asia; a marked diminution in Britain's status as a great power; and heightened internal tensions involving the Celtic nations, the black immigrant community and large sections of the industrial working class. Britain in the 1980s was a struggling country. At the same time, a kind of national pride served to moderate these disruptive forces. A continuing sense of its long and fascinating history helped Britain to remain, to some degree, a stable and peaceful society.

KENNETH O. MORGAN

CHRISTOPHER HARVIE

8. *Revolution and the Rule of Law*

(1789–1851)

Reflections on the Revolutions

In 1881 the young Oxford historian Arnold Toynbee delivered his *Lectures on the Industrial Revolution,* and in so doing made it as distinct a 'period' of British history as the Wars of the Roses. This makes it easy, but misleading, to conceive of an 'age of the dual revolution'—political in France and industrial in Britain. But while the storming of the Bastille was obvious *fact,* industrialization was gradual and relative in its impact. It showed up only in retrospect, and notions of 'revolution' made less sense to the British, who shuddered at the word, than to the Europeans, who knew revolution at close quarters. A Frenchman was in fact the first to use the metaphor—the economist Adolphe Blanqui in 1827—and Karl Marx gave the concept general European currency after 1848.

This makes the historian's task awkward, balancing what is significant now against what was significant then. The first directs us to industrial changes, new processes developing in obscure workshops; the second reminds us how slowly the power of the pre-industrial élites ebbed, how tenacious religion proved in the scientific age. Only around 1830 were people conscious of substantial and permanent industrial change; it took another twenty years to convince even the middle class that it had all been for the better.

Should there not be a simple factual record of developments? In theory, yes. But the age of the 'supremacy of fact' was so ever-changing and obsessively individualistic that recording and assessing facts was another matter. There was no official population Census until 1801; before then there had been real controversy about whether the population of Britain was growing or shrinking. Although the Census subsequently developed into a sophisticated implement of social analysis, covering occupations and housing conditions, this was as gradual a process as the systematic mapping of the country, carried out by the Ordnance Survey in stages between 1791 and the 1860s. The ideology of *laissez-faire* and actual government retrenchment adversely affected statistical compilation, as fewer goods or businesses were regulated or taxed. (Continental autocracies were, by comparison, enthusiastic collectors of data about their little industrial enterprises.) So controversy still rages over some elementary questions—notably about whether industrialization did the mass of the people any good.

At this point, modern politics casts its shadow. Toynbee's contemporaries agreed with Karl Marx that capitalist industrialization had, by 1848, failed to improve the condition of the working class. After 1917 Soviet Russia seemed to demonstrate a viable alternative: 'planned industrialization'. But the costs of this, in human life and liberty, soon became apparent and, with the 'developing world' in mind, liberal economists restated the case for industrialization achieved through the operation of the free market. Even in the short term, they argued, and faced with the problem of providing resources for investment, British capitalism had increased both investment and living standards. The results of this vehement dispute have been inconclusive. They have also been restricted in their geographical context, considering that British economic development had direct, and far from fortunate, effects on Ireland, India, and the Southern States of the USA.

If there are problems with statistics and context, there is also the question of consciousness. Industrialization as a concept was only germinating in the 1820s. Whatever the governing élite thought about economic doctrines, as magistrates and land-owners their watchword was stability, their values were still pre-industrial. But by 1829 the trend to industrialization became, quite suddenly, unmistakable. Only eleven years after the last of Jane Austen's novels a raucous new voice pictured the 'Signs of the Times' in the *Edinburgh Review*:

We remove mountains, and make seas our smooth highway; nothing can resist us. We war with rude nature; and by our resistless engines, come off always victorious, and loaded with spoils.

Thomas Carlyle summed up, vividly and emotionally, a plethora of contemporary impressions: the change from heroic to economic politics that Sir Walter Scott had described in the Waverley novels, the planned factory community of Robert Owen's New Lanark, the visionary politics of desperate handloom weavers, the alarm and astonishment shown by European visitors. Only a

'A *voluptuary* under the horrors of digestion'. George IV, as Prince of Wales in 1792, surrounded by evidence of his extravagances—unpaid gambling debts (despite £161,000 voted by Parliament in 1787 to bail him out) and visible through the window his opulent London residence of Carlton House. A cartoon of a favourite victim by James Gillray, 1757–1815, the most brilliant and merciless of British caricaturists.

few months later, his word was made iron in George Stephenson's *Rocket*.

But can we gain from such images a consistent set of concepts which are relevant both to us and to the age itself? G. M. Young, its pioneer explorer, in *The Portrait of an Age* (1936), saw his actors 'controlled, and animated, by the imponderable pressure of the Evangelical discipline and the almost universal faith in progress'. But Young's history—'the conversation of the people who counted'—was pretty élitist history, which neglected the mass of the people—miners and factory hands, Irish cotters, and London street arabs—or identified them solely as 'problems'. The perception, at its most acute in Tolstoy's *War and Peace*, that great movements stem from millions of individual decisions reached by ordinary people, was lacking. Few of the British contemporaries of his French and Russian soldiers shared the views of 'the people who counted': as far as we know, only a minority of them saw the inside of a church, and from what they wrote and read they had little enough faith in progress. Yet, however constrained their freedom of action, the decisions of those subjected to the 'monstrous condescension of posterity' are crucial. We have to attend to them.

E. P. Thompson, who coined this phrase, has argued that a continuing frame of interpretation did exist: the law. No matter how partial its administration—and in the eighteenth century this was often brutally apparent—'the rule of law' was still regarded as a common possession. This claim remained valid after the industrial impact. In 1832, as a young MP, Thomas Babington Macaulay argued in favour of political reform to protect the rule of law from the exercise of arbitrary power: 'People crushed by law have no hopes but from power. If laws are their enemies, they will be enemies to law . . . ' Let the law 'incorporate' new groups, and these would defer to the state system. This philosophy balanced the 'revolutionary' consequences of industrial changes, and the frequent attempts to create from these a new politics.

The evolution of law, moreover, provided a model for other social and political changes. 'The most beautiful and wonderful of the natural laws of God', in an Oxford inaugural lecture of 1859, turned out to be economics, but they might as well have been jurisprudence or geology. Personal morality, technical innovation, the very idea of Britain: the equation of law with progress bore all these together on its strong current.

Among all classes, the old morality—bribery and unbelief, drinking, wenching, and gambling—gradually became regarded as archaic if not antisocial. As well as 'vital religion', rationalist enlightenment, retailed from Scotland or France, and cheaper consumer goods indicated that life could be longer and more refined. Where Samuel Pepys had regarded his Admiralty subordinates' wives as legitimate fringe benefits, James Boswell,

People. A family group by John Harden of Brathay Hall, 1826. Harden, 1772–1847, was a talented amateur artist who lived in modest comfort in the Lake District, then a notable centre of English intellectual life: Wordsworth, de Quincey, and Arnold of Rugby were neighbours. His paintings convey a perceptive impression of 'English Biedermeier' middle-class life.

equally amorous, agonized about his wife and family, foreshadowing new moral imperatives—whether engendered by the evils of corruption or slavery, proletarian unrest, the French, or the wrath of the God so dramatically depicted by William Blake.

The onus of proof was on the status quo. Did it elevate? Did it improve? The English traveller, who in 1839 was appalled to find that the Hungarians had no sailing boats on their waterways when their Muslim neighbours had *dhows* on the Danube, was typical in regarding this, whatever the reasons for it—the interests of oarsmen and horsemen, the free transport entitlement of Hungarian nobles, sheer loathing of everything Turkish—as a case of 'sinister interests' blocking reform and progress.

Neither 'progress' nor the rule of law were inevitable but had to be fought for, against internal and external enemies: 'old corruption' and new disaffection at home, powerful rivals abroad. Progress meant moral development, not economic or political manipulation—the values expressed, say, by the hero of Mrs Craik's *John Halifax, Gentleman* (1852):

Nothing that could be done did he lay aside until it was done; his business affairs were kept in perfect order, each day's work being completed with the day. And in the thousand-and-one little things that were constantly arising, from his position as magistrate and landowner, and his general interest in the movements of the time, the same system was invariably pursued. In his relations with the world outside, as in his own little valley, he seemed determined to 'work while it was day.' If he could possibly avoid it, no application was ever unattended to; no duty left unfinished; no good unacknowledged; no evil unremedied, or at least unforgiven.

The rule of law was an English tradition, but its role as an ideology of 'efficient' government had in part been created on Britain's internal frontiers. Dragging their country out of its backwardness, the Scots had used their distinctive legal institutions as instruments for consolidating landed capital, for exploring and ordering 'civil society'. In Edinburgh, Adam Smith, William Robertson, Adam Ferguson, and David Hume wove economics, history, sociology, and philosophy together with jurisprudence to produce the complex achievement of the Scots Enlightenment. Figures such as Patrick Colquhoun, James Mill,

Lord Kames, Hugo Arnot, and Lord Monboddo, in Edinburgh
a 1748 engraving by John Kay. The judges Kames and Monboddo (1714–99) were also, respectively, an economist and sociologist and a pioneer of linguistics and evolutionary thinker, representatives of the 'enlightenment' which drastically modernized Scots society after 1745.

and the 'Edinburgh Reviewers' transmitted its values south. Ireland's contribution was quite different. 'The Law', Dean Swift had written, 'presumes no Catholic to breathe in Ireland.' Protestant law had, by definition, to be coercive. Not surprisingly, Ireland saw the creation of Britain's first state-organized police force, in 1814.

Although legal campaigns helped to end the serfdom of Scots colliers and salt-workers in 1799, and the British Empire's slave trade in 1807, Scots and English cottars benefited little from their role in the 'improvement' of their countryside. Law was more than ever the tool of property: a function which unified the local élites of a still-disparate society when assault from Europe threatened. The clan chiefs and lairds who had rallied to the French-backed Charles Edward in 1745 were now landowners who had no common cause with revolutionaries. Jacobinism was as alien to them as Jacobitism. But the ensuing use of law to enforce national solidarity and safeguard economic changes was to face it with its most formidable test.

Industrial Development

A greybeard in 1815, who could remember the panic in London as the Jacobites marched through Manchester in 1745, would be struck by one important international change—the reversal in the positions of Britain and France. This was not simply the result of over twenty years of war culminating in victory at Waterloo, but of consistent industrial development and the take-over of important markets. British blockade destroyed the economy of the great French seaports: grass grew in the streets of Bordeaux, and meanwhile Britain annexed something like 20 per cent of world trade, and probably about half the trade in manufactured goods.

Industrial development did not follow a predetermined, predictable route to success. The process was gradual and casual. Adam Smith regarded industry with suspicion; even in the 1820s, economists doubted whether technology could improve general living standards. Britain had certainly advanced in the century which followed Gregory King's estimate, in 1688, that mining, manufacturing, and building produced a fifth of the gross national income of England and Wales. (The *British* figure would be less, as it included backward Scotland and Ireland.) By 1800, estimates put the British 'manufacturing' figure at 25 per cent of national income and trade and transport at 23 per cent. This sort of growth, however, was not beyond French capabilities. What marked Britain off were qualitative changes, notably in patterns of marketing, technology, and government intervention—and, at 33 per cent of national product in 1800, her capitalist agriculture. While revolution retarded French farming by enhancing peasant rights, in Britain feudal title became effective ownership, the key to commercial exploitation.

In 1745 France's population, at 21 million, was double that of Britain. Her economy, thanks to royal patronage and state control, had not only a huge output but was technologically inventive and grew as rapidly as Britain's. But technology in Britain was developed by new requirements, while in France it was checked not only by government interference but by the bounty of traditional resources. France still produced ample wood for charcoal: British ironmasters had to turn to coal. France had a huge woollen industry integrated with peasant farming; in Britain, enclosure and growing agricultural efficiency set limits to such domestic industries, and encouraged the building of large industrial plants which needed water or steam power or systematized production. Above all, Britain had already won the trade war by the 1770s, pushing France out of the Spanish territories, out of India and Canada—with even the loss of her American colonies soon made good by the rise of the cotton trade.

In 1801, the first official Census found that England had 8.3 million people, Scotland 1.63 million, Wales 587,000, and Ireland 5.22 million. This settled the debate on population: it seemed to have risen by about 25 per cent since 1750, a rate of increase 50 per cent greater than the European norm. Debate still continues about why. The death-rate fell some time before 1750 (as a result of improved food supplies and better hygiene, and a diminution in the killing power of epidemics) and this was then reflected in a rising birth-rate as the greater number of surviving children entered breeding age.

In Britain, increased manufacturing activity, and the vanishing of the family farm, made children a valuable source of income. 'Away, my boys, get children,' advised the agricultural writer Arthur Young, 'they are worth more than they ever were'. In Ireland, population growth surfed along on a different wave: the desire of landlords for greater rents, and the cultivation of potatoes from the 1720s on. The latter increased the nutritive output of a patch of land by a factor of three; the former realized that a rising population on additional farms meant that each acre might yield three times its rent. The population consequently doubled in the fifty years between 1780 and 1831.

Population (*in millions*)

	1780 (est.)	1801	1831	1851
England	7.1	8.30	13.1	16.92
Wales	0.43	0.59	0.91	1.06
Scotland	1.4	1.63	2.37	2.90
Ireland	4.05	5.22	7.77	6.51
Total UK	12.98	15.74	24.15	27.39
England (as %)	54.7%	52.7%	54.2%	61.8%

A recent calculation has suggested that in the early nineteenth century British agriculture was 2.5 times more productive than that of France, itself much more efficient than the rest of Europe. The result was that a population on the move from country to town, and at the same time increasing, could be fed. In 1801 about 30 per cent of the mainland British lived in towns, and 21 per cent in towns of over 10,000 population—a far higher percentage than in any north European country. Industrial towns, however, accounted for less than a quarter of this figure.

Sir David Wilkie, 'The Irish whiskey still' of 1840. A romanticized view of rural Irish society before the famine, a period which, ironically, saw Ireland's greatest anti-liquor campaign under Father Mathew. Notice the good health of the peasants, and the potatoes in the lower left-hand corner.

Their inhabitants were outnumbered by the numbers living in seaports, dockyard towns, and regional centres. London, already a metropolis without parallel, had around 1.1 millions, over a third of the entire urban population.

Otherwise, population was still fairly evenly distributed. The counties were still increasing in absolute numbers. The 'Celtic fringe' still accounted for nearly half (45 per cent) of United Kingdom population: Dublin (165,000) and Edinburgh (83,000) still followed London in the great towns league; Cork and Limerick were larger than most manufacturing towns. The complex organization of such regional centres reflected the predominant roles of local gentry, clergy, farmers, and professional people, and the result of decades of increasing trade.

Trade more than industry still characterized the British economy. Continental towns were—or had only recently ceased to be—stringently controlled, their trade limited and taxed in complex and frustrating ways. The medieval gates of little German cities still swung shut at nightfall to keep 'foreigners' from their markets. But in Britain, by contrast, there were scarcely any impediments to internal commerce, while 'mercan-

Old Hetton Colliery, near Sunderland, by Thomas Hair *c*.1840. This big pit is fairly typical of the deep mines sunk in the northern coalfield to cope with the escalating demand in the early years of the nineteenth century. The standard (4 feet 8½ inches) gauge railway connecting it with the sea was laid out by George Stephenson and two of his locomotives can be seen in the foreground.

tilist' governments had positively encouraged the acquisition of 'treasure by foreign trade'. The eighteenth century had seen important changes. Seemingly perpetual war in the Channel and the attraction of large-scale smuggling, centred on the Isle of Man, had shifted commerce routes north. Liverpool rose on grain and slaves, then on cotton, Glasgow on tobacco and linen, then on cotton and engineering. Gradually, their entrepôt function was being changed by the opening up of efficient transport links to their hinterland, and its transformation by manufacturing industry.

Trade and distribution provided the central impulses for industrialization. No other European country had 30 per cent of its population in towns, to be fed, clothed, and warmed, or controlled such vast overseas markets. The institutions through which British merchants handled all this—which the law allowed, if not encouraged them to set up—provided a framework in which increases in productivity could be translated into profit, credit, and further investment. At home, an expanding 'respectable class' provided a market for clothes, cutlery, building materials, china; this 'domestic' demand grew by some 42 per cent between 1750 and 1800. But in the same period the increase in export industries was over 200 per cent, most of this coming in the years after 1780.

Besides agriculture, three sectors were dominant—coal, iron, and textiles. The first two provided much of the capital equipment, infrastructure, and options for future development; but textiles made up over 50 per cent of exports by value in 1750, and over 60 per cent by 1800. Cotton, insignificant in 1750, was dominant with 39 per cent in 1810. Coal output doubled between 1750 and 1800, as steam pumps enabled deeper and more productive seams to be mined, and horse-worked railways bore coal ever-greater distances to water transport. Iron production, boosted by war demand, by the use of coal instead of charcoal for smelting, and by the perfecting in the 1780s of 'puddling' and 'rolling' wrought iron, rose by 200 per cent between 1788 and 1806. But textiles were the power which towed the glider of industrialization into the air.

Wool had always been England's great speciality, though linen, dominant on the Continent, was expanding under government patronage in Ireland and Scotland. Cotton rose largely through its adaptability to machine production, and the rapid increase in the supply of raw material that slavery in the American south made possible. The new machinery was primitive. But rising demand meant that resistance to its introduction by the labour force was overcome. John Kay's fly-shuttle loom (which doubled a weaver's output), destroyed when he tried to introduce it in the 1730s, was taken up in the 1770s, along with James Hargreaves's hand-operated spinning jenny (a multiple-spindle wheel) and Richard Arkwright's water-powered spinning frame. The last, and the great factories it required, spread from the Derbyshire valleys to Lancashire and Scotland. Before competition brought prices down—by two-thirds between 1784 and 1832—huge fortunes could be made. Arkwright's shrewd exploitation of his patent rights brought him £200,000 and a baronetcy. Sir Robert Peel, calico printer and father of the future Tory premier, ended up by employing 15,000. Robert Owen reckoned that between 1799 and 1829 his New Lanark mills netted him and his partners £300,000 profit *after* paying a 5 per cent dividend. For some twenty years a modest prosperity extended, too, to the handloom weavers, before the introduction of power-looms and the flooding of the labour market with Irish immigrants and, after 1815, ex-servicemen. This turned the weavers' situation into one of the starkest tragedies of the age.

Cotton technology spread to other textiles—speedily to Yorkshire worsteds, slowly to linen and wool. But it also boosted engineering and metal construction. Powerful and reliable machinery had to be built to drive thousands of spindles; mills—tinderboxes otherwise—had to be fireproofed with metal columns and joists. In 1770, Arkwright used millwrights and clockmakers to install his mainly wooden machinery at Cromford. But mill-design and machine-building soon became a specialized job, with water-wheels of up to 150 horsepower, complex spinning mules (a powered hybrid of the jenny and the frame, spinning very fine 'counts') and the increased use of steam-power.

James Watt patented his separate-condenser steam engine in 1774, and its rotative version in 1781. By 1800, cotton mills were its chief users, as it supplied reliable and continuous power for mule spinning. In its turn, the increasingly sophisticated technology required by the steam engine enhanced both its further application—to locomotives in 1804, to shipping in 1812—and the development of the machine-tool industry, particularly associated with Henry Maudslay and his invention of the screw-cutting lathe. This (and its associated invention, the micrometer) made possible the absolutely accurate machining of parts. From now on, machines could reproduce themselves and be constructed in ever-greater complexity. The standards of the

New Lanark mills and village, on the upper Clyde, in 1818, the time of
Robert Owen's experiments. The mills built by Owen's father-in-law, David
Dale, in the 1780s, are the central five-storey range of buildings; next to *immediate
left* the school (1817), and then *left foreground* the institute (1816) and
community centre, both built by Owen, which attracted many influential
visitors from overseas.

eighteenth-century clockmaker were no longer an expensive
skill, but part of the conventional wisdom of mechanical engineering.

The creation of a transport infrastructure made for a golden age
of civil engineering, too, as men such as Brindley, Smeaton,
Telford, and Rennie strove to exploit water-carriage and horsepower as efficiently as possible. In a parallel exploitation of
wind-power, sailing ships became so sophisticated that they
remained competitive with steam until the 1880s. The country's
awful roads were repaired and regulated, and in some cases built
from scratch, by turnpike trusts, even by government. It took
nearly a fortnight to travel from London to Edinburgh in 1745,
two and a half days in 1796, and around 36 hours by coach or
steamer in 1830. Building on the steady growth of river navi-
gation in the seventeenth century, 'dead-water' canals using
pound locks were being built in Ireland in the 1730s. But it was
the duke of Bridgewater's schemes to link Manchester with a
local coalfield and Liverpool, 1760–71, that showed the importance of water transport for industrial growth. Bridgewater's

The canal system in the early nineteenth century

engineer, Brindley, devised 'narrow' canals to prevent water loss in the 'dry' Midlands, and during the peace of 1764–72, when money was cheap, companies of gentry, merchants, manufacturers, and bankers managed to link all the major navigable rivers. Such private enterprise could pay, in the case of the Oxford canal, up to 30 per cent in dividend, but the average was about 8 per cent. The next boom, in the 1780s, pushed the system beyond what was commercially feasible, but Britain now had a transport network without parallel in Europe, while the unity of 'improvers', agricultural and industrial, in this cause overcame many of the barriers to further co-operation.

Reform and Religion

The British government did not play, or wish to play, a positive role in industrialization; as the Corn Laws of 1815 were to show, neither did it abstain in the interests of *laissez-faire*. But increasingly it observed principles which were more or less systematic, and less unfavourable to industrial capitalists than they were to any other class—except, of course, landowners, who were frequently capitalists themselves in mining, transport, and property development. The axioms of Blackstone and Burke: of continuity, the division of powers, the interpenetration of government, economy, and society—and above all the notion of government as a self-regulating mechanism—complemented the mechanics of classical economics, the discoveries of science, and even the cultivated deism of the upper classes.

But the ideal required renovation. Corruption and inefficiency had taken their toll at the time of the American War, and although the spectacle of mob violence—particularly in the Gordon Riots of 1780—made respectable reformers more circumspect, reform was an admitted necessity. The messages of Adam Smith and John Wesley had, in their various ways, seen to that. The problem was, how could it be kept within constitutional bounds? Attempts such as the Association movement to make politics more principled and symmetrical simply exposed the ramifications of 'interest' and downright corruption. The 'vast rotten borough' of Scotland, where only 4,000-odd electors returned 45 placemen MPs (only one man in 114 had the vote, compared with one in seven in England), got its reward in the patronage distributed by its 'managers' the Dundas family, notably in the East India Company and the Admiralty. Ireland's 'free' Parliament, after 1782, was still an institution for which no Catholic could vote.

The opinion of the great manufacturing towns had to be articulated by pressure groups such as the General Chamber of Manufacturers, because of the gross maldistribution of political power. In 1801 the 700,000 people of Yorkshire had only two county and 26 borough MPs, while the 188,000 people of Cornwall had two county and 42 borough MPs. Dissenters and

Thomas Telford's 'stream in the sky'—the Pont–cysyllte aqueduct—carried the Llangollen canal 124 feet over the Dee in a cast-iron trough only 10 feet wide. It was probably the most spectacular piece of engineering of the early industrial revolution.

Catholics were allowed to vote after 1793 but could not sit in Parliament. On the other hand, so restricted was the impact of politics, and so expensive the business of getting on in it, that for some exclusion was a positive benefit. Although their overall numbers were in decline, the elaborate family relationships of the Quakers (who could not 'marry out' and remain in the sect) underpinned widely scattered enterprises ranging from iron and lead-smelting works to banks and railways. The liberal-minded Unitarians, who 'believed in one God at most', were energetic leaders of provincial enlightenment in science and education.

Somewhat different was the Evangelical revival. Populist and traditional high church in origin, this drew inspiration from the religious heritage of the seventeenth century—exemplified by Bunyan, and broadcast by John Wesley—and from the devotional literature of such as William Law. In contrast to 'Old Dissent' and Calvinist 'election', it stressed that grace was available to those who directed their life by biblical precept. It was respectable without being exclusive, ecumenical and diffusely 'enthusiastic' (many who were to become its severest agnostic and high-church critics started as devout Evangelicals)—a faith of crisis, valid against atheistic revolution, unfeeling industrial relationships, and brutal personal behaviour. Pitt drank and Fox gambled, but both were susceptible to the sort of pressure which well-placed Evangelicals could exert. The Evangelical revival was politically conservative, yet it soon flowed into peculiar channels. In 1795 the 'Society of Methodists' founded by Wesley left the Church of England because they could no longer accept conventional ordination. Tories they remained, but further Methodist groups such as the Primitives (who seceded in 1811) became more autonomous and more radical. Methodism was northern—'the real religion of Yorkshire'—elsewhere the Baptists and Congregationalists expanded in industrial towns whose élites were frequently Unitarian or Quaker. George Eliot described dissenting values in her 'political novel' about 1832, *Felix Holt* (1867):

Here was a population not convinced that Old England was as good as possible; here were multitudinous men and women aware that their religion was not exactly the religion of their rulers, who might therefore be better than they were, and who, if better, might alter many things which now made the world perhaps more painful than it need be, and certainly more sinful.

'Vital religion' accomplished a religious revolution in Wales. In 1800 over 80 per cent of the population still adhered to the established Church whose mid-eighteenth century missionary efforts, the 'circulating schools', had increased literacy (in Welsh) and enthusiasm beyond the point where it could sustain it. Into the vacuum flowed Calvinistic Methodism and the other non-conformist bodies; by 1851, Wales was 80 per cent chapel-going. In Scotland, the established Presbyterian Church, which controlled education and poor relief, was practically a subordinate legislature. Controlled by the landowners and their worldly, liberal clergy, it was coming under increasing assault not only from independent Presbyterians, but from those, usually Evangelicals, who wished to transfer power to the congregations. In Ireland, the dissenting tradition was initially liberal, its leaders comparing their legal disadvantages with those of the Catholics. But the events of the 1790s, and the recrudescence of Evangelical fundamentalism was ultimately to intensify the divide between the Protestant north-east and the rest of the country.

The Wars Abroad

The French Revolution was greeted with general enthusiasm in Britain. At worst, it would weaken the old enemy; at best it would create another constitutional state. Charles James Fox,

James Watt, Joseph Priestley, the young Wordsworth, and Coleridge all celebrated it; Robert Burns was inspired to write 'Scots wha' hae'—which had obvious contemporary implications. Even the government was slow to echo Edmund Burke's severe censure in his *Reflections on the Revolution in France*, published in November 1790, while it still seemed a modest constitutional movement. Although Burke expressed what the establishment felt, especially when Paris lurched leftwards in June 1791: remove customary deference and force would rule. Reform should be permitted only on terms which retained the basic political structure. Burke both attacked France and dramatized Blackstone's defence of the British political system. The establishment became really alarmed by the Anglo-American radical Tom Paine's reply, *The Rights of Man* (1791–2), with its bold proposals for individualist, democratic reform. Burke may himself have started what he tried to avoid. If the *Reflections* sold 19,000 copies in six months, *The Rights of Man* sold 200,000—an incredible total for a society still only semi-literate. Pamphleteering had not demonstrated this range and impact since the Civil War.

'The breaking of the line' at Trafalgar, 21 October 1805.
In contrast to most eighteenth-century naval battles, which were broadside exchanges, Nelson's ships (sailing from *right* to *left*) broke through the French line at right angles and then engaged in the destructive close-quarter melee at which they excelled.

The government was alarmed by two things above all—the impact of French notions of 'self-determination' on Britain's Low Country client states, and the contagion of ideas. The European monarchies, with even greater grounds for concern, abandoned the gentlemanly rules of eighteenth-century war in summer 1792 and treated the French as rabid dogs to be shot. The French reciprocated with the notion of war as a popular crusade: 'a nation in arms'. In Britain, the diplomatic threat worked on the political threat: warnings to France increased the conviction of some optimistic revolutionaries in Paris that war would lead to a British revolution. On 1 February 1793 France declared war.

Britain was unprepared. The army had only 45,000 men; scarcely a tenth of the battle-fleet could put to sea. Moreover, the war was quite different from earlier Anglo-French conflicts. The new style of army, the intensity of the revolutionary attack, the competence of France's new commanders: together these put Britain's allies in trouble from the start. By 1797 Austria had been knocked out and Britain stood alone against Bonaparte's Armée d'Angleterre.

Three things preoccupied the government in those early war years: the threat of invasion, the cost of war, and the problem of combating internal dissension. The French made three invasion attempts, once via Wales and twice via Ireland. A landing in Pembrokeshire in 1797 found no support, but in autumn 1798 a force commanded by General Humbert landed at Killala in Mayo and, with local allies, campaigned for two weeks until defeated. The government hoped to defend the mainland by fortifying the coast with Martello towers, embodying the Militia (the home defence force), and extending the Militia Acts to Scotland and Ireland. All this gave ceaseless headaches to the part-time local officials involved. As subsidies to allies were running into tens of millions by 1795, taxation had to be radically increased and included, after 1799, the innovation of an income tax levied at 2s. (10p) in the pound. Finally the government acted drastically against groups which sought peace or solidarity with the French. 'Pitt's reign of terror' in 1793–4, supplemented by the local activities of magistrates, industrialists, and patriotic societies, destroyed many of the radical societies. The repression was particularly fierce in Scotland, where Lord Braxfield's brutal Doric humour arbitrarily upheld 'the most perfect constitution ever created'.

Braxfield's sarcasms—on being told by one of his victims that Jesus was a reformer, his reply was 'Muckle be made o' that. He waur hangit tae!'—symbolized the end of the upper-class libera-

lism of the Scottish enlightenment. Thirty years of fairly constant
repression followed, wielded by Pitt's Scottish lawyer allies, the
Dundas family.

In Ireland, the reversal was even more drastic. War led Pitt to
pressurize the Irish Parliament into granting Catholics voting
rights in 1793, in an attempt to win them from enthusiasm for
'godless' France. But the non-sectarian radicalism of the United
Irishmen rapidly grew. By 1798, it was countered in Ulster by the
ultra-Protestant Orange Lodges and by the local violence of a
Catholic peasantry bitterly resentful at Protestant privileges, and
in part influenced by French-trained priests imbued with
revolutionary ideals. Shortly before Humbert landed there was a
vicious, though short-lived, outburst in Wicklow, enough to
convince the Protestant ascendancy of its isolation. In 1800
Ireland followed the example of the Scots in 1707, and entered
into political union with England.

Apart from the brief interlude of 1801–3, the 'wars abroad'
lasted until 1815. By then, Britain had spent £1,500 million on
war; yet the effects were ambiguous and curiously limited. The
war was soon erased from popular memory. Britain was an
armed camp for much of the time: there were constant drafts into
the militia, and at any stage about a sixth of the adult male
population may have been under arms. Compared with France,
few of these actually served abroad, although many—around
210,000—died. What was in France a demographic set-back—her
population increased by 32 per cent, 1800–50, compared with
Britain's 50 per cent—had a different, smaller impact on Britain.
Yet British naval supremacy was never challenged after 1805, and
through blockade it destroyed much of French industry, whose
most dynamic sectors were based on the trading ports.

Adam Smith had written that war would distort demand and
create a 'seller's market' among certain types of labour. It
proceeded to do so. The iron trade boomed not only in its
traditional base of the West Midlands, but in central Scotland
and also in South Wales, where Merthyr Tydfil expanded
twenty-fold in population between 1790 and 1820—a raw, remote
city (accessible, incredibly, by canal) in a country whose largest
mid-eighteenth-century town, Carmarthen, had contained
scarcely 4,000 people. As blockade throttled her rivals, Britain's
ever more commanding lead in textiles reached the stage where
her manufacturers were clothing French armies. The huge naval
dockyards of Chatham, Portsmouth, and Devonport were further
expanded and became pioneers of mass production. Their
creations, the sailing warships, were dramatically improved;

steam-power, when it took over in the 1850s, was almost a lesser revolution.

The navy, in fact, typified many of government's problems. The wretched condition of the sailors provoked mutinies at Spithead and the Nore in 1797. These had little political content; the mutineers, however aggrieved, remained overwhelmingly patriotic. They were dealt with by a mixture of coercion and concession—as indeed were the well-organized dockyard workers. Elsewhere, government reacted ambiguously to attempts to remedy working-class distress. The Combination Laws of 1799 treated trade unions like revolutionary societies and outlawed them; government also successfully opposed attempts to secure legal minimum wages and restore older industrial relationships, even when these were backed by manufacturers (on the whole smaller ones). Such measures, and the depressions which resulted from the diversion of investment into government funds and the trade war, ensured that average real wages stagnated between 1790 and 1814. Yet the relatively generous poor relief scales adopted by many rural parishes after the 1790s—the so-called Speenhamland system—continued a traditional entitlement to relief, and undoubtedly mitigated even sharper social conflicts.

For most of the war Britain avoided European involvement, and paid subsidies instead to the members of the various coalitions she assembled, first against revolutionary France, then against Napoleon. This was simply a refinement of the mercenary principles of eighteenth-century wars. Only between 1811 and 1814, when she sent her own troops to the Peninsula, did her army take on a European role. The gains in other areas, however, were immense; her hold over India was strengthened, and she achieved effective dominance, through Singapore, of the Dutch East Indies; she conquered Ceylon between 1795 and 1816, took over South Africa from the Dutch, and established a claim on Egypt. Informally, she secured a trading hegemony over the former Spanish colonies of Central and South America.

Although Britain was victorious, the war's imprint on Europe was predominantly French. Wherever Napoleon's armies went, they left (or their opponents copied) the laws, the measurements, the administration—and above all the nationalistic ethos—of the revolution. The map had been totally changed. Before 1789, Britain had been part of a continental community. David Hume and Adam Smith were as much at home in Paris as they were in Edinburgh, and rather more, perhaps, than they were in London. After 1815, Britain, despite the economic progress which attracted hundreds of foreign visitors, remained at a distance from European life.

At home, war and depression polarized political ideas into 'revolutionary' and 'loyalist'. 'Pitt's reign of terror', patriotic societies, and church-and-king mobs pushed democratic thinkers, earlier commonplace enough, either into obscurity or into alliance with genuinely oppressed groups like the Irish or the working class. The 'Jacobin tradition' became as sensitive to industrial and economic change as it had been to the 'evils' of established government. A diffuse, volatile blend of everything from anarchism to religious millenarianism, it continued to mark working-class movements up to and including Chartism.

Paradoxically, however, the relentlessly practical approach of the governing élite, and the role of repression in exalting state power over contractual ideas of politics, conjured up its own radical rival. Evangelicalism, in the hands of William Wilberforce and the Clapham Sect, aimed at converting the élite; but so too did the reiterated schemes of Jeremy Bentham, a wealthy lawyer who believed, more or less, that society could be governed through a set of self-evident principles analogous to those of economics. Of these, the most easily grasped was 'utilitarianism'—that social action should aim at producing 'the greatest good for the greatest number'. The sworn foe to all ideals of 'social contract', Bentham opposed the French Revolution, and tried to interest successive British governments in his schemes, particularly of law and prison reform. He was probably more successful than he thought, but frustrations drove him towards the democratic reformers and by 1815 he was supporting universal suffrage. The 'philosophic radicals', as Bentham's disciples were called, offered the combination of institutional reform with political continuity—and, after 1815, offered it to both sides, as they built up a following of moderate working-class leaders. From this stemmed both a centralized pattern of state action, and a theory of public intervention, which remained powerfully influential for the rest of the century.

Benthamite theory saw local authorities raising rates and taking executive action in appropriately-sized districts. They would be supervised by salaried inspectors reporting to a central board. 'Old corruption' and popular profligacy would thus be supposedly checked; local responsibility would be retained. But, in fact, the officials were dominant. Bentham and his acolytes, the Mills, father and son, and Edwin Chadwick, may have been converted to democracy, but they were reluctant to let the people's representatives do more than veto the officials' actions.

The London scavenger: engraving, after a Daguerrotype by Beard, in the *Morning Chronicle*, 1848. Almost as much as Henry Mayhew's careful interviews (he was the real pioneer of the art) these early photographs capture the complicated if frequently sordid lives ot the 'tribes' of casual workers in the capital.

Not surprisingly, their most spectacular successes were gained in British India.

Law had shifted into a class pattern. Working men, accustomed to fight disabilities in the courts, lost traditional rights and had their independent action constrained. The alarm of the propertied classes gave teeth to hitherto ineffective sanctions. The 'making of the English working class' was, at least in part, a reaction to a combination of war, industrialization, and repression: it meant a hostility to inequitable law. There was little respect for 'the Thing' (the undeclared confederacy of the rich to exhaust the poor) in William Cobbett; practical ignorance of it, in Robert Owen. Even the Benthamites thought the legal establishment a 'vast sinister interest'. Although ultimately, only the Irish stood out against it, the triumph of the rule of law, like Waterloo, proved 'a damn close-run thing'. It was probably only possible because popular expectations of it endured long enough to be sustained by a new wave of constitutional agitation.

Roads to Freedom

> Men of England, wherefore plough
> For the Lords who lay ye low?
> Wherefore weave with toil and care
> The rich robes your tyrants wear?
> . . . . . .
> Shrink to your cellars, holes and cells;
> In halls ye deck another dwells.
> Why shake the chains ye wrought? Ye see
> The steel ye tempered glance on ye.
> Shelley, *To the Men of England*

The post-war Tory government after 1815 encountered a new set of literary radicals. Coleridge and Wordsworth, gathered to the bosom of the forces of order, were succeeded by Byron and Shelley. Lord Liverpool's administration of 1812–27 was in fact a pretty bourgeois affair, made up of minor gentry, the sons of doctors and merchants, and even (in the case of George Canning) an actress. Although condemned as reactionary—which some of its members certainly were—it sat edgily on the right centre. It was liberal (by the standards of Restoration Europe) abroad, and conciliatory at home. But it inherited a fearsome post-war slump and racking industrial tensions, on top of a war debt to be paid for, and demobilized servicemen to be settled. It was scarcely aided by an able Whig opposition, which lacerated it through the medium of the new literary reviews, and a rich culture of popular protest, from the 'unstamped' newspapers of Henry Hetherington and Richard Carlile to the bucolic radicalism of William Cobbett and the visionary millenarianism of William Blake. The landed interest pressed for, and obtained, the maintenance of subsidy on grain through the Corn Law of 1815; this probably staved off, for over a decade, discontent among those of the working population who tilled the land. But it was all at a cost. Even more than in 1811–12, the threat to order came from the new industrial towns, where the end of the post-war boom caused widespread unemployment and a steep fall in wages. The consciousness of the workers, more of their *industrial* than of their class position, had steadily sharpened since 1800, and the local representatives of government, industrialists and Justices of the Peace, felt their isolation acutely.

Do the fears that these gentry frequently expressed—of Jacobin mobs baying at their gates—and the explicitly revolutionary ideas of some leaders of the working classes, add up to a real threat to overthrow the regime, which was only narrowly averted? They might have done, had action been co-ordinated, had a common economic cause existed to bind industrial workers to the parliamentary radicals and the skilled trades of the capital, and had the governing classes really lost their nerve. But this would have been very difficult to achieve. London was not an 'absolute' capital like Paris; there were few vital levers of power to be grasped—had the London radicals mobilized *en masse*.

London did not move with the provinces. The parliamentary opposition disowned and deprecated violence, and the Home Office under its repressive head, Viscount Sidmouth, and his local agents cowed resistance—but at a price. The climax came in Manchester on 16 August 1819, when the local magistracy ordered the yeomanry to apprehend speakers at a huge but peaceful reform demonstration in St. Peter's Fields. The soldiers turned on the crowd and eleven were killed at 'Peterloo'. Both the desire of radicals for revenge and the penetration of the radical movement by government spies and *agents provocateurs* were responsible for further outbreaks in the following year—a weavers' rising in Scotland and the 'Cato Street conspiracy' to assassinate the Cabinet in London. Repression—the gallows and transportation—was sharp, savage, and effective, but in the long term it strengthened constitutional resistance and steadily discredited the government.

The government itself looked askance at unbound industrialization. Moving towards free trade, systematic administration, and a reformed penal code, it still depended on the agricultural interest, and feared further working-class violence. Sir Walter Scott, its supporter, regretted the shift of industry to the towns, since he believed that in country mills the manufacturer 'exercised a salutary influence over men depending on and intimately connected with him and his prospects'. He probably had Robert Owen and New Lanark in mind. Propagandizing for self-governing industrial communities, Owen wanted to put a brake on industry and, through spade-cultivation, make agriculture again a great employer. His 'new moral world' fitted into the atmosphere of social peril and Utopian salvation which had been pervasive since the end of the war.

> The Strongest Poison ever known
> Came from Caesar's Laurel Crown.
> Nought can deform the Human Race
> Like to the Armour's iron brace.
> When Gold & Gems adorn the Plow
> To peaceful Arts shall Envy bow.

Artisans did not need to understand the artisan genius William Blake's cosmology to appreciate the message. The future must have seemed to many as apocalyptic as the huge but enormously detailed and didactic paintings of John Martin, which had a great vogue as engravings in the mid-1820s.

The Whig contribution to the political battle was, however, effective enough. In 1820 George IV's attempt to divorce his consort led to the royal family's dirty linen being washed in the courts. Henry Brougham, a leading contributor to the *Edinburgh Review*, championed Queen Caroline (not the most promising of martyrs) against king and ministry, to the plaudits of the public. Then in August 1822 Castlereagh, who as Foreign Secretary had managed to extricate Britain from the conservative powers represented in Metternich's Congresses, killed himself. The way was open for the more liberal side of the Liverpool government to show itself.

Castlereagh's successor at the Foreign Office, George Canning, sided with the American president Monroe in 1823 in guaranteeing the new republics of South America—and incidentally confirmed Britain's privileged access to a vast new market. Two years later the ministry repealed the Six Acts and anti-trade union legislation, and in 1826 it ended the 'management' of Scotland by the Dundases. The duke of Wellington's administration passed Catholic Emancipation in 1829. It bowed to Daniel O'Connell's expert management of Irish public opinion, and to the threat of a national uprising when O'Connell was elected as MP for County Clare in 1828 but, as a Catholic, was debarred from taking his seat.

Only parliamentary reform remained to be implemented, but here a direct party issue was involved. Pressure groups—the trade unions, the Scots, the Irish—could be bought off with judicious concessions. Reform, however, would mean a triumph for the Whigs, with all that meant in terms of parliamentary command and patronage. In 1828 the duke had dug his heels in, under pressure from his 'Ultras', but in the following year they parted from him over Catholic Emancipation. Meanwhile in the country agitation grew, and the Whigs did not scruple to encourage their radical rivals. Pressure rose to a peak after the Whigs under Earl Grey and Lord John Russell won the election which the death of George IV occasioned in 1830. When their Reform Bill was rejected by the Lords, well-organized 'Political Unions' held monster rallies in the cities; rioters attacked Nottingham Castle and the bishop's palace in Bristol, both seats of anti-Reform peers; in Merthyr riots were followed by the execution of a workers' leader, Dic Penderyn. In April 1832 the Lords gave way—by nine votes—much to the relief of Grey's government, which had shown its otherwise conservative nature by the brutal suppression of farm labourers' discontent— the 'Captain Swing' riots—in southern England.

Coping with Reform

Despite the near-revolutionary nature of the reform agitation, the act of 1832 incorporated the most potentially troublesome sectors of industrial and commercial power, but did little more. Scotland's electorate shot up from 4,579 to 64,447 (a 1,407 per cent increase), but that of Ireland increased by only 21 per cent; 41 large English towns—including Manchester, Bradford, and Birmingham—got representation for the first time, but the average size of an English borough electorate—and these returned almost half (324) of the total of 658 MPs—remained under 900. The 349 electors of Buckingham still returned as many MPs as the 4,172 electors of Leeds. England, with 54 per cent of the population, continued to return 71 per cent of the Commons. Before 1832 it had returned 74 per cent. 'Virtual representation', of interests rather than people, remained a principle, and Parliament continued to be dominated by the landed interest for almost a further half-century.

   Some conservatives now feared a Benthamite assault on the aristocracy and the Church. But there were few doctrinaires in Parliament, and the reforming zeal of the Whigs rapidly waned. Humanitarians got their way in 1833 with the abolition of slavery in the British Empire and the regulation of children's work in textile factories by the Factory Inspectorate. The Poor Law Amendment Act of 1834, which its architect Edwin Chadwick saw as the basis of a systematic and economical reconstruction of English local government, remained, however, an isolated monument—as much hated by the people as were its symbols, the gaunt Union Workhouses or 'bastilles'.

The Times, too, was loud in abuse of the New Poor Law, feeling perhaps that philosophical radicalism had gone far enough. For 1834 was a traumatic year. Ireland was quiet for once, the Whigs edging towards an understanding with O'Connell, which lasted for the rest of the decade, but on the mainland the 'alternative society' of the still-inchoate working class reached its apogee. The growth of trade unions, led by men such as John Doherty; the arguments of the 'unstamped' press; the frustration of radicals with the Reform Act; the return to politics of Robert Owen—all combined to produce a project for a Grand National Consolidated Trades Union which would destroy the capitalist system through a 'grand national holiday' or general strike. After this, society would be reorganized on a co-operative basis, with money values calculated in terms of hours of labour performed. Government counter-attacked in March with the victimization of six Dorset labourers—the 'Tolpuddle Martyrs'; the GNCTU undertook too many protests and strikes, which its organizers could not co-ordinate. Owen pulled out in August and effectively brought the movement to an end. On 16 October Parliament accidentally burned down; six months earlier this might have appeared more than simply symbolic.

The Whig triumph really came with local government reform. Scottish burgh councils, hitherto self-elected, were put under a rate-payer franchise in 1833; reform of the English towns followed two years later. In the larger towns, Whigs and radicals came into the fruits of office, and by and large stayed there. But the government was now badly split. In November 1834 the Tories, now under Peel and more or less pledged to work within the framework of reform, took office. A false dawn, this: the Whigs were back in April 1835, but under the deeply conservative Melbourne. When they fell from power in 1841 Peel seemed more acutely to reflect the spirit of gradualist reform, an outlook shared with the young queen's serious-minded consort, Albert of Saxe-Coburg-Gotha.

Peel, however, was threatened from two sides. Manufacturers, concerned at falling profits, demanded lower wages, and believed that they could only get them if the price of bread was reduced (bread was the staple diet of the working class—they ate about five pounds of it per head per week). This could only be done by permitting the free import of grain, in other words by repealing the Corn Law of 1815. Radicals, frustrated by Whig backsliding, climbed on to the bandwaggon and grabbed the reins. Richard Cobden, a none-too-successful cotton merchant with transatlantic interests, John Bright, a Quaker carpet manufacturer from Rochdale, and James Wilson, the Scottish journalist who founded the *Economist* in 1843, became leading figures in the Anti-Corn Law League, inaugurated at a meeting in Manchester in October 1838. The League both represented, and in part created, the commercial-minded individualistic middle class—what the Germans called (and still call) 'Manchestertum'. By petitions, demonstrations, the mobilization of nonconformity, the imaginative use of the new penny post (1841), it created a widespread animus against the territorial aristocracy, and against Peel himself.

Peel had, in fact, followed most of the precepts of political economy in his public finance: duties on imports were drastically reduced, the Bank of England reorganized, railway promotion allowed to have its free enterprise head (despite the predilection of William Gladstone, the President of the Board of Trade, for outright nationalization). But the Leaguers acted with the fury of the desperate. They realized that their prosperity was borne on the back of an increasingly mutinous labour force. An extremely unorthodox Manchester cotton-master, the young German Friedrich Engels, watched the successive waves of discontent breaking against the mill-walls, and prophesied:

The moment the workers resolve to be bought and sold no longer, when, in the determination of the value of labour, they take the part of men possessed of a will as well as of working power, at that moment the whole Political Economy of today is at an end.

Engels's chosen instruments were the ultimate in economic depressions, and the power of the organized working class expressed in Chartism.

'I cares nothing about politics neither; but I'm a chartist a London scavenger told Henry Mayhew, the pioneer social investigator, in 1848. The People's Charter, with its celebrated six points—manhood suffrage, the ballot, equal electoral districts, abolition of property qualifications for MPs, payment for MPs, and annual Parliaments—achieved the same immediate impact as the French Revolution and Daniel O'Connell's campaigns in Ireland. But this only gave a superficial and episodic unity to an immensely complex, highly localized movement. Formally it was ultra-democratic (although only as far as men were concerned—a

Cottages. A cramped and squalid 'miners' row' of two-room cottages
at Nitshill colliery, near Glasgow, which was representative of
most rural labourers' accommodation.

proposal for female suffrage was an early casualty). In its most
dramatic nation-wide phase it was also short-lived, lasting from
1838 to 1842. But organization, and heterodoxy, bubbled away in
the regions, influenced by the local economic predicaments,
political traditions, and the character of the leaders. The division
between 'physical-' and 'moral-force' leaders was complicated by
attitudes to the established parties, to the drink question,
Ireland, property, and education. In Scotland and the English
Midlands, leadership came from small tradesmen with a sprink-
ling of business and professional men. In Yorkshire it was
militant, following heavy unemployment and the impact of the
New Poor Law, but participated with the Tories in their
campaign for factory reform. The 'frontier towns' of industrial
Wales had already seen plenty of 'collective bargaining by riot',
so it was possibly not surprising that a huge protest demonstration at Newport, on 4 November 1839, ended as a bloody
confrontation with the military. Fourteen were killed, but
subsequent trials led to transportation to Tasmania, not the
gallows.

Peel was more humane and tactful than Melbourne in 1831 or
Liverpool in 1819, and his policy succeeded. The economic boom
of 1843 and 1844 sapped Chartism; its last revival in 1848
reflected the agony of Ireland rather than the ambitions of the
English artisans, or any desire to emulate events in Europe. Late
Chartism was more experimental and variegated, as well as more
Irish. Feargus O'Connor projected land settlement schemes,
Owenite and socialist ideas came back, along with ideas culled
from European revolutionaries, many of whom ended up as

exiles in Britain. But however fascinating intellectually the friendship of Julian Harney and Ernest Jones with Marx and Engels, the mass movement was dead. Old Chartists remained active in single-issue movements such as temperance, co-operation (the Rochdale Pioneer store of 1844 had Chartist origins), or trade unionism. Others emigrated. Many former Chartists ended up quite respectably integrated into mid-Victorian local government.

'Unless the Lord build the City . . . '

In 1832 an appalling cholera epidemic, sweeping through Europe from the Middle East, probably killed 31,000 in Britain; in 1833 Parliament voted a £30,000 grant to elementary education, and John Keble preached at Oxford on 'national apostasy'. These events merely coincided with political reform—Parliament spent more time and money on the stables of Windsor Castle than on the education grant—but were important determinants of the direction that subsequent state action took, and the way in which the early Victorians rationalized their social position.

Cholera dramatized the problem of rapid urban growth, though its impact could be as deadly in the countryside. The new industrial towns were small in area, and densely packed, as walking to work was universal. Urban land usage accorded with economic power: the numerically tiny property-owning class, possibly less than 5 per cent of the population in a cotton town, often occupied 50 per cent of the land area. Working people lived where factories, roads, canals, and, later, railways allowed them to. The results were squalid—nineteenth-century towns smoked and stank—and, for the workers, expensive both in terms of rent and of human life. A tolerable house might take a quarter of a skilled man's weekly income, and few families were ever in a position to afford this. As a result, not only did slums multiply in the old inner-city area—the rookeries of London, the cellar-dwellings of Liverpool and Manchester, the 'lands' of the Scottish burghs, 'China' in Merthyr Tydfil—but new regionally-specific types of slum were created by landlords and speculative builders—the 'back-to-backs' of Yorkshire and the tiny 'room and kitchen' or 'single-end' flats in which 70 per cent of Glasgow families lived by 1870.

If housing was bad, sanitation was worse. Better-off citizens could combine to create commissions to provide water and sewerage, light the streets, and provide some sort of policing, but if anything, this worsened the plight of their poorer neighbours. A middle-class area's new water-closets all too often drained into the working class's water supply.

Epidemics were the working class's revenge. Surrounded by masses of the very poor in the shape of servants and tradespeople (whom they usually ignored) the wealthy suddenly became intensely vulnerable. A. C. Tait, a future Archbishop of Canterbury, for example, lost five of his seven children to scarlet fever in Carlisle in 1856. In 1831 the government forced local notables to serve on temporary boards of health, in order to combat cholera. In 1840 Edwin Chadwick, concerned at the numbers driven into pauperism by the death of the breadwinner and ill-health, conducted on behalf of the Poor Law Commissioners an *Inquiry into the Sanatory Condition of the Labouring Population*, published in 1842. As a result of this, and subsequent agitation, not to speak of the threat of another cholera outbreak, an act of 1848 gave municipalities powers to set up local boards of health, subject to three Public Health Commissioners, among them Chadwick himself. Besides the Benthamites, other forces had been mobilized—some Chartists and radicals, but probably more Tories, professional men, and philanthropists. Exemplifying the movement as a whole was Lord Ashley. The future earl of Shaftesbury could be a prejudiced low-church Tory—Macaulay referred to his style as 'the bray of Exeter Hall'—but he inherited Wilberforce's skills at manipulating public, and élite, opinion to secure effective government intervention. In the 1840s and 1850s these skills were used to help miners, factory hands, poor emigrants, and slum-dwellers. Some have argued that administrative reform took on a dynamic of its own, independent both of parliamentary action and ideology. 'The Tory interpretation of history' (as this view has somewhat unfairly been called) contrasted the power of officials—'the men on the spot'—and enthusiasts like Ashley virtually to create their own laws with Parliament's indifference to social conditions. But this is only a partial explanation of the reform process. Standards of conduct among officials varied from department to department, and between individuals. Some were dedicated to the point of self-sacrifice, others reflected the easy-going ethos of a civil service still recruited by patronage. Anthony Trollope, as a senior official of the Post Office, still found time to hunt twice a week, and turn out a steady 1.7 novels per annum—one of which, *The Three Clerks* (1857), gives an engaging picture of a backwater of the unreformed civil service, and Trollope's own sour observations on its reformers.

As this was the golden age both of 'local self-government' and of professional evolution, the strongest initiatives came from the great cities, and from a new generation of largely Scottish-trained doctors, who were making the transition from lowly surgeon-apothecaries into a self-governing profession. Liverpool appointed the first Medical Officer of Health in 1847; the City of London, a 'square mile' rich in every variety of social peril, appointed the dynamic Dr John Simon a year later. By 1854 the appointment of Medical Officers of Health was compulsory, and proved critical not only in getting the cities to undertake major water, drainage, and slum clearance schemes, but to ensure that regulations on building and overcrowding were enforced.

The new industrial society brought into question the organization of education. Opinions on this differed: the Evangelical Hannah More believed that to inculcate religion but preserve order, children should learn to read but not write. Adam Smith, fearing the intellectually stultifying impact of the division of labour on the working class, sought to mitigate it by state education. Although this existed in Scotland, as a result of the Calvinist reformation of the Kirk, there was no English equivalent. Before the 1800s, there were grammar schools, frequently of pre-reformation origin, independent or 'adventure' schools, and charity schools. These varied enormously in quality, and could never accommodate an expanding and youthful population, let alone service the new urban areas and improve standards. Around 1800, however, opinion—including even that of George III—swung towards education as a prophylactic against revolution—partly through the appearance of new, cheap, and thus seductive forms of teaching. The 'monitorial' systems of Lancaster and Bell, whereby senior pupils learned lessons by rote and then instructed their juniors, led directly to the foundation of the British and Foreign Schools Society in 1808, and the National Society in 1811. These two attempts at national coverage, however, coincided with the exacerbation of hostilities between their respective sponsors, the nonconformists and the established Church; religious animus continued to take precedence over educational criteria for nearly a century.

Religious antagonisms in the reform of the endowed, or 'public', schools were internal to Anglicanism, and less fierce. The schools' condition, peculiarly wretched in the last years of the eighteenth century, had improved even before the radical Broad-Churchman Thomas Arnold began his career at Rugby in 1829. His reforms, in fact, paralleled the essentially conservative political settlement of 1832, but lasted far longer. A 'liberal education' (Latin and Greek) remained dominant among those destined for the universities, but it was elevated from a totally meaningless ritual for young aristocrats into the subject-matter of competitive advancement, through scholarships and, at Oxford and Cambridge, college fellowships, for middle-class boys. Their goals were the prizes of subsidized entry into the professions, but their function was more profound: to act as bell-wethers guiding other boys from the commercial middle class into a sanitized version of the values of the territorial aristocracy. By the time he died in 1842, Arnold was being imitated at the other older public schools, and the movement proceeded, aided by the expansion of the railway system and, in 1857, by Thomas Hughes's remarkably successful *Tom Brown's Schooldays*.

The remodelling of the public schools provided a paradigm for a new generation of reformers, many of whom had been educated there. Unlike the Benthamites, they developed no highly-integrated programme, but rather sought to convert institutions accessible only to the aristocracy and the Anglican clergy to serve the whole of society. This ideal of 'nationalization' with its corollary, the 'incorporation' of the working class into 'political society', was expressed in 1848 by the Christian Socialist followers of F. D. Maurice—including Tom Hughes—in their attempt to make the Church of England an arbiter between capital and labour. They were not alone. In Bradford William Edward Forster, a young radical woollen manufacturer, formerly a Quaker, wrote:

Unless some concessions be made to these masses, and unless all classes strive earnestly to keep them better fed, first or last there will be a convulsion; but I believe the best political method of preventing it is by the middle class sympathising with the operatives, and giving themselves power to oppose their unjust claims by helping them in those which are reasonable.

Forster's wife was the daughter of Arnold of Rugby, the sister of Matthew Arnold, inspector of schools and poet. The 'intellectual aristocracy' of high thinking and moderate reform was already shifting from evangelical religion to political intervention.

Arnold, the public schools, and most of the politicians belonged to the Broad Church or liberal Anglican tradition, whose principles envisaged the Church as partner of the State, a relationship to which theological doctrine was strictly subordinate. The Evangelicals exalted religious sanctions, but their simple theology was being corroded by liberal assaults, which seemed to reach a climax with the Reform Act of 1832. Clergymen feared that a tide of Benthamite, and hence atheistic, reform would be unleashed; John Keble in his Oxford sermon declared a clerical resistance which would be founded on the apostolic traditions of the Church of England. 'Tractarianism', or the Oxford Movement, did not oppose liberalism through social reform or through 'high-church' ceremonial. It was a conservative, intellectual appeal to Anglican tradition. After twelve years it split, in 1845, when some of its leaders, including John Henry Newman (partly in reaction to low-church persecution, partly out of sheer intellectual conviction) decided that nothing separated them from Rome, and 'went over'. Although its enemies forecast otherwise, the Oxford Movement served to strengthen the spirit of Anglicanism both through devout laymen such as W. E. Gladstone and through its influence on religious education and architecture. The Broad Church, being posited on a more sociological appreciation of religion, was in difficulties when it appeared that less than a fifth of the English attended their parish church. The unique religious Census of 1851 showed that only about 35 per cent of the English population went to Sunday service, and—although there were intense regional variations here—half of these 'sat under' dissenting ministers. In 1848 and after, the Broad Church Christian Socialists tried energetically to reach out to working men, but for every working man convinced by the theology of the group's leader, F. D. Maurice, ten were impressed by the novels of his colleague Charles Kingsley, and many more helped practically by the work of J. M. Ludlow for the trade unions and E. V. Neale for the infant co-operative movement.

Anglicans at least possessed a tradition, wealth, and breadth of manoeuvre denied to the nonconformists. Sectionally divided and always treated with suspicion by the ruling classes, several of their leaders—notably Jabez Bunting of the Methodist Conference—tried to integrate themselves through their conservatism. Political radicalism tended to be the hallmark of rural or mining area Dissenters—the change in South Wales was particularly drastic—or of urban élites such as the Unitarians or the Quakers. Only in the 1850s, after the success of the Corn Law campaign, did dissent begin to flex its muscles, align itself with the Liberal Party, and demand either improvements in its own civic status or—in the programme of the 'Liberation Society' (founded in 1844)—the dismantling of the established Church. Organized dissent came to play a major—and troublesome—institutional role within Liberalism, but it was a wasting asset, as the steady trickle of wealthy nonconformists over to the Church of England showed.

In Scotland the controversy over patronage came to a head in the 'ten years' conflict' of 1833–43, which ended with the 'Disruption' of the established Kirk and the creation of a new independent 'Free Church'. The secular role of the Kirk rapidly crumbled—a statutory poor law was enacted in 1845—but religious politics continued to obsess the Scots middle class for the rest of the century.

'The ringing grooves of change'

The 1840s remained, however, a decade of crisis, even in terms of classical economics. British industry was still dominated by textiles, and the market for them was both finite and subject to increasing competition from America and Europe. The industry was overcapitalized, and the adoption of each new invention meant that the return on capital decreased; each commercial depression was steeper and longer lasting than the last. Real wages increased only slowly, probably not sufficiently to counter the precipitate decline of the handwork trades and the high marginal costs of urban life. To Karl Marx, surveying Britain through the descriptions of his mill-owning friend Friedrich Engels, this was all part of one pattern. Capitalism was doomed to choke on its own surplus accumulations of capital; its increasingly underpaid labourers would, in the next economic depression, rise decisively against it. He would have echoed Shelley's challenge:

> Rise like Lions after slumber
> In unvanquishable number—
> Shake your chains to earth like dew
> Which in sleep had fallen on you—
> Ye are many—they are few.

In the 1840s events in Ireland seemed to bring the revolution perceptibly nearer. The potato blight of 1845, 1846, and 1848 destroyed the basis of the country's population growth; between 1845 and 1850 up to a million died of the consequences of malnutrition, two million emigrated between 1845 and 1855. The poor Irish immigrant, prepared to work for wages far below the English norm, had already been seen as an explosive force; Carlyle had written in *Chartism* (1839):

Every man who will take the statistic spectacles off his nose, and look, may discern in town or country . . . [that] the condition of the lower multitude of English labourers approximates more and more to the Irish competing with them in all markets. . . .

British engineers of the railway age, a posed group by John Lucas, ostensibly set in autumn 1849 in a hut on the edge of the Menai Straits during the hoisting into position of the tubular wrought-iron spans of Robert Stephenson's Menai Bridge (in background) on the Crewe–Holyhead railway. Stephenson is seated centre, and Isambard Kingdom Brunel on the far right. Joseph Locke (seated second from right) completed the triumverate of great railway engineers. All three died in their mid-fifties, worn out by overwork, in 1859–60.

That this did not happen was substantially due to a dramatic industrial development which simultaneously soaked up surplus supplies of labour and capital and transformed them into a new and more varied economy. Its principal—and psychologically most spectacular—instrument was the railway.

Railways of various primitive types had since the early seventeenth century carried coal from mine to port or river; by 1800 there were perhaps two hundred miles of horse-worked track scattered throughout the country, built to various gauges and patterns, with wooden and later with iron rails. Cast iron was used from the 1770s, wrought iron 'edge-rail'—much more reliable—from the 1790s. Steam traction then appeared in two forms: stationary low-pressure engines dragged wagons up inclines, and light high-pressure 'locomotive' engines moved themselves on the rails. In 1804, Richard Trevithick demonstrated the locomotive in Wales, and it was soon adopted in the

Railways in the nineteenth century 1825–1914

northern coalfield, where 'viewers' like George Stephenson were building large-capacity edge-railways whose demands stretched the capabilities of horse traction, as coal production doubled between 1800 and 1825. Throughout Britain by 1830, 375 miles of line, authorized by Parliament, had been built.

The commercial boom of the mid-1820s gave the next boost, with the promotion of the Liverpool and Manchester Railway.

Cotton production had almost doubled between 1820 and 1830, and Manchester's population had risen by 47 per cent. Transport of the necessities for both was checked by the monopolistic Bridgewater Canal; a large-scale competitor was necessary. Its demands almost exceeded the technology available: only on the eve of its completion, and under pressure of an open competition, was an efficient enough locomotive produced by the Stephensons. The difference between the award-winning *Rocket* (1830) and the production-line *Patentee* (1834), however, was almost as great as that between the *Rocket* and its clumsy if reliable precursor, the *Locomotion*. Locomotive design did not subsequently change for half a century.

In the 1830s, railway development was buoyed up by another speculative boom. By 1840 nearly 2,400 miles of track connected London with Birmingham, Manchester, and Brighton. Some of the new lines were prosperous; others, overcapitalized and faced with penal land and legal charges, ran into trouble. There were few enough rules in the early days of joint-stock companies, and the reputation soared of those who succeeded in turning 'scrip into gold', such as George Hudson, 'the Railway King' who controlled a third of the system by 1845. Hudson made his attractive profits by paying the dividends of existing lines with capital raised for new branches; when the great mania of the 1840s, which he helped promote, faltered in 1848, he was exposed and fled the country—but not before mileage had risen to over 8,000, and the network had been extended from Aberdeen to Plymouth.

But the railway age produced its heroes as well: the self-taught Stephenson and his brilliant son Robert, Joseph Locke, Daniel Gooch, and the polymath Isambard Kingdom Brunel, whose vast projects—the seven-foot-gauge Great Western Railway, the pioneer iron-and-screw steamer *Great Britain*, and the 18,000 ton sea-leviathan *Great Eastern*—fascinated the public as much as they terrified his unfortunate financial backers. 'What poet-race', G. K. Chesterton would later ask, 'shot such cyclopean arches at the stars?' Such men—Carlyle called them 'captains of industry'—were more attractive entrepreneurs than the cotton-masters, and Samuel Smiles was subsequently to make them paragons of 'self-help'.

This new transport system had been created in less than a score of years, and without any modern construction techniques. The 'navvies'—of whom 250,000 were said to be at work in 1848, powered by beer and beef—created the huge earthworks which characterized early British railways. The image of the British working man in the 1830s had been of the pathetic factory slave or starving cotton-weaver. In the 1850s it was provided by the brawny labourers who ran up the Crystal Palace in six months, and who were shipped to the Crimea to make good—with railways and camps—the incompetence of the military. The railways had cost an unprecedented amount of money, however: by 1849 no less than £224.6 million had been invested. In 1849 total receipts remained low at only £11.4 million; although they rose by 1859 to £24.4 million, railways were never more than a modest and reliable investment, and in the case of some companies they were far from that. Until 1852, they made more money from passengers than freight and the subsequent expansion of goods traffic was obtained to a great extent by a systematic process of buying over their chief competitors, the canals, whose owners, having hitherto enjoyed inflated profits, were little inclined to see themselves beggared by competition. By the mid-1850s, strategic sections of the canal network were in railway ownership, and traffics were ruthlessly transferred to rail. Already, in the most dynamic area of industrial growth, the conspiracy of capitalists denounced by Adam Smith had become a fact.

Politics and Diplomacy: Palmerston's Years

The railway boom coincided with a dramatic shift in politics. The harvests of 1842, 1843, and 1844 had been good; grain was plentiful and costs low. Then in 1845 the harvest was wrecked by bad weather, and the first blights hit the Irish potato crop. The arguments of the Anti-Corn Law League seemed confirmed. Peel attempted to carry free trade in Cabinet, failed, and resigned, only to come back when the Whigs could not form a ministry. In February 1846, he moved a package of measures abolishing duties on imported corn over three years. He thus bought—or hoped to buy—the support of the gentry through grants towards the poor law and local police forces. But his party was deeply split and only a minority supported him when he was censured on Irish coercion in May. In the ensuing election Russell came back with a Whig ministry, and Whigs and later Liberals dominated politics thereafter. Badly weakened by the shift of the Peelite élite, which included Gladstone, Aberdeen, and Sir James Graham, into the ambit of the Whigs, the Tory gentry now found themselves led by the ex-Whigs Lord Derby and Lord George Bentinck, and the exotic ex-radical Benjamin Disraeli. The

W. P. Frith, 'The Railway Station' (1862). In fact Brunel's Paddington, a scene architecturally not much changed today, but used as the setting for the sort of 'all human life is there' painting in which Frith excelled. Vast numbers of copies were reproduced.
Note the absence of working-class people apart from 'railway servants'.
This Great Western broad-gauge train probably didn't carry 'parliamentary' carriages (only one a day was obliged to do so).
Rail travel was for the fairly well-off until the 1870s.

Tories stood firm as a party, but held power for only five of the next thirty years.

There was a greater degree of party management, centred on the new clubs of St. James's, the Reform and the (Tory) Carlton, both founded in 1832, but to conceive of politics shading from left to right means imposing the criteria of a later age. National party organizations were as unknown as party programmes. Public speeches were rare. Leaders—still predominantly Whig magnates—would drop a few hints to their closest colleagues, often their relatives, about policy just before elections (which took place every seven years). Prospective candidates travelled to likely seats, issued addresses, and canvassed for the support of local notables, only 'going to the poll' if promised respectable support.

Huge expenses made contested elections the exception rather than the rule. The territorial nobility were impregnable in their many surviving 'pocket boroughs'. A vote—delivered in public—against, say, Blenheim Palace at Woodstock, was still an almost suicidal move for a local farmer or tradesman. Counties, likewise, were dominated by the great families. The medium-sized boroughs were more open but expensive; their electors sometimes reached the levels of corruption depicted at Eatanswill in Dickens's *Pickwick Papers*. The newly-enfranchised great

towns could sometimes elect active if impecunious men—
Macaulay sat for Leeds—but more often favoured affluent local
businessmen, who usually bore most of the cost of the contest.
Some things, however, remain familiar today: England was more
conservative, the 'Celtic fringe' more radical.

Although Wellington's brief caretaker ministry of 1834 proved
the last occasion on which a duke became first minister, power
lay with the landed interest, in which the Whigs were still as well
represented as the Tories, although in many cases the elevation
to this status was recent, a tribute to the flexibility of the élite.
Peel and Gladstone—both Oxford double-firsts—were only a
generation removed from provincial industry and commerce,
and even more remarkable was the rise of Benjamin Disraeli,
adventurer and novelist, stemming from a religion whose
members were only to obtain full civil equality in 1860.

Ministries spent little time over domestic legislation, but
much more over foreign and service affairs—not surprisingly,
since the latter claimed more than a third of the estimates.
Neither navy nor army had changed much since 1815. The navy
bought its first steamer, a tug called the *Monkey*, in 1822. With
enormous reluctance, others were ordered in 1828, the Lords of
the Admiralty feeling that 'the introduction of steam is calculated
to strike a fatal blow at the supremacy of the Empire'. Paddles
meant a loss of broadside guns, and sailing ships could keep
station for years, so Devonport was still launching all-sail
three-deckers in 1848, although the successful use of screw-
propulsion on smaller ships was numbering the days of the
sailing fleet. The old long-service army of about 130,000 men—42
per cent Irish and 14 per cent Scots in 1830—poorly paid and
wretchedly accommodated, kept the peace in Ireland and the
colonies. In many small campaigns it advanced Britain's spheres
of influence and trade in India, and in the 'Opium War' of
1839–42 in China, although now on behalf of free-trading
merchants rather than the fading Chartered Companies.

Britain's withdrawal from European commitments was
reflected, too, in her diplomacy. After the defeat of Napoleon, the
Continental conservative leaders, above all Tsar Alexander I of
Russia, tried to establish a system of co-operation in Europe
through regular congresses of the great powers. But even in 1814
British diplomats preferred security to be achieved by the
traditional means of the balance of power, even if this meant
resurrecting France as a counterweight to Russia. For much of the
time between then and 1848, a tacit Anglo-French *entente*
subsisted, though it was disturbed in 1830 when Catholic

Belgium detached itself from Holland, and looked as if it might fall into the French sphere of influence. The solution to this was found in Belgian neutrality, and a new royal family with close links with Britain—all guaranteed by the Treaty of London (1839), whose violation by Germany in August 1914 brought the long peace to an end.

Other problems between Britain and France were less easily settled, as they were linked with the steady decline of the Turkish Empire, which Britain wished to maintain as a buffer against Austria and Russia in the Balkans. For much of this period, the dominant figure was Palmerston, who, coming late into foreign affairs in 1830 at the age of forty-six, burrowed himself into the grubby premises of the Foreign Office in Whitehall (which at the zenith of its power had a staff of only forty-five) and stayed there as the dominant force for over thirty years—aggressively patriotic, but still, within limits, liberal. In 1847, however, the most celebrated British politician in Europe was not Palmerston but Cobden, the apostle of free trade. He was fêted in capital after capital, and his hosts were sure of one thing—the conservative monarchies were doomed, and the day of liberalism would shortly dawn.

Early in 1848, Marx and Engels drafted the *Communist Manifesto* in London, prophesying, on behalf of a small group of German socialists, a European revolution, to be led by the workers of those countries most advanced towards capitalism. Paris rose up against Louis Philippe on 24 February, then Berlin, Vienna, and the Italian states erupted. But Britain did not follow. There was a momentary panic when the Chartists brought their last great petition to London on 14 April; 10,000 special constables were sworn in; the telegraphs bought over for the week by the Home Office. The constables were potentially more worrying than the Chartists, as middle-class volunteer forces had spearheaded the Continental risings. But their loyalty was absolute; revolutions were something that happened elsewhere. The Chartists dispersed from Kennington Common; Parliament laughed the great petition out.

But there was no repetition of 1793 either. The republican government in Paris wanted to maintain co-operation with Britain, acted firmly against its own radicals, and did not try to export revolution. Palmerston wanted no change in the balance of power, but favoured constitutional regimes and an Austrian withdrawal from Italy. This moderation was scarcely successful, and Britain was unable to guarantee any of the gains that the liberals briefly made. A combination of peasant support bought by land reform and Russian aid, which crushed Hungary and gave Austria a free hand elsewhere, brought the *anciens régimes* back to power—but Austria was now prostrate and the Russians worryingly dominant in Eastern Europe.

Incorporation

Repeal of the Corn Law, the handling of the 1848 emergency, and the rapid expansion of the railways not only made the economic situation more hopeful but underpinned it with a new political consensus. The agricultural interest had been checked, but its farming efficiency enabled it to ride out foreign competition. At the same time the bourgeoisie realized that it had both to co-operate with the old élite in controlling the industrial workers, and to concede enough to the latter to stave off political explosions. In this context (particularly compared with textiles), railways, steamers, and telegraphs were all useful and glamorous, attractive advertisements for industrialization. Functionally, they brought together land, commerce, and industry. And they made lawyers in particular very rich.

By the 1850s the law 'incorporated' the working class—or, at least, their leading members. The 'New Model' trade unions of skilled workers, such as the Engineers and the Carpenters, pressed not for drastic state intervention but for contractual equality. They acted not through public demonstrations but through diplomatic pressure on MPs of both parties. Their procedures and iconography rejected the oaths and mysticism of the old quasi-conspiratorial societies for an almost pedantic legalism, concerned with defending their respectability at the top of the working class.

Economic and social theory moved towards the idea of 'incorporation'. Classical economics had earlier been subversive and pessimistic: one strand of it, in the hands of Marx, remained so. But John Stuart Mill in his *Logic* of 1840 and his *Political Economy* of 1848 reconciled utilitarianism with gradual reform and sympathy for the aims of moderate working-class leaders. Mill found to his surprise that the *Logic*, with its substantial borrowings from the French sociological tradition of Saint-Simon and Auguste Comte, became the orthodoxy of the older universities, which were recuperating from the traumas of the Oxford Movement. But the 'Saint of Rationalism' himself had, in his enthusiasm for the English Romantic poets, gone far to make his blend of utilitarianism, ethical individualism, and reformist 'socialism' acceptable to reformers within the establishment,

An industrialized town depicted in *Contrasts* (1840), by A. W. N. Pugin, in which the great Gothic revival architect attacked classical architecture, religious heterodoxy (the places of worship of no less than nine denominations are shown), and the heartlessness of industrial society with its grim, machine-like buildings. The gaol in front is a version of Bentham's 'Panopticon'.

who broadcast it in the high-minded literary reviews which burgeoned around the mid-century.

In the eyes of the candidates for political incorporation, 'the rule of law' was far from absolute. A. V. Dicey, who applied the phrase to nineteenth-century government, was himself to write in the 1860s: 'John Smith *qua* John Smith cannot be suppressed, but John Smith *qua* artisan can.' But he expected that the extension of the franchise would end such inequities. As, by and large, it did.

Who then remained 'without the law'? The Irish had been wounded too deeply. 'Repeal of the Union' was O'Connell's bequest to a new generation of patriots. Although the Catholic middle class, like the Scots, proved anxious to find niches in the British establishment, Irish nationalists were made more aggressive by the famine, and could in the future count on the aid of their embittered emigrant brethren in America. Settlers in the colonies may have prided themselves on their transplanting of British institutions, but as the Colonial Office was aware, settler notions of law found no place for the rights of the natives. High and low churchmen complained when the courts upheld the vague and all-embracing formulas of the Broad Church estab-lishment. They could not dislodge it but they could indelibly affect the skyline of Victorian cities and the practice of piety.

The intellectuals accepted the notion of political and social evolution—Tennyson's 'freedom slowly broadens down/from precedent to precedent'—long before Darwin's *Origin of Species* appeared in 1859. Although no friend to liberalism, Thomas Carlyle's commendations of self-reliance and the work ethic gave individualism an almost religious quality. John Stuart Mill became a pillar of the mid-Victorian Liberal Party, eccentric only in his desire to extend 'incorporation' to the half of the population whom politics ignored—women (whose slow progress to civic and legal equality started, however, to accelerate during the 1850s). Two more troubled intellects were difficult to pin down. John Ruskin, 'the graduate of Oxford' whose *Modern Painters* was the sensation of 1843, combined reverence for aristocracy with increasingly subversive views on the economy and the environment; though his directly political impact was to be minimal compared to that of Robert Owen. No one savaged the law's delays and inequities more energetically than Charles Dickens, yet no one worried more about the results of revolution and lawlessness. The Circumlocution Office, the Tite Barnacles, Jarndyce *versus* Jarndyce, were balanced by Slackbridge, Madame Defarge, and Bill Sikes, though Dicey got it just about right when, on balance, he put Dickens alongside Shaftesbury as a force pushing public opinion towards 'positive' reforming legislation.

Militant dissent and old radicalism had their own world-view, remote from that of the establishment, but its tentacles reached out towards them. The middle class read 'industrial novels,' such as Disraeli's *Sybil*, in the 1840s, anxious about and intrigued by conditions in the great towns, trying to personalize their problems and reconcile them with individualist morality. But Mrs Gaskell in *Mary Barton* and Charles Kingsley in *Alton Locke* could not provide any such assurance; the only effective solution for their most heroic characters was emigration. Dickens's savage Carlylean satire on Manchester, *Hard Times*, wavered and collapsed when it came to considering any better future for the inhabitants of Coketown.

But few of the Coketown people had time or money to read about what the literati thought of their plight, and little enough was known about what they read, although it was obviously affected by the co-option of the literary radicals by a middle-class public. Henry Mayhew, the pioneer social investigator of the *Morning Chronicle*, just about carried on the journalistic tradition of Cobbett and Hazlitt into the 1860s; Dickens, from the same Bohemian milieu, shifted away from it. We know that the 'labour aristocracy' in the trade unions read what their betters wanted

Crystal Palace, 1850. Using a horse-operated crane to raise the wrought-iron cross beams of the central avenue of the Crystal Palace. Joseph Paxton's design was a pioneer work of prefabrication; workers are already glazing the roof from trolleys. Site work started in August 1850, and was completed by May 1851.

them to read; that the religious kept their Bibles and their *Pilgrim's Progress*; but what of the 'roughs', and 'tavern society'? A folk tradition survived and developed in the fishing ports, among the weavers, and on the farms. Later in the nineteenth century, an American professor discovered two-thirds of the great traditional English ballads still being sung in the 'Farmtouns' of north-east Scotland, where the more plebeian 'bothy ballads' acted as a means of spreading information about farmers among the ploughmen and carters, and the 'Society of the Horseman's Word' conserved a primitive, but effective, trade unionism.

In his novel *Except the Lord* (1953) about the mid-Victorian youth of a radical politician, Joyce Cary takes his hero, Chester Nimmo, into a fairground tent. A troupe of actors are performing *Maria Marten, or the Murder in the Red Barn*, a staple of nineteenth-century melodrama, loosely based on an actual murder which occurred in 1830—the eve of 'Captain Swing'. This was Nimmo's reaction:

The drama that we saw, and that millions had seen, was a story of the cruellest hurt of many inflicted by the rich on the poor. Throughout the play everything possible was done to show the virtue, innocence and helplessness of the poor, and the abandoned cruelty, the heartless self-indulgence of the rich.

And this was one among hundreds of such plays. I have wondered often how such propaganda failed to bring to England also, as to France, Italy, Germany, almost every other nation, a bloody revolution, for its power was incredible. As I say, it was decisive in my own life . . .

Cary, a subtle and historically aware novelist, seems to have sensed here a resentment and grievance deep enough to be concealed by the respectability and self-help of formal working-class politics but for which political 'incorporation', the repetitive rows of sanitarily adequate workmen's dwellings, the increasingly opulent chapels, the still-locked Sunday parks, offered no consolation.

H. C. G. MATTHEW

9. *The Liberal Age*

(1851–1914)

Free Trade: an Industrial Economy Rampant

THE Great Exhibition of 1851 celebrated the ascendancy of the United Kingdom in the market-place of the world, though many of the Continental exhibits, especially those from the German states, gave British manufacturers pause when the high quality of their technology was examined. The Exhibition, sponsored by the court and organized by the aristocracy, reflected Britain's commitment to economic progress and hence to Liberalism. It touched an enthusiastic nerve in the popular mind. For many ordinary people, it was the first occasion for a visit to London, an exhausting but exhilarating long day-trip on one of the special trains which brought visitors from all over the country. The success of the Exhibition astonished contemporaries. Figures for attendance were published daily in the press; by the end, over six million tickets had been sold, and on one day over 109,000 persons visited the 'blazing arch of lucid glass', Joseph Paxton's Crystal Palace which housed the Exhibition in Hyde Park. Its substantial profits were later used to build the museums at South Kensington. The huge crowds were well behaved and openly monarchic. Members of the propertied classes congratulated themselves: the nervous, brittle atmosphere of the 1840s was giving way to the calmer tone of the 1850s, which by the 1860s had become positively self-confident. A street ballad sold at the Exhibition emphasized the curious blend of artisan self-reliance, free-trade internationalism, and monarchic chauvinism which was to define the language of much of British public life for the rest of the century:

> O, surely England's greatest wealth,
> Is an honest working man. . . .
> It is a glorious sight to see
> So many thousands meet,
> Not heeding creed or country,

Each other friendly greet.
Like children of one mighty sire,
May that sacred tie ne'er cease,
May the blood stain'd sword of War give way
To the Olive branch of Peace.

But hark! the trumpets flourish,
Victoria does approach,
That she may long be spared to us
Shall be our reigning toast.
I trust each heart, it will respond,
To what I now propose—
Good will and plenty to her friends,
And confusion to her foes.

The tone of ballads such as this explains the popularity of Henry Temple, Lord Palmerston. When Lord Aberdeen's coalition government of 1852 foundered into war against Russia in the Crimea (1854–6) and then disintegrated when the ineptitude of the war effort was revealed, Palmerston emerged from its ruins as Prime Minister. He held this post, leading the Liberal coalition, with one short interruption until his death in October 1865. Palmerston personified the bombastic self-confidence of Britain as the only world power, and succeeded in being simultaneously an aristocrat, a reformer, a free-trader, an internationalist, and a chauvinist.

The society which the Great Exhibition of 1851 revealed was given more statistical analysis in the Census of the same year. Two facts captured the public imagination. For the first time, more people in the mainland of the United Kingdom lived in towns—albeit often quite small ones—than in the countryside: a dramatic contrast with the past and with any other economy. The free-trade movement accompanied rather than anticipated the commitment of the British economy to manufacturing, transport, and service industries with an urban base. That dream of the Liberal Tories of the 1820s, that the economy could be somehow held in balance between agriculture and industry, was forgotten with the free trade dawn. Agriculture remained easily the largest single industry and indeed increased its competence and output markedly in the 1850s and 1860s. But the growth of population was in the towns, and labourers left the land for the cities. When agriculture faced its crisis in the 1870s with the opening of the North American prairies, there were relatively few left to defend it. The 'Revolt of the Field' in the 1870s was a motley affair as out-of-work labourers struggled to organize themselves as wages fell and magistrates and farmers brought in the troops to harvest the crops. By the 1850s, Britain—especially northern and midland England, South Wales, and southern Scotland—was thus, through the working of Adam Smith's 'invisible hand' of world trade rather than by any conscious political decision, committed to a ride on the roller-coaster of international capitalism, a ride where the travellers could not see beyond the rise or dip ahead of them: no one had been there before. An urban nation had no precedent: perhaps that was why the British dwelt so tenaciously on rural images and traditions.

The other statistic of the 1851 Census that caught the attention of contemporaries was its revelations about religion. It was the only Census ever to attempt to assess religious attendance, or the lack of it. There were difficulties about the statistics, but the main emphasis was indisputable and surprising: England and Wales were only partly church-going, and Anglicans were in only a bare majority of those who attended. Of a total population of 17,927,609, the church-goers were:

Church of England	5,292,551
Roman Catholics	383,630
Protestant Dissenters	4,536,265

Of potential church-goers, over five and a quarter million stayed

The best of artisan housing. The model estate laid out by the Cadburys at Bournville, photographed in 1879.

Working-class housing, probably not the worst, at Staithes, Yorkshire, characteristic of the sort of slum that some councils demolished under the Housing Act of 1890.

at home. The Census was a triumph for non-Anglicans. Their claim to greater political representation and attention was now backed by that most potent of all mid-Victorian weapons, so approved of by Mr Gradgrind, Charles Dickens's Lancastrian manufacturer: 'a fact'.

England in the 1850s was thus increasingly urban, perhaps increasingly secular, certainly increasingly non-Anglican in tone. Mid-Victorian politics reflected these tendencies, all of which pointed towards Liberalism.

Between 1847 and 1868, the Tories (the rump of the party left as protectionists after the 1846 split) lost six general elections running (1847, 1852, 1857, 1859, 1865, 1868). It is clear that the Tories lost these elections; it is less easy to say who won them. Majority governments relied on support from four main groups: the Whigs, the radicals, the Liberals and the Peelites (the followers of Sir Robert Peel in 1846). This support was always liable to disintegration. The classic mid-Victorian political pattern was as follows: a coalition government was made up of all or most of the above groups, compromising and bargaining until they could agree no more and a point of breakdown was reached: the government would go out of office without dissolving Parliament; the Tories would then form a minority government, during which the non-Tory groups would resolve their differences, defeat the Tories, force a dissolution, win the general election, and resume power. This overall pattern explains the minority Tory (Derby/Disraeli) ministries of 1851–2, 1858–9, 1866–8.

The political system between 1846 and 1868 thus excluded the Tories from power, while allowing them occasional periods of minority office. During the same period, the majority coalition first formed by Lord Aberdeen in 1852 gradually fused itself into 'the liberal party', though even when it became regularly referred to by that name in the 1860s it remained fissiparous and liable to disintegration. At the executive level, the Whigs, the Peelites, and Lord Palmerston predominated. To a considerable extent they ruled on sufferance. That great surge of middle-class political awareness exemplified in the Anti-Corn Law League in the 1840s had made it clear to politicians that the old political structure could be maintained only if it came to terms with middle-class expectations. The series of great budgets introduced by the Peelite Chancellor of the Exchequer, William Ewart Gladstone, in the years 1853–5 and 1859–65 went far towards meeting these expectations fiscally. The manufacturing classes wanted free trade: Gladstone saw that they got it.

'Free trade' of course meant much more than simply the abolition of protective tariffs. 'Free trade' or *laissez-faire* were shorthand terms exemplifying a whole philosophy of political, social, and economic organization. John Stuart Mill's *Principles of Political Economy*, first published in 1848, the handbook of mid-Victorian liberalism, put the point in a nutshell: '*Laisser-faire*, in short, should be the general practice: every departure from it, unless required by some great good, is a certain evil.' The presumption was that the State should stand aside. The division which Mill and others made between 'the State' on the one hand and society on the other was based on the assumption that the individual could and should stand alone. Individualism, self-respect, self-reliance, and the organization of voluntary and co-operative societies, these were the keynotes of mid-Victorian liberalism. Thus the economy should be self-regulating, and the individual whether consumer or producer, holding his copy of Samuel Smiles's *Self-Help* (1859), should be free to make what way he could in it.

This view of individualism gained from the widely popular writings of the social evolutionists. Charles Darwin's *On The Origin of Species* (1859) was not a bolt from the blue: it fitted naturally into, as well as transcending, a corpus of writing on evolution. The concept of evolution, and consequently of 'progress', whether on the individual, national, or global level, came to permeate every aspect of Victorian life and thought. Because evolution was determined by laws of science (a view usually described as 'positivism'), man's duty was to discover and obey such laws, not meddle with them. Hence most positivists (such as Walter Bagehot, editor of the influential weekly *Economist*, and Herbert Spencer, author of many works on sociology) were strong *laissez-faire* supporters.

If the individual was to make his way productively, he or she must be prepared and equipped with knowledge: the availability of knowledge and the freedom to comment on it was thus central to a liberal society. Moral choices must be informed choices: self-awareness and self-development in the context of human sympathy were the themes of the novels of George Eliot (Mary Ann Evans) and her own life was a testimony to the trials as well as the liberation of the free spirit in mid-Victorian society.

The abolition in 1855 and 1861 of the 'Taxes on Knowledge' (the stamp duties on newspapers, and the customs and excise duties on paper) epitomized the sort of liberal legislation which was particularly prized. The repeal of these taxes made possible the phenomenon which was both the epitome and the guarantor of liberal Britain—the liberal metropolitan and provincial press. The 1850s and 1860s saw a spectacular expansion of daily and Sunday newspapers, especially in the provinces, overwhelmingly liberal in politics and in general outlook. By 1863, there were over 1,000 newspapers in Britain, the vast majority of very recent foundation. For example, in Yorkshire in 1867, 66 of the 86 local newspapers had been founded since 1853. In London, the *Daily Telegraph*, re-founded in 1855 as a penny daily and as the flagship of the liberal press, had a circulation of almost 200,000 in 1871, far outstripping *The Times*. The new provincial press took its tone from the *Telegraph*, and that tone was unabashedly and enthusiastically progressive. A typical example is this leader commenting on Gladstone's tour of the Newcastle shipyards in 1862:

When we pull a political pansy for Lord Derby [the Tory leader], and tell him 'that's for remembrance', it is because the violent fallacies and frenzies of Protection are not to be forgotten simply because they are forgiven . . . With ten years' honour upon her green laurels, and the French treaty [of free trade signed in 1860] in her hand—the emblem of future conquests—we have enshrined Free Trade at last in a permanent seat.

By the 1860s, free trade—in its specific sense of an absence of protective tariffs—had become a central orthodoxy of British politics, almost as entrenched as the Protestant succession. The triumph of the classical political economists was complete, in the sense that the cardinal tenet of their faith was established as a political principle so widely accepted that only a deliberately perverse or self-confessedly unreconstructed politician would deny it. Front-bench Tory politicians quickly took the view that if their party was again to become a majority party, they must accept that protection was 'not only dead but damned', as Disraeli said. Tory budgets became as impeccably free-trading as Liberal ones.

Outside the area of fiscal policy, there was less agreement about how far 'free trade' should go. Pressure groups within the Liberal movement in the 1850s and 1860s promoted a large range of 'negative' free-trade measures: the abolition of established Churches, the abolition of compulsory church rates, the abolition of religious tests for entry into Oxford and Cambridge and public offices, the removal of restrictions upon the transfer or use of land, the end of a civil service based on patronage. In addition to these, there was in the 1860s a general movement in the constituencies for further parliamentary reform—a demand welcomed by some but not all of the Liberal MPs. The Liberal Party legislating on such matters was not really a 'party' in the modern sense of the word. It was rather a loose coalition of complex, interlocking allegiances, the most basic of which was its commitment to a free-trading economy. Within the coalition nestled many reforming interests, especially of a religious sort. A great religious revival in the 1860s added to the number of religious activists within the Liberal Party, and to the enthusiasm with which they both aired their opinions and worked for the party's success. Roman Catholics, nonconformists, and even secularists found voices within this broadly-based movement for progress—the voices were given a common accent by their hostility to Anglicanism and the established Church. Non-Anglicanism was, throughout the century, perhaps the most important social reason for voting Liberal. Paradoxically, however, the leadership of the coalition was uniformly Anglican, though of a moderate and reforming kind. There was, therefore, considerable dispute between the leadership of the coalition and its more militant supporters about the speed of reform. On the whole, the leadership—Palmerston, Lord John Russell, Gladstone—wanted moderate reform which would strengthen the Anglican Church overall, while the radical rank and file wanted step-by-step reform which would lead to the eventual disestablishment of the Anglican Church. Both groups could thus agree on limited measures such as the abolition of compulsory church rates while disagreeing on the ultimate ends of their policies. The crowning success of this sort of approach to politics was the disestablishment of the Anglican Church in Ireland in 1869.

The participation of the articulate members of the working classes within the Liberal Party, especially at the constituency level, was of great importance. In the 1830s and early 1840s, the six points of the Chartists had constituted a demand which, in terms of the politics of the day, could not be incorporated by the classes holding political power. By the late 1850s, radical movement for constitutional reform, often led by ex-Chartists, demanded only changes in the franchise, and of these, enfranchisement of the male head of each household at most ('household suffrage'). It was not difficult for political leaders in both parties, but especially in the Liberal Party, to come to terms with such requests. They also had their own reasons for wanting to change the system. Some Tories wanted to change it because their experience from 1847 onwards showed that they could not win a general election within the existing system. Some Liberals, including Gladstone and Lord John Russell, wanted to make marginal extensions to the franchise so as to include more liberal artisans, sturdy individualists who would support the Liberals' programme of retrenchment and reform. Some radicals, such as John Bright, wanted a 'household suffrage' to give a more full-blooded basis to Liberalism, though even they were quick to point out that they did not want votes given to what was known as 'the residuum' (that is, paupers, the unemployed, the 'thriftless', men with no property at all). Some Liberals such as Robert Lowe, radical enough on ordinary legislation, distrusted any change leading to 'democracy' as they believed the 'intelligent class' would be swamped by it. Some Tories such as the future Lord Salisbury feared a household suffrage would lead to an attack on property through increased direct taxes such as the income tax. Some Whigs saw no reason to change a system which always returned non-Tory Parliaments.

Palmerston reflected the views of this last group, and won a great election victory in 1865 without a pledge to franchise reform. He died that autumn. Russell, his successor as Prime Minister, brought in with Gladstone in 1866 a very moderate reform bill dealing mainly with towns, on which their ministry broke up, some of their party withdrawing support because the bill did too much, others because it did too little. The third of the Derby/Disraeli minority Tory administrations then brought in its own bill for the towns, thus selling the pass of the anti-reformers' position. Reform of some sort became certain: the Liberals had begun their customary regrouping when Disraeli unexpectedly announced his acceptance of a household suffrage amendment: the bill then passed, in a form a great deal more

The Forth Bridge under construction 1888–9.
Completing the railway network, which reached its zenith in the 1890s.

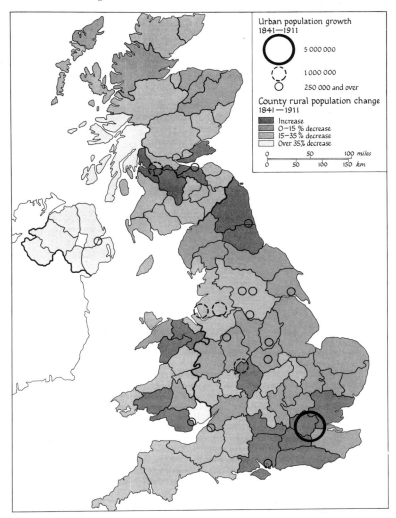

Urban population growth 1841–1911

dramatic and sweeping than the Russell–Gladstone bill of the previous year. The franchise system of 1832 was ended: the parameters of urban politics until 1918 were established (similar voting privileges were granted to men in the counties in 1884–5). In an extremely confused situation in 1868, the Liberals seemed to reconfirm their 1865 election position as the dominant party by winning the general election with the huge majority of 112. In fact, the 1867 Reform Act had changed the rules of the political game in such a way that a majority Tory government again became possible—but it was to be a Tory government under Disraeli in 1874 which made no serious attempt to reverse any of the main Liberal achievements of the previous thirty years, certainly not the centre-piece of free trade.

The early years of Gladstone's first government (1868–74) were the culmination of these reforming pressures: by 1874 many of the demands of mid-century Liberalism were fulfilled. In addition to disestablishing the Irish Church, the Liberals in the 1860s and early 1870s had abolished compulsory church rates, the 'taxes on knowledge', religious tests for Oxford and Cambridge, and the purchase of commissions in the army; they had legislated on Irish land, and on education for England and Scotland; they had opened the civil service to entrance by competition and they had made capitalism relatively safe for the investor by introducing limited liability—all this in addition to their preoccupation with free trade finance, proper government accounting, minimum budgets, and retrenchment.

Though there was the usual tug and tussle of political bargaining, this great reforming surge had not been seriously opposed. Even the establishment of the Anglican Church—whose defence *in toto* had been a central rallying point of Toryism in the first half of the century—had been ended in part clearly and efficiently: what had in the 1830s been merely a radical dream had by the 1870s become reality, and almost without apparent struggle. The Tories' ultimate card, the unelected House of Lords, had been played in only a limited way—to delay repeal of the paper duties, to delay church rate repeal, the ballot, and the abolition of religious tests at the universities. The propertied and labouring classes had collaborated in a great clearing of the decks of the Liberal ship of state.

The advent of 'free trade' as the prevailing ethos coincided with an economic boom, lasting from the early 1850s to the early 1870s. Contemporaries saw the first as causing the second; economic historians have been more sceptical. The removal of tariff barriers probably had only a marginal impact on the British economy, but the ascendancy of 'free trade', in its larger sense of a national commitment to economic progress, was closely related to an entrepreneurial enthusiasm which all classes seem to have shared. The mid-century boom was not, in percentage terms, very spectacular, and it was linked to a mild inflation. But it was none the less extremely important, for it seemed to show that the 'condition of England' question which had been so much a preoccupation of the 1820–50 period could be solved—was being solved—by market forces working within the existing social and political structure. Even the distress caused by the 'cotton famine' of the 1860s in Lancashire—when the cotton mills were cut off by the American Civil War from their traditional source of raw material, the plantations in the Southern States—produced little prolonged political reaction, and the propertied classes congratulated themselves that local initiative and voluntary subscriptions had seemed to be sufficient to allow the Westminster government to avoid accepting any direct responsibility for the sufferings of the Lancastrian work-force (though in fact a government loan scheme had also been important).

Compared with any other country, the British economy in the period 1850–70 was extraordinary in its complexity and in the range of its products and activities. It was strong in the basic raw materials of an early industrial economy—coal and iron—and it increased its world ascendancy in these two commodities as Continental countries imported British coal and iron to supply the basic materials for their own industrialization. An energetic manufacturing sector pressed forward with a huge range of items, from ships and steam engines through textiles to the enormous variety of small manufactured goods which adorned Victorian houses and, by their export in British ships, 'Victorianized' the whole trading world. This intense industrial activity rested on a sound currency and on a banking system which, though it had its failures, was comparatively stable and was, especially from the 1870s, gaining an increasingly important role in the economy.

A Shifting Population: Town and Country

This surge of economic progress produced a nation and an economy whose preoccupations were by 1870 largely industrial and urban. The growth of towns, which some had thought in 1851 could hardly be continued, intensified. By 1901, only one-fifth of the population of England and Wales lived in what may be called 'rural areas'; that is, 80 per cent of the population was urbanized, a far greater proportion than in any European country, and one which remained little changed until the 1970s. By 1901, there were seventy-four towns with over 50,000 inhabitants and London, 'the metropolis' as Victorians called it, grew from 2.3 million in 1851 to 4.5 million in 1911 (or 7.3 million if we

Victorian eclecticism: Birmingham advertisements at the time of the 1868 general election. Note the anti-papal broadsheets at the bottom of the illustration.

include all its suburbs). The most rapid growth was not in the already established 'industrial revolution' cities, such as Liverpool and Manchester, but in the clusters of towns around the industrial heartland, towns such as Salford. These areas of urban sprawl went to make up what Patrick Geddes, the late-Victorian theorist of town planning, called 'conurbations', that is large areas of industrial and urban land in which several cities merge to form what is really a single non-rural unit. By 1911, Britain had seven such areas, at a time when no European country had more than two. These were: Greater London (7.3 million), south-east Lancashire (2.1 million), the West Midlands (1.6 million), West Yorkshire (1.5 million), Merseyside (1.2 million), Tyneside (0.8 million), and central Clydeside (about 1.5 million)—all this in a nation with a population of only 40 million on the mainland in 1911. Some towns, such as the iron and steel town of Middlesbrough, grew from virtually nothing to a population of 120,000 in half a century. Most of these conurbations contained a significant Irish community, and their politics consequently tended to be more 'orange and green' than elsewhere. At the end of the century London and Leeds also absorbed large Jewish communities, the victims of an Eastern European 'rural depopulation' as ferocious as the Irish famine.

Urban growth at this sort of pace was, of course, to be a common phenomenon in underdeveloped countries in the twentieth century, but in the nineteenth it had no precedent. It is not easy to generalize about these towns. Styles and standards of architecture varied enormously, from the indestructible stone tenements of Glasgow, through the 'back-to-back, two-up, two-down' little houses in the mining towns, often built of poor-quality brick, to the decorous suburbs of the lower and upper middle classes. A common feature of this housing was that it was almost all leased or rented—owner-occupiers were rare, though becoming more common by the end of the century. Some towns were well planned by civically-minded local councils, with parks, libraries, concert halls, and baths; others were left to the mercy of the speculative builder.

These growing towns were dominated by the railways, which created for the first time a nationally integrated economy. They transformed the centres of towns by the space which their stations and marshalling yards took up, they made it possible for better-off people to live away from the town centre by providing cheap transport from the suburbs, and they covered everything with soot. Filth and noise characterized Victorian cities—filth from the trains, the chimneys of factories and houses, and the horses, noise from the carts and carriages and horses on the cobblestones. When motor transport began to replace horses in the early twentieth century, everyone noticed how relatively quiet and clean town centres became. But noise, filth, and bad housing are relative to what people are accustomed to: it was only slowly that the demand for improvement in urban life became a powerful one. For many Victorians, production was its own justification, a view well expressed by Florence, Lady Bell, in her book *At The Works*, a classic study of a classic industrial town, Middlesbrough, a town given over to one pursuit and one only, the making of iron:

In default of a romantic past, of a stately tradition, the fact of this swift gigantic growth has given to Middlesbrough a romance and dignity of another kind, the dignity of power, of being able to stand erect by its sheer strength on no historical foundation, unsupported by the pedestals of Time . . . And although it may not have the charm and beauty of antiquity, no manufacturing town . . . can fail to have an interest and picturesqueness all its own . . . Tall chimneys, great uncouth shapes of kilns and furnaces that appear through the smoke of a winter afternoon like turrets and pinnacles . . . Twilight and night are the conditions under which to see an ironmaking town, the pillars of cloud by day, the pillars of fire by night.

The dynamism of the towns was, in the twenty years after the Great Exhibition, and partly inspired by the machinery exhibited at it, mirrored in the countryside. 'High farming'—capital spending on fertilizers, drainage, buildings, farm machinery such as reapers and threshers, roads linking with the new railways—apparently belied the argument that free trade spelt doom for the countryside, and led to considerable modernization, moral as well as physical, and even in the countryside there were fears for the continuance of traditional religion, as many turned to nonconformity and some to materialism.

An energetic and aggressive farming generation won the profits which maintained the sedate, leisured, county society depicted in Anthony Trollope's novels of Barsetshire. In 1868, 80 per cent of food consumed in the United Kingdom was still home-produced. But despite 'high farming', many areas, especially in Ireland and Scotland, remained woefully under-capitalized, the foot-plough and hand-winnowing still being common in the north and west Highlands in the early twentieth century.

In the 1870s, a series of bad harvests, the opening of the North American prairies, faster and cheaper shipping thence and from the overseas wool-growing areas, led to 'the great depression'. Only milk, hay, and straw production were not open to harsh foreign competition. In particular, the price of grain, the characteristic product of the eastern side of the country, fell dramatically, but farmers, especially the smaller ones, were slow to accept the permanence of this fall, or to adapt to the new demand for dairy products. The pastoral west was less severely affected. The significance of agriculture in the economy declined as towns grew, a decline made swifter by the depression: in 1851 agriculture accounted for 20.3 per cent of the national income, in 1901 only 6.4 per cent, and the majority of British food and agricultural raw materials such as wool were imported—a fact which was to be of considerable strategic importance. Cries for the protection of agriculture received little response, even within the Tory Party—certainly not to the point of an alteration to the fiscal system of free trade. Some Liberal land reformers—for whom protection was axiomatically ruled out—advocated smallholdings (the 'three acres and a cow' campaign of 1885) as a solution; the establishment of the Crofting Commission (1886)

Varieties of agriculture. '*High farming' (above)* involved heavy capitalization: this steam plough, built by John Fowler of Leeds, was fuelled by straw. In many Celtic areas, improvements were minimal: these crofters in Skye *(below), c.*1885, are using wooden foot-ploughs to prepare the soil for potatoes.

for the Scottish Highlands, empowered to establish crofting communities free from landlord interference, was the only substantial achievement on the mainland, though a notable one in its long-term results.

The attraction of higher wages for fewer hours in the towns, mechanization in the 1850s and 1860s, depression in the last quarter of the century, all led to extensive rural depopulation—a great exodus mostly to the Scottish and English towns, some to the coalfields (especially in Wales), some to the colonies, some to the army. Between 1861 and 1901 the decrease in the total of rural male labourers in England and Wales was just over 40 per cent; the total of women, less easily employable in the towns, decreased less dramatically, leaving a marked imbalance of the sexes in the countryside, though many unmarried women found their way into domestic service in the towns aided by such agencies as the Girls' Friendly Society.

All this left rural society demoralized and neglected, with the passivity characteristic of communities in decay. Thomas Hardy's novels, whose span of publication (1872–96) covered almost exactly the years of the agricultural depression, captured majestically the uncontrollable and distant forces which seemed to determine the fate of the country communities and their inhabitants. Hardy wrote of country habits and traditions which had passed away but, though historical in form, the novels had a contemporary overtone. *The Mayor of Casterbridge* described the fate of Michael Henchard, a corn merchant whose failure to adapt to new methods of trading brought him to ruin. Hardy observed of him at the moment of his financial crash: 'The movements of his mind seemed to tend to the thought that some power was working against him.' The 'general drama of pain' which the Wessex novels depict was the disintegration of a civilization. Surveying his novels as a whole in 1895 Hardy observed: 'The change at the root of this has been the recent supplanting of the class of stationary cottagers, who carried on the local traditions and humours, by a population of more or less migratory labourers, which has led to a break of continuity in local history, more fatal than any other thing to the preservation of legend, folk-lore, close intersocial relations, and eccentric individualities. For these the indispensable conditions of existence are attachment to the soil of one particular spot by generation after generation.' Fortunately, Cecil Sharp, Marjorie Kennedy-Fraser, and other folklore and folk-song and dance historians recorded something of the quality of British rural life before it was wholly lost.

The breaking up of country customs was encouraged by Whitehall and Westminster. Educational measures—for example the 1872 Scottish Education Act—worked to Anglicize the Gaelic-speakers of Scotland and Ireland and the Welsh-speakers of Wales, and to equip the peasantry for urban life. Between 1850 and 1900 rural change and education policy dealt those languages a powerful and in Scotland almost a fatal blow. In Wales, however, local initiative secured the teaching of Welsh in schools from 1889.

In some areas, there was a good deal of movement between town and country, as migrant workers left the towns for the harvest, and poaching by the inhabitants of small towns in the surrounding countryside was common. Some industrial workers, especially coal-miners, lived in villages with moors and fields at their doors and their sports such as whippet and pigeon racing had rural associations. Middle-class people took advantage of low land values to buy up a country place. For the financially sharp members of the propertied classes, the countryside became an expensive playground, a place for 'week-ending'; but for many urban-dwellers in the great cities it became a remote, even dangerous, place populated by a curious people with antique accents, clothes, and manners. Oscar Wilde's comedy, *The Importance of Being Earnest* (1895), caught the metropolitan tone:

The agricultural depression. Farm labourers evicted at Milbourne St. Andrew, Dorset, in 1874, for belonging to Joseph Arch's National Agricultural Labourers Union.

LADY BRACKNELL. . . . land has ceased to be either a profit or a pleasure. It gives one position, and prevents one from keeping it up. That's all that can be said about land.

JACK. I have a country house with some land, of course, attached to it, about fifteen hundred acres, I believe; but I don't depend on that for my real income. In fact, as far as I can make out, the poachers are the only people who make anything out of it.

LADY BRACKNELL. A country house! . . . You have a town house, I hope? A girl with a simple, unspoilt nature, like Gwendolen, could hardly be expected to reside in the country.

None the less, the image of a happy rural past lingered in the town-dweller's mind: regardless of class, whenever he (or she) could, he lived in a house with a garden, and perhaps rented an allotment: he recreated the country in the town while ignoring the reality of its sufferings. Architecture and town-planning increasingly reflected nostalgia for the village, culminating in the Bournville experiment of Cadbury's, the Quaker employers, and in the 'Garden City' movement at the end of the century.

The Masses and the Classes: the Urban Worker

The urbanization of the mass of the population and the decline of rural areas not surprisingly had profound social consequences for all classes of the population. The greatest fear of the propertied classes in the first half of the century had been of a revolutionary working class or classes: that no such class emerged is perhaps the most striking feature of the second half of the century. Most industrial labourers left no memorial save the products of their labours: the details of their lives, their aspirations, hopes, beliefs, likes, dislikes, habits, and enthusiasms are largely lost. In the empire, detailed reports on all such things were drawn up with all the efficiency of the trained civil servant fascinated by an alien race, but at home it was only at the end of the century that systematic observation of the living customs of the British urban poor began. Henry Mayhew's impressionistic *London Labour and the London Poor: a Cyclopaedia of the Condition and Earnings of those that will work, those that cannot work, and those that will not work* (1861–2) made a start, but an unsystematic one, and one which was not followed up. What we do know suggests highly complex and varied patterns of life, with regionalism and religion often playing an important part.

The standard of living of some members of the labouring population began to increase quite fast. Between 1860 and 1914 real wages doubled. The years of particularly rapid growth were the boom years of 1868–74, and the period 1880–96; during the latter period real wages went up by almost 45 per cent. By the 1880s, for the first time in the century, a significant number began to enjoy leisure time. Some money (though not much) was coming to be available for more than the essentials of food, housing, and clothing. Strikingly, this surplus coincided not with a rise but with a fall in the birth-rate, which affected the propertied classes from the 1870s, the working classes, mirroring their social superiors, a little later. The extra cash was thus not absorbed by extra children. This was a startling and unprecedented development which falsified the predictions of the classical political economists from Malthus to Marx, that the labouring classes were condemned to subsistence levels of living through the 'iron law of wages' because any surplus wealth would be absorbed by extra children. Control of family size opened the way to the relative prosperity of the British working class since the 1880s. How and why this happened is hardly known. Men and women married later; they may have made some use of the rather unreliable birth-control devices popularized from the 1870s; women may have used abortion as a regular means of birth-prevention.

The term 'working classes' (the Victorians almost always used the plural) of course covered a wide spectrum. Charles Booth's survey of *Life and Labour of the People in London,* begun in the late 1880s, found six main categories: 'high-paid labour'; 'regular standard earnings'; 'small regular earnings'; 'intermittent earnings'; 'casual earnings'; and what Booth called the 'lowest class'. 'Regular standard earners' made up the largest group—as much as the total of the other five categories put together—and it was this group of men and women which particularly reduced the size of their families, saw their real incomes rise, and began to be aware of their potential power within the economy.

The growing prosperity of the 'regular standard earners' led them to join trade unions as a means of safeguarding their gains and of negotiating for better wages and conditions of work. The unions of the mid-century were for the most part rather narrowly-based 'craft unions', made up of men who jealously guarded the privileged and hard-won ascendancy among their fellow employees given them by their qualifications through apprenticeship or their responsibility for skilled machine-working. The steady demand for skilled labour reinforced the influence and status of the craft unions, and some technical developments, for example in the building of iron ships, expanded rather than diminished their importance. In the 1870s and especially in the 1880s these began to be supplemented to include many more of the workmen in regular employment. Rising living standards made this possible, for trade union membership was quite expensive. The unions existed not only, or even chiefly, for purposes of wage negotiation, but also for a wide variety of 'self-help' benefits and the trade unions were closely linked to, and sometimes synonymous with, the Friendly Societies. The first of these benefits for any self-respecting workman was the burial benefit—the avoidance of a funeral paid for by the workhouse—but many unions also had sickness and unemployment benefits, for the State as yet offered no help for victims of temporary calamity, still less did it assist those more permanently disadvantaged, save for the ultimate safety net of the workhouse.

Trade union activity grew in a context which seems most curious to the post-1945 observer. The twenty years after 1874 were characterized by a sharp and substantial deflation—that is, prices (and, to a lesser extent, wages) fell. On the other hand, *real* wages, for those in regular employment, rose. But this was hard for trade unionists to come to terms with: a man will hardly believe that an employer who reduces his wages may still be leaving him better off. The new trade unionism was thus concerned to defend working-class wages: it was a reaction, as much as a positive force. It had little ideology except for the

Respectability at leisure. The crowd at Tottenham Hotspur v. Sunderland, 20 January 1912. Note the formality of dress: stiff collars, ties and even a few bowler hats.

concept of solidarity. Some socialists played a part in the most publicized strikes of the period—the strike at Bryant and May's match factory in 1888, and the London Dock Strike for the 'dockers' tanner' in 1889, both of which attracted much middle-class interest, probably because they both occurred in London under the noses of the radicals. But these were not typical strikes (indeed the London Dock Strike was not conducted by a union: the union was formed *after* the strike finished); nor should the role of the 'socialists' who led them, such as John Burns, be over stressed. Even most of the trade union leadership was staunchly Gladstonian: Karl Marx and his works were virtually unknown, outside a small circle, in the country where he had spent almost all his working life; the writings of the socialist groups which sprang up in the 1880s reached only a tiny audience. Indeed, the resistance of the working classes to socialist ideas made them the despair of middle-class intellectuals.

If the trade union was the institutional expression of a growing working-class self-awareness, shared leisure activities, especially for the male wage-earner, further encouraged this sense of solidarity. Watching Association Football—a game founded by public schools and university amateur clubs, but essentially professional by the mid-1880s—became the regular relaxation of males (and almost without exception only males) in industrial towns from Portsmouth to Aberdeen. In the last quarter of the nineteenth century a football club was established in every self-respecting industrial town. Some of these teams reflected the religious schisms of the cities (Catholic Celtic and Protestant Rangers in Glasgow, Catholic Everton and Protestant Liverpool on Merseyside). All of them encouraged a local patriotism, enthusiasm, and self-identification on the part of the followers, which was the envy of many a political organizer. Football was the product of a highly-organized urban society: the regularity and complexity of the Cup (from 1871) and League (from 1888) competitions, the need for sustained as well as immediate interest, the budgeting for the weekly entrance fee and, perhaps, train fare for the away match, the large, self-regulating crowds, all reflected a disciplined and ordered work-force, content to pay for its leisure watching *others* play for a club organized usually by local businessmen. Sustaining attention over the whole of the football 'season' gave the working man something of the wider perspective of time familiar to his agricultural counterpart from the climatic seasons.

The growing popularity of the much lengthier, more idio-syncratic and socially integrative game of cricket, organized through the County Championship from 1873, defies any such simple explanation; it was, perhaps, a testimony to the survival of individuality despite industrialization and the division of labour. W. G. Grace, the Gloucestershire physician whose autocratic command of the pitches and players of the day allowed him to set many batting, bowling, and fielding records still hardly surpassed, became almost as much of a national hero as Fred Archer, the champion jockey in 1874–86. Grace's great and much-caricatured beard caused him to be confused in the popular mind with Lord Salisbury—a confusion probably of some advantage to the latter.

Travel for the working class had hitherto taken place in the context of a desperate search for new employment or accommodation. By the 1880s it was starting to be recreational: the trip to the seaside organized individually or by the firm on one of the new Bank Holidays became for many an annual excursion. Resorts—Blackpool, Morecambe, Scarborough, Southend, Eastbourne, Portobello—rose to meet the demand and to stimulate it further. For the holidays of the working classes were almost always spent in towns: 'the beach' meant the pier, sideshows,

The seafront at Blackpool. The complete urbanization of the Blackpool seafront in the 1890s reflected the priorities of its clientele, chiefly Lancastrian textile workers.
By 1911 there were over 4,000 landladies in Blackpool.

and bathing cabins, backed by hotels, boarding houses, and shops. Radicals and socialists in the 1890s attempted to broaden this tradition through rambling and cycling clubs which made trips into the countryside, but the appeal of these was more to the lower middle class than to the working class.

The development of a popular press and the rapid nation-wide communication made possible by the electric telegraph encouraged the other great working-class recreation: betting, especially on horses, and, through the nascent pools industry, on football. Betting offered the pot of gold at the end of the rainbow: leisure could be fun, but it might also be profitable—though, of course, it rarely was.

The more prosperous sections of the working classes thus began to share a little the prosperity and expectations which the industrial revolution had brought the propertied classes half a century earlier. Diets improved a little, with meat, milk, and vegetables in addition to bread, potatoes, and beer. The quality of housing was a little better; houses and people were cleaner as soap became cheaper and generally available. Books, photographs, the odd item of decorative furniture, began to adorn the regularly employed workman's home. Respectability, in the sense of having the use of money to demonstrate some degree of control of living style, some sense of settled existence, some raising of the horizon beyond the weekly wage packet, became a goal, encouraged by the spread of hire-purchase companies, which managed much of the spending of the working classes' surplus.

The rise in the standard of living of the wage-earning population was important, but it must be kept in perspective. The second half of the nineteenth century was punctuated by short-term dislocations of the economy in each decade. Many contemporaries believed that the years from the mid-1870s to the mid-1890s constituted a 'great depression', when profits fell. As we have seen, this phrase is certainly true with respect to agriculture. With respect to industry as a whole, it was a period of readjustment rather than depression, but for the working person 'readjustment' usually meant misery. It was during the 1880s that the word 'unemployment' was given its modern meaning.

Religion, in the sense of church-going, played little direct part in the life of most working people in the towns. 'It is not that the Church of God has lost the great towns; it has never had them,' wrote A. F. Winnington-Ingram (an Anglican clergyman) in 1896. Protestant churches both Anglican and nonconformist were unsuccessful in persuading rural labourers to continue as

Cycling, 1885. The bicycle offered women freedom of movement and an escape from the chaperone.

church-goers as they entered the towns, and they failed to reach the majority of those born in towns, despite the indirect allurements of charitable hand-outs and the provision of education in Sunday Schools, and the direct approach of missions, revival crusades, and the Church and Salvation Armies. In London in 1902–3 only about 19 per cent of the population regularly went to church, and those that did came largely from the socially superior areas. The figures would probably be a little better in provincial cities and considerably better in small towns. Only the Roman Catholics attracted significant working-class attendance: their organization was geared to this, and they skilfully appealed through church social organizations and clubs to the Irishness as much as to the Catholicism of their congregations.

This is not to say that the working classes were wholly ignorant of religion. 'Rites of passage' (especially weddings and funerals) remained popular even when secular alternatives became available. Nor do non-church-goers appear to have been actively hostile to religion except when it took on a Romish or ritualistic form and became linked with the abrasive relations between Irish immigrants and the host community. Rather, especially in the case of Anglicanism, they resented a religion so obviously linked to the status and power of the propertied classes. Not going to church, in a society whose articulate members so strongly advocated the practice, was a protest as well as a sign of indifference.

Clerks and Commerce: the Lower Middle Class

For the middle classes, the decades after 1850 offered a golden age of expansion. In 1851 the middle class was a fairly small and reasonably easily identified group: the professions, business men, bankers, large shopkeepers, and the like. The gulf between this group and the working classes was deep. By the end of the century, a far more complex pattern had emerged. A large, intermediate group, which may be called the lower middle class, was called into being by economic change. The service sector of the economy had become much greater and more complex. As the British economy became gradually as much commercial as industrial, it created a vast army of white-collar workers to manage and serve in the retailing, banking, accounting, advertising, and trading sectors. The management of factories passed from a paternal family tradition to a new class of professional managers, and the bureaucracies of manufacturing industry grew swiftly. The civil service, both local and central, began to expand rapidly as government spent more on new responsibilities, especially on the education system created by the Act of 1870. Shops, offices, and telephone exchanges offered new opportunities for the employment of women. London was particularly affected by the changes which created a vast army of City workers, trained at the new polytechnics, commuting by train or by the new underground railways from the suburbs being built on what was then the edge of the city, or from towns

One of the national telephone company's London exchanges, 1900. Women's employment benefited from the expanding service sector: by 1911 there were 14,000 female telegraph and telephone operators, 183,000 teachers, 475,000 shop assistants, and over a million domestic servants.

such as Croydon which developed rapidly from the 1870s as dormitories for City clerks. Suburbanization was the characteristic innovation of city life in the second half of the century: rows of neat houses, terraced or semi-detached, with small gardens, often both at front and rear of the house, testified to the successful propertied aspirations of this new society.

These were families which had done well out of the Liberal age: Liberalism called for individual achievement, and this class had responded. It valued merit, competition, respectability, efficiency, and a sense of purpose. It respected achievement, money, and success. Uncertain of its own position in the social order, it responded to those confident of their own right to command: it respected hierarchy. In this, it differed considerably from the sturdy individualism of Liberals in the 1850s, sustained by the pre-industrial ethos of 'the good old cause' and the rallying cries of the seventeenth century; its search for a secure place in the social order made it the vehicle by which the Conservatives became a party with a stake in the cities. In some places, particularly in small towns with a nonconformist tradition such as the market towns of Wales and Scotland, it ran the town, and the self-confidence this gave it, together with its nonconformity, helped to keep it Liberal. In large towns, it tended to act as a collaborating class, offering the aristocracy and the upper middle class the means of power in exchange for recognition and status.

The *Daily Mail*, founded by the Harmsworth brothers in 1896, with its highly efficient national distribution, soon had the provincial press on the run, and was the archetypal reading matter for the lower middle class; initially liberal–imperialist in tone, it crossed over to the Unionists during the Boer War. 'By office boys for office boys', Lord Salisbury contemptuously remarked of it and its clientele.

The Propertied Classes

The upper middle classes divided into two. Those working in the professions—doctors, lawyers, the clergy of the established church, civil servants of the administrative grade—shared a common background of education at university and, increasingly, at one of the public schools. In many towns, they lived more exclusively than in the first half of the century, moving out of the town centre to imposing villas in the suburbs. The habit of sending children away to boarding school increased the national outlook of this class and weakened the roots of its individual members in the localities. The spirit of Thomas Arnold of Rugby, as interpreted and modified by his successors, pervaded the outlook of the professions. Education through a syllabus dominated by Greek, Latin, and ancient history, moralized at by Broad-Church Anglicanism, 'fitted for life' by incessant games (rugby football in the winter, cricket and athletics in the summer) designed to occupy every idle moment, the ethos of the professional classes was worthy but sterile. Increasingly designed to provide men to run an empire, it neglected the needs of an industrial state.

The manufacturing middle class was to some extent affected by this. Instead of sending their children early into the family firm, manufacturers increasingly sent them into the educational process designed for the professional classes. Sons of the owners of cotton mills and shipyards learnt Greek and rugby football, and not, as their German counterparts were doing, science and accounting. Sons educated in this way often showed little interest in returning to manufacturing life, and the preservation of the entrepreneurial and manufacturing ethos which had been one of the chief motors of industrial progress in the first half of the century became increasingly difficult. Such men found commerce more congenial than industry, and went into the expanding banking sector where the sweat and gore of the factory floor and labour relations were sterilized into columns of figures.

The British economy came to rely more and more on the competence of such men. A huge balance of payments deficit on imports and exports of commodities began to open (£27 million in 1851, £134 million by 1911). This was turned into an overall surplus by 'invisible earnings'—the profits of banking, insurance, shipping, and the income from British capital invested abroad. Income from services (£24 million in 1851, £152 million in 1911) and from overseas dividends (£12 million in 1851, £188 million in 1911) seemed to become the vital elements in British prosperity, and with them came a middle class whose chief expertise was in handling money, not men or products.

This important development in British social and economic life was as unplanned as the earlier phase of manufacturing industrialization. It was the product of that industrialization in two ways. As the 'workshop of the world' sold its products abroad, it stimulated other economies which cried out for capital they could not themselves supply. Competition with such economies, and depression in some sectors of manufacturing in the 1880s, lowered the rate of profit on British manufacturing, and the 'invisible hand' thus pointed the way to the expansion of the service industries.

Again, this tendency must not be exaggerated, nor its novelty over-stressed. The easy fusion of land, industry, and commerce was a well-established English tradition. It had prevented the aristocracy becoming a caste in the Continental style, and it had offered the reward of status to the manufacturer. Some took this reward, others, especially nonconformists, did not seek it. Manufacturing and manufacturers remained a powerful force in England. But the primacy of manufacturers, 'the monarchy of the middle classes', so much expected and feared in the first half of the century, did not occur. In part this must be explained by the extent to which the aristocracy neutralized the political and

Styles of education.
(*Above*) nature study in
an Elementary School,
c.1908 and (*below*) a
dormitory in Christ's
Hospital (public
school) in the late
nineteenth century.

social effects of 'trade' by absorbing it.

The middle classes were Protestant, and actively so. They were increasingly important within the hierarchy of the Anglican Church and the universities: the latter now catered largely for them as the passing of professional and civil-service examinations became required through the series of reforms consequent upon the Northcote–Trevelyan Report of 1854. Respectability, the need to maintain the house, and to pay the servants and school and university fees, encouraged restriction in the size of middle-class families from the 1870s, that is, rather earlier than the same phenomenon among the working classes.

Smaller families were also sought by middle-class women who were beginning to expect more from life than the privilege of breeding children and running the household. Women, thus partially liberated, played an important role in charities, churches, local politics, and the arts, especially music. With great difficulty, some forced themselves upon the universities (they were allowed to attend lectures and take examinations, but not degrees), and from the late 1870s women's colleges were founded at Oxford, Cambridge, and London. The professions remained barred to women, but a few succeeded in practising as doctors. The upper levels of nursing were, however, the nearest most women could get into a professional career.

Pomp and Circumstance

The aristocracy (and gentry) was only partly affected by these changes. Of the three great classes in British social life, it probably changed the least in Victoria's reign. The aristocracy was, as the socialist writer Beatrice Webb observed, 'a curiously tough substance'. It continued to wield considerable political power, supplying much of the membership of both political parties at Westminster, occupying almost all the upper posts in the empire, running local government in the counties, and officering the army—the navy was less socially exclusive. The aristocracy and gentry gained from prosperous farming in the 1850s–1870s, and lost by the agricultural depression; but it recovered some of its losses by skilful investment in urban land, and by the windfall of urban expansion, as what had been agricultural lands of declining value made their owners wealthy as suburbs were built upon them. The British aristocracy had always been involved in industrialization, especially in the development of mining, canals, and railways. It now shrewdly associated itself with the new wave of commercial expansion: most banks and insurance companies had a Lord to add tone to the managerial board. It also shored up its fortunes by astute marriages, notably with the new aristocracy of wealth in the United States: the best-known example was the marriage of the ninth duke of Marlborough to Consuelo Vanderbilt. By these means, many of the great aristocratic estates were preserved despite agricultural decline. But they were playthings as much as engines of wealth, and came to be treated as such. The aristocracy came to be known to the urban population chiefly through their representation in the popular press and magazines as men and women of leisure: racing, hunting, shooting and fishing in the country, gambling and attending the season in London. In a population for which leisure was becoming increasingly important, this did not make the aristocracy unpopular. The court led the way. The gravity which Albert applied to court life in the south was applied with equal pertinacity to the serious business of recreation in the north. Victoria and Albert's development of Balmoral on Deeside in the 1850s, their obvious and highly publicized enjoyment of peasant life and lore, their patronage of Sir Edwin Landseer, the hugely popular artist of rural slaughter, made Scotland respectable, and likewise similar moors and mountains in the north and west of England and in Wales. The court linked itself to the Romantic movement, now in its declining and consequently most popular phase, and by doing so re-established its popularity and represented the control of nature by an urban civilization. *The Monarch of the Glen*, Landseer's portrait of a stag, one of the most reproduced of all Victorian paintings, is not monarch of all he surveys, but a stag at bay, within the gun sights of the stalker: no glen was safe, nature was tamed.

Victoria and Albert's life at Balmoral was enjoyable but high-minded: duty to the peasantry was consistently emphasized. The Prince of Wales, Victoria's son Edward who succeeded her in 1901, was merely hedonistic. A series of scandals alarmed his mother but gratified the press by the copy they yielded. The Prince with his coterie of rich friends such as Sir Thomas Lipton, who made a fortune from the new retail trade in groceries, epitomized the 'plutocracy'. The evangelicalism and tractarianism which made such a mark on the aristocracy in post-Regency days and which made Palmerston's dandyism in the 1850s and 1860s seem conspicuously out of place, appeared to give way to ostentatious consumption and a general moral laxity. Some aristocrats, such as Lord Salisbury, the Tory Prime

Reality behind the ideal.
Prince Albert Stag Hunting, by Sir Edwin Landseer.

Minister, continued the old fashion of simple living despite magnificent surroundings, with a household noted for its religious tone. But Salisbury, the last Prime Minister to wear a beard, was becoming an anachronism by his last decade, the 1890s. Arthur Balfour, his nephew and successor as Prime Minister, was seen as a free-thinker. Balfour and Edward VII characterized the new fashion—the one apparently sceptical, the other openly sybaritic.

Despite the marked difference in style between Victoria and her son, the monarchy—the apex of the court and of polite society generally—flourished under both. Victoria in her long reign (1837–1901) jealously guarded its prerogatives which increasingly she saw as best safeguarded by a Conservative government. Her long disappearances from public life after Albert's death in 1861 were unpopular, and made possible quite a serious republican movement stimulated by the Paris Commune, which was headed off with some skill by the Liberal Party leadership in the early 1870s. It was the absence and idleness of the monarch that caused widespread adverse com-

The retailing revolution centred on chains of food shops, such as Sainsbury's and large department stores with credit offered, such as Peter Jones, *c*.1900.

ment, not her presence. In a rapidly-changing society with important elements strongly receptive to the appeal of hierarchy, the monarchy, carefully presented by the growing mass-communications industry, seemed something of a fixed point, with its emphasis on family, continuity, and religion. Walter Bagehot in his classic study, *The English Constitution* (1867), pointed out that the English 'defer to what we may call the *theatrical show* of society . . . the climax of the play is the Queen'. The monarchy helped to legitimize power: it is 'commonly hidden like a mystery, and sometimes paraded like a pageant', as it was with great success at the Jubilees in 1887 and 1897. The obvious ordinariness of Victoria herself, her well-publicized sufferings ('the widow of Windsor', bravely performing her duties), and the fact that she was a woman, old and often ill, pointed up the contrast between human frailty and the majesty of institutions, much increasing respect for the latter.

The monarchy represented the timeless quality of what was taken to be a pre-industrial order. In an increasingly urbanized society, it balanced the Industrial Revolution: the more urban

Britain became, the more stylized, ritualized, and popular became its monarchy, for the values which it claimed to personify stood outside the competitive egalitarianism of capitalist society.

'A Great Change in Manners'

Britain (with the exception of Ireland) between the 1850s and the 1890s was a society of remarkable order and balance, given its extraordinary underlying tensions of industrial and social change. Though political rioting did not altogether disappear, it became infrequent enough to encourage widespread comment. Crime on the mainland, both in the form of theft and of acts of violence, declined absolutely as well as relatively—an extraordinary development in a rapidly-expanding population, firmly contradicting the adage that industrialization and urbanization necessarily lead to higher rates of criminality. The Criminal Registrar noted in 1901 that, since the 1840s, 'we have witnessed a great change in manners: the substitution of words without blows for blows with or without words; an approximation in the matters of different classes; a decline in the spirit of lawlessness.' This largely self-regulating society relied on voluntary organizations—the Churches, the Friendly Societies, a vast network of charitable organizations—to cater for spiritual and physical deprivation. In one important area—education—it was already admitted by the 1860s that voluntary effort by the Churches could not supply an elementary education system adequate to the needs of an industrial state, and in 1870 the Liberal government passed an Act to set up Education Boards with a duty to build board schools where there were no church schools (though children were not *required* to attend them until 1880, and had to pay to do so until 1891). Local initiative, especially in London and some of the northern manufacturing towns, grafted on to the elementary schools a quite effective and wide-ranging system of technical education for teenagers and even adults—but because it depended on the imagination of each school board, this system was patchy and in no way matched its German equivalent. Manufacturing towns, notably Manchester and Birmingham, set up civic univerisities much less orientated towards a classical education for those entering the traditional professions than Oxford and Cambridge. Government responsibility for education was seen by contemporaries as one of Mill's exceptions to the rule, not as the start of a wider acceptance of responsibility for social organization.

'The Angel in the House'. This rather contrived photograph (1865) reflects a striving for gentility, but also captures something of the loneliness of many middle-class women.

'Villa Tories': the Conservative Resurgence

By increasing the electorate from 20 per cent to 60 per cent of adult men in the towns, and to 70 per cent in the counties, the Reform Acts of 1867 and 1884 posed problems for politicians. Household suffrage presented them with a much larger, though by no means universal, body of voters (far short of a universal suffrage, even for men) and elections were by secret ballot, whereas previously each individual's vote had been published.

For the Liberal coalition, accustomed never to losing general elections, the question was, could their amorphous system of informal alliances continue to be successful? It was a question posed the more starkly when Gladstone's first government disintegrated in the traditional Liberal style in 1873–4, and then, untraditionally, lost the election, thus yielding power to the Tories for the first time since 1846. The Liberals' response was twofold. In certain urban areas, and especially in Birmingham, where Joseph Chamberlain was the dominant political figure, a tight 'caucus' system of party organization was introduced. The 'caucus' was a group of self-appointed local notables, often nonconformist business men, and usually strongly critical of the Liberal Party leadership as being too cautious and too aristocratic. The National Liberal Federation, formed in 1877, attempted to give a degree of bureaucratic unity to the sundry local caucuses. On the other hand, the Liberal leadership, still predominantly aristocratic, reacted with alarm. Spanning the two groups was the commanding figure of W. E. Gladstone, son of a Liverpool (originally Scottish) corn merchant, but educated at Eton and Christ Church, Oxford; himself strongly Anglican but in the later phases of his career sympathetic to nonconformist aspirations, he was thus able to appeal to a wide spectrum of Victorian society. Gladstone had no 'caucus' to back him up: he aspired to a national rather than a local basis of power. He appealed over the heads of the local organizations to the body of Liberal opinion at large, and his means was the political speech and pamphlet. The new and vast network of national and provincial newspapers, linked by the telegraph, allowed for the first time an instant national debate: a politician's speech could be on the breakfast table of every middle-class household in the land the morning after it was given. Thus in the general election campaign of 1868, in his campaign against the Disraeli government's supine reaction to massacres of Christians by Turks in Bulgaria in 1876, and in his campaign against the moral and financial delinquency of the imperialistic exploits of the Conservatives in 1879–80 (the 'Midlothian Campaign'), Gladstone blazed a new trail in an attempt to create a great popular front of moral outrage. 'The Platform' became the characteristic form of late Victorian politics: Gladstone invented a new forum of political debate, and his contemporaries, both Liberal and Tory, were obliged to join in.

The 1867 Reform Act brought the Tories new opportunities. Accustomed, almost habituated to losing, they began to win. In 1867 the National Union of Conservative and Constitutional Associations was founded, and in 1870 a Central Office began to improve the co-ordination of electoral strategy. The target for the Tories was the boroughs: to obtain political power they had to enlarge their base from the counties to the expanding towns and

All in a day's play. Edward VII and friends with the day's bag of pheasants at Sandringham, the king's favourite retreat in Norfolk.

suburbs. This they did with very considerable success in the 1870s and 1880s. Under the leadership of Disraeli they won the general election of 1874 convincingly; under the leadership of Salisbury after Disraeli's death in 1881 they became the predominant party. They achieved this by linking an essentially hierarchic, aristocratic, and Anglican party with the aspirations of the expanding middle and lower middle classes in the great cities: the Tories became the party of property and patriotism. Disraeli saw that political success was becoming as much a question of presentation as of policy. In famous speeches in Lancashire and at the Crystal Palace in 1872, he portrayed the Liberals as unpatriotic, a danger to property, a threat to the institutions of the nation, betrayers of Britain's world and imperial interests. In a more positive vein, he advocated a policy of social reform, supposedly of particular appeal to such members of the working classes as had recently become voters. The themes of these speeches—especially the patriotic ones—were quickly taken up by other Conservatives. They were the prototype for most Tory election addresses for the next century.

The early years of the Conservative government of 1874–80 were marked by a burst of social reforms mostly promoted by R. A. Cross, the Home Secretary: artisans' dwellings, public health, Friendly Societies, river pollution, the sale of food and drugs, merchant shipping, trade unions, factories, drink licensing, and

'The Widow of Windsor' at Balmoral, with John Brown, in the late 1860s.

education were all the subject of legislation. Many of these reforms were 'in the pipeline' and owed a strong debt to the Peelite–Liberal traditions which had also motivated the previous Gladstone government. They affected middle-class perhaps more than working-class interests and because the social measures were permissive rather than compulsory their effect was more limited than might have been expected (for example, by 1880, only ten of eighty-seven Welsh and English towns had decided to implement the Artisans' Dwellings Act). None the less, these reforms were important in Conservative mythology. They showed that the Tories could be a party which dealt effectively with urban questions, and they offered the basis for the claim that 'Tory democracy' was a reality. Contrasted with German conservative answers to the problems of urban life, they appeared integrative, conciliatory, and constructive.

But the real interest of Conservatism was the consolidation of an urban middle-class base: working-class support was a bonus.

The bogy of Liberal lack of patriotism was only partially successful, for the Tories' claim to be the party of competent imperialism was severely dented by their mishandling of events in South Africa and Afghanistan in the late 1870s, and by the high costs of their military exploits. It was hard simultaneously to be imperialists and to appeal to the middle-class virtue of financial retrenchment: a self-contradiction which Gladstone's Midlothian speeches skilfully exposed.

The Tories lost the 1880 general election, borne down partly by Gladstone's oratory, partly by the trade recession of that year. The succeeding Gladstone government of 1880–5 was the nadir of Liberalism, the party restless, the Cabinet divided. In imperial affairs, Tory claims seemed borne out: hesitation and confusion led to a series of disasters, culminating in the death of Charles Gordon at Khartoum in 1885. Too habituated to the way the 'official mind' of the colonial office thought to decline to extend imperial responsibilities, the Liberals occupied territory while declaring their regrets: electorally, they lost both ways, alienating anti-imperialists by doing too much, and imperialists by seeming reluctant. In domestic affairs, Gladstone's determination to control and reduce expenditure made positive reform difficult. In marked contrast to 1868–74, the government was noted for only one great reform, the county franchise reform of 1884. The enfranchisement of agricultural labourers was expected to deliver the county seats into the Liberals' hands and Salisbury used the blocking power of the House of Lords to extract a great prize as a 'tit-for-tat': a redistribution bill allowed the boundaries of borough seats to be drawn much more favourably to the Tories. Thus the Tories were able to use a Liberal reform to create a political structure of single-member, middle-class urban and suburban constituencies on which the basis of their subsequent political success has since consistently rested.

The effect of this was to make the Liberals increasingly dependent on the 'Celtic fringe', the Irish, Scottish, and Welsh MPs. The concerns and priorities of these three countries thus moved on to the centre of the British imperial stage.

Ireland, Scotland, Wales: Home Rule Frustrated

That there was an 'Irish problem', nobody could deny: what it was, hardly anybody could agree. Disraeli caught the tone of metropolitan bewilderment:

I want to see a public man come forward and say what the Irish question is. One says it is a physical question; another, a spiritual. Now it is the absence of the aristocracy, then the absence of railroads. It is the Pope one day, potatoes the next.

Irish agriculture was overwhelmingly the country's largest industry and was overwhelmingly owned by Protestants, who mostly, contrary to popular myth, lived on or near their estates. It flourished in the boom of the 1850s and 1860s and achieved a modest degree of technical improvement, but it remained, compared with England, grossly under-capitalized. Ireland could not produce her own capital, and could not attract much from England. Her economy could not sustain her population: unknown numbers moved to the mainland, where no town of any size was without its Irish community; between 1841 and 1925 gross 'overseas' emigration included four and three-quarter million to the USA, 70,000 to Canada, and more than 370,000 to Australia.

The legacy of the 1798 rebellion, the failure of Daniel O'Connell's attempt in the 1830s and 1840s to repeal the 1800 Act of Union, and the catastrophe of the famine of 1845–6, produced the Fenian Irish independence movement of the 1860s which attempted risings in the USA and in Canada and in Ireland. In 1867 it astonished England by a series of bomb explosions, notably one at Clerkenwell Prison in London, in which over one hundred innocent persons were killed. The Fenian movement in no sense represented Irish opinion generally, but the danger that it might come to do so encouraged Liberal politicians, especially Gladstone, to concessionary action. Disestablishment of the Anglican Church in Ireland in 1869, the Land Act of 1870, and an abortive educational reform in 1873 (rejected by the Irish members themselves) were intended to show that Westminster could give the mass of the Irish what they wanted. But these reforms were not enough. Isaac Butt's Home Government Association flourished, and the Liberal Party, hitherto the dominant party in Irish politics, was on the run. The agricultural depression from the early 1870s to the mid 1890s greatly worsened the situation. Charles Stewart Parnell (like Butt, a Protestant) became leader of the Home Rule Party in 1877, a position he held until his ruin in a divorce scandal in 1890. Parnell was prepared to exploit every political situation without reluctance or embarrassment—but even this tougher line was to some extent outflanked by the Land League which sought personal ownership of the land for the peasantry. Parnell, somewhat ambivalently, became its president in 1879. The Land League—a potent blend of 'physical force' Fenians and 'moral

Gladstone on the stump, addressing a crowd in Warrington, Lancashire, from his election train in 1885.

force' Parnellites fused into a popular front of nationalistic Catholicism—fought a sustained campaign against evictions in the 'Land War' of 1879–82 at the height of the depression, meeting them with violence and their perpetrators with 'boycotting' (named after Captain Charles Boycott, whose nerve cracked when faced with social and economic ostracism). Violence in the Irish countryside, and the murder in 1882 of the Irish secretary, Lord Frederick Cavendish, Gladstone's nephew by marriage, astonished and appalled the propertied classes in England which, as we have seen, had become accustomed to a very low level of violent crime.

The Gladstone Government of 1880 met this crisis on the one hand with coercion and on the other with concession, in the form of the 1881 Land Act, which gave much to the peasants, but did not give them ownership. The Home Rule Party increased its hold on Ireland (helped by the county franchise reform of 1884) and at the election of December 1885 won 86 seats, thus holding the balance of power between the Liberals and Tories at Westminster.

Gladstone cut the Gordian knot by coming out for Home Rule; a private appeal to Salisbury to treat the question on a bipartisan basis was rejected. Gladstone's decision was quite consistent with the main thrust of Liberal thinking, but its timing recognized political necessity: only once subsequently, in 1906, were the Liberals to gain power without the need for the support of Home Rule MPs in the lobbies. Most Liberals championed devolution and the rights of nations 'struggling rightly to be free', as Gladstone put it; it was hard to deny in 1886 that Ireland had proved itself to be such a nation. The question was, was its nationality to be recognized or crushed? Moreover, the moderate Home Rule Bill produced by Gladstone in 1886 did not grant independence, though it was the argument of its opponents first, that despite Parnell's assurances it would in the long run lead to Irish independence, and, second, that it gave no safeguard against 'Rome Rule' to the Protestant population, mostly concentrated in Belfast, the industrial capital of the province of Ulster.

This complex series of events led to a major crisis in British politics. The Liberal Party, faced with Gladstone's Home Rule Bill in the summer of 1886, split: 93 MPs, most of them Whigs under Lord Hartington but with some radicals under Joseph Chamberlain, voted with the Tories against the bill, thus bringing down the Liberal government and introducing twenty years of Conservative (or Unionist, as the anti-Home Rule Coalition was called) hegemony. With the Liberal-Unionists (the defectors from Liberalism) went a significant proportion of the Liberal press and almost all those landed aristocrats who traditionally paid most of the party's electoral expenses. This loss of influence and money was probably of more importance to the Liberals than the actual numbers of defecting MPs, though in the Lords the Liberals were now a tiny minority.

The split of 1886 weakened the party, but left Gladstone in control of it and of the National Liberation Federation, a hold he consolidated at its Newcastle meeting in 1891 when he accepted its radical programme. Home Rule thus shackled Liberalism to Gladstone. Before 1886, Ireland blocked the way to the passage of second-rank measures, so Home Rule was necessary as well as right. But after 1886, Home Rule was impossible, given the existence of the House of Lords. Home Rule thus both stimulated Liberals to battle for the right, and condemned them to a generation of frustration.

Naturally enough, events in Ireland affected Scotland and Wales. In both, disestablishment of the Church also became a political issue, and both experienced land campaigns. These had little of the violence characteristic of parts of Ireland, though in the Isle of Skye troops were used in 1882 to suppress crofter demonstrations. Certain Liberals in both countries demanded 'Home Rule All Round' and this movement, buoyed up by the cultural renaissance that Wales and Scotland shared with Ireland in the late nineteenth century, achieved considerable influence in the late 1880s and 1890s. Unlike Ireland, however, the Liberal Party was able to contain within itself the quasi-nationalistic movements in Scotland and Wales, partly because the dominant industrial sector in Scotland and the growing predominance in Wales of the South Wales coalfield bound those countries far more intimately than Ireland to the imperial economy; in southern Scotland and South Wales Liberal imperialism trumped nationalism.

With the Liberal Party split, and unable to reunite despite various attempts in the late 1880s, the Tories consolidated their hold. They were not active reactionaries. Salisbury made no attempt to reverse the Liberal achievements of the 1850s–1870s which at the time he had so bitterly opposed. Their position and their alliance with the Liberal-Unionists depended on preventing things being done, not on doing them. Thus though some legislation was passed, particularly the establishment of elected County Councils in 1888, a measure to improve working-class housing in 1890, and, later, the Education Act of 1902, which went some way to establishing a system of secondary education, the Unionist hegemony of 1886–1905 was not a period of legislative significance, nor was it intended to be. The urban electorate which the Tories essentially relied upon wanted the continuation of the Liberal state of the 1850s and 1860s, without the new accretions to Liberalism such as Home Rule. It rejected Gladstonian Liberalism, not because it had turned its back on the gains of the free-trade years in the mid-century, but because the Gladstonian Liberals seemed to have progressed too far beyond the objectives of that period. The anti-Gladstonian coalition thus relied heavily on Home Rule to keep the coalition together and to keep the Liberals out. It ventured beyond its anti-Home Rule stance at its electoral peril, as it was to find out in the early years of the twentieth century. The continuing Liberal commitment to Home Rule helped in this. The short Liberal minority government of 1892–5 (Gladstone's last administration, with Rosebery as its Prime Minister after his retirement in 1894) spent much effort upon the second Home Rule Bill, which it succeeded in passing through the Commons only to see it thrown out by the Lords. The Liberals could mount a disparate majority made up of the English counties, Scotland, Wales, and Ireland, but they could not sustain it or repeat it. The Unionists won convincingly in 1895 and confirmed their majority in 1900, taking advantage of temporary successes in the South African war to hold the 'Khaki election'.

Reluctant Imperialists?

The Unionist case against Home Rule had always had an imperial dimension: imperial power must not be devolved, the very circumstances of the passing of the Act of Union in 1800 showing the strategic importance of Ireland, which Home Rule would again put at risk. In the last third of the century, imperial issues became much more of a public preoccupation; we must now look at their effect on Britain's position in the world.

The British did not as a whole look for increased direct imperial authority, and pressure groups for its extension were of little popular significance. Indeed, in the old areas of white settlement, they successfully sought to devolve authority, passing the Dominion of Canada Act in 1867 and the Commonwealth of Australia Act in 1900. Yet the last forty years of the century saw the annexation of vast areas of land in Africa, the Far East, and the Pacific. In 1851 Britain was the world's trader, with an overwhelming dominance of world shipping, which continued even when Britain's dominance in manufactured goods was declining after 1870. British interests were thus to be found wherever there was trade, even though British imperial authority might not be *formally* present. *Informal* imperialism thus preceded formal annexation: nothing could be less true than the adage, 'trade follows the flag'. In almost every case, it was the opposite. As Joseph Conrad's novels illustrate, there was no creek, however distant, without its British representative, organizing the shipping of paraffin oil and local goods.

In East and Central Africa, the first European presence was often religious, as evangelical medical missionaries such as David Livingstone preached the gospel, healed the sick, and exposed the inhumanity of the inland slave trade. H. M. Stanley's 'rescue' of Livingstone in 1871, skilfully self-publicized, became one of the great adventure stories of Victorian times, and greatly increased interest in 'the dark continent'.

In some areas, British attempts to trade were supported by arms—a notable example being the opium monopoly of the Indian government and general free-trading access which was forced upon the Chinese government by the British in a series of

*The expansion of
the British Empire
1815–1914*

'opium wars' culminating in the treaty of Tien-tsin (1858), the
most disreputable of all Britain's imperialistic exploits, because
it was a considered and consistent policy, not the accidental
result of a local crisis. Governmental involvement of an oblique
sort was sometimes used to develop small beginnings through
the device of the Chartered Company—a trading company with
governmentally guaranteed rights to trade and administer an
area; Nigeria, East Africa, and Rhodesia all came under eventual
British rule in this way, for when a Company went bankrupt (or
effectively so—Cecil Rhodes's British South Africa Company
never paid a dividend before 1920 and was taken over in 1923)
the British government had little option but to assume its
administrative responsibilities.

In addition to this huge and largely informal network of trade
was the centrepiece of India, 'the chief jewel in the imperial
crown', now no longer so profitable, but the assumed focal point
of British thinking about security outside the European context.
Following the Indian mutiny of 1857–8, the old East India
Company was wound up, and its territories came under direct
British administration. In 1876, at the express wish of the queen,

an Act was passed at Westminster which declared her 'Empress of India'.

To safeguard India, and the route to that subcontinent, various annexations were made. In the vicinity, Burma and Malaysia were annexed, largely at the urging of the government of India and Calcutta, which conducted its own programme of imperialism with the systematic approach characteristic of everything it did, and quite dissimilar to the haphazard methods of London. On the route, Egypt and the Sudan came under British control, and imperial expansion in East and South Africa was at least partly affected by Indian considerations. This simple statement of course disguises an extremely complex narrative with respect to each of these annexations. The most controversial annexations were in Egypt and South Africa, and some attention should be given to these.

The route to India had made security in the eastern Mediterranean, especially against Russia, a long-standing British preoccupation. Between 1854 and 1856 the British and French, with some assistance from Piedmont-Sardinia, had sent substantial fleets and armies to prop up Turkey. The Crimean War had a

The free-trade empire. Calcutta Harbour, *c.*1880.

complex series of causes, but the root one was Russian aggrandizement against the sprawling and feeble Ottoman Empire. The performance of Britain and France, the two most 'advanced' European nations, against 'backward' Russia was disappointing and in certain respects inept, although the supply by sea of large armies at a considerable distance created new problems. The newspaper-reporting by telegraph of the hardships of the troops starkly illustrated the problems and the paradox of war-making by a liberal state, and Florence Nightingale made a name for herself as the 'lady with the lamp'. The immobility of the campaign, which consisted largely of a series of sieges, bloodily resolved in the Crimea and in the area of Kars in Asiatic Turkey, looked forward to the 1914–18 war. Turkey was successfully defended, and the British thus shored up the Ottoman Empire of which Egypt was a part.

The hope was that Turkey would reform and behave like a modern, liberal state. This hope was not fulfilled. By the 1870s, Turkey was again disintegrating, and under attack from Russia. The Disraeli government of 1874–80 continued the Crimean policy of defending Turkish integrity: the Liberal opposition under Gladstone argued that this was no longer feasible and supported the division of much of 'Turkey in Europe' into separate, Christian states. The 'Concert of Europe' present at the Congress of, Berlin in 1878 reached agreement on this and Disraeli returned to London bringing 'peace with honour' and the imperial gain of the island of Cyprus, thought to be of strategic importance for the Eastern Mediterranean, but in fact useless as a naval base.

As Turkey disintegrated, so Egypt became increasingly self-reliant, organizing the building of the Suez Canal, opened in 1870, and of great importance to Britain's links with India. The inflow of capital to build the canal destablised Egypt, which began to disintegrate socially and politically. In 1875 Disraeli bought the Khedive's large holding in the shares of the company which ran the canal. Thus when Egypt reached the point of bankruptcy, and a military coup was attempted, Britain had not only a general strategic interest in the situation but also a direct financial one. After attempts to find alternatives, Gladstone reluctantly invaded and occupied Egypt on behalf of the canal's creditors in 1882, and the British remained until 1954, though the country was never formally annexed and was thus similar in status to the theoretically independent princely states in India. Formal annexation of the rebellious Sudan naturally followed in a series of campaigns in the 1880s and 1890s, the Mahdi, the slayer of the maverick Gordon in 1885, being finally and ruthlessly crushed by Kitchener at the battle of Omdurman in 1898. Turkish decay thus drew Britain into becoming the major power in the Eastern Mediterranean and in North-eastern Africa.

Events in South Africa were not dissimilar, but were complicated by the presence of the Boers. The Cape was occupied in 1795 to safeguard the route to India. The security of the hinterland, whither the Boers had trekked in the 1830s, affected the Cape. Various plans for incorporating the Boers in a federation were suggested, and confederation was imposed upon the Boers by the Disraeli government in 1877 at a moment when the Boers were weakened by the Zulus. Incompetent generalship (a feature of British military operations in South Africa) led to the death of 800 British troops at Isandhlwana, one of the very few occasions in colonial wars in which spears triumphed over guns. This was, of course, only a temporary set-back, and the Zulus were liquidated at Ulundi (1879). The Boers then wished to regain their independence. After a short war when the defeat of a small group of British soldiers at Majuba Hill in 1881 gave a propaganda value to the Boers out of all proportion to its military significance, an ill-defined agreement was reached: the Transvaal and Orange Free State to have independence, but under British suzerainty. Increasing exploitation of diamonds and the discovery of gold in the Transvaal in 1886 transformed the situation. In financial terms, Southern Africa became literally Britain's chief imperial jewel.

The influx of capital directed by men such as Cecil Rhodes destabilized the rural economy of the Boers, as it had that of Egypt. The Transvaal, like Egypt, went bankrupt, but the Boers, under Paul Kruger, retained strict political control. An attempt by Dr Jameson, a crony of Rhodes, to encourage a rising by the Uitlanders (the British in the Transvaal without political rights) failed in 1896. Alfred Milner, the new High Commissioner, asserted British rights over the Boer republics and determined to break Kruger by war. Milner goaded Kruger into attacking Cape Colony in 1899, and what was expected to be a short, limited war began. The Boers, however, were well stocked with German arms; the British, used to fighting colonial wars against undisciplined natives without guns, proceeded ineptly, and a series of disasters followed before weight of armaments captured the main Boer cities in 1900. The war seemed over, and Chamberlain, the Colonial Secretary, persuaded Salisbury to hold the 'Khaki election', easily won by the Unionists. But the Boers refused to accept defeat, and harassed the British with guerrilla tactics. The British replied by burning Boer farms, clearing the veldt, and systematically herding Boer families into 'concentration camps'. High death-rates in the camps led to radical protests in Britain. 'When is a war not a war?' asked Sir Henry Campbell-Bannerman, Rosebery's successor as Liberal leader, answering himself: 'when it is carried on by methods of

The First Welsh Regiment in camp on the veldt during the Boer War.
'We're foot-slog-slog-slog-sloggin' over Africa
Foot-foot-foot-foot-sloggin' over Africa—
(Boots-boots-boots-boots-movin' up and down again!)
There's no discharge in the war!'

barbarism in South Africa'. In 1902, peace was negotiated: Milner had failed in his aim of smashing the social and political structure of Afrikanerdom.

The fin-de-siècle *Reaction: New Views of the State*

The Boer War was immensely expensive, costing far more than all Britain's other imperial exploits in the nineteenth century put together. It failed to smash the Boers, but it did smash the Gladstonian system of finance, raising government expenditure to a new plateau from which it never descended. The war also put into stark and dramatic popular form a number of concerns which were already preoccupying the intelligentsia. The war showed the strength and loyalty of the empire, for the white colonies sent troops to help, but it also showed its weaknesses. The empire seemed over-extended and under-coordinated. The British navy was no longer pre-eminent. The French navy was being joined as a threat by the Germans, the Italians, the Americans, and the Japanese. The policy of 'splendid isolation' began to look dangerous. Imperial rivalry had meant that in the 1870s–1890s France had usually seemed Britain's most likely enemy and Germany her most likely friend. Germany's navy plan of 1898, and her bid for 'a place in the sun' which coincided with her encouragement to Kruger during the Boer War, now made Germany seem a potent threat, the contemporary feeling about which is well captured in Erskine Childers's classic spy story *The Riddle of the Sands* (1903). Naval security in the Indian Ocean and the Pacific was gained by the Anglo-Japanese alliance of 1902. This attempt to limit imperial responsibility was followed up by agreements (*Ententes*) resolving imperial differences with France in 1904 over North Africa and with Russia in 1907 over Persia. The Boer War thus led to a 'new course' in British foreign policy. For while these *Ententes* were formally about extra-European areas, their real importance came to lie within Europe; although they were not alliances, they committed Britain, to some extent, to the side of the Franco-Russian alliance against Germany and Austria in the rising tension in Europe. What that extent was, was not yet clear.

Anxieties about world security raised by the Boer War also popularized discussion about Britain's relative economic position, for it was up on that that national strength ultimately rested. The overwhelming superiority of the British economy of the 1850s was much diminished. The USA, Germany, France, and

Russia were now all substantial industrial powers, with the first two superior to the British in certain sectors of their economies. Britain was now one among several, no longer the unaccompanied trail-blazer. Yet for the most part British society and government behaved as if nothing had changed. The liberal state of the 1850s and 1860s, with its precepts of free trade, minimal government spending, an economy autonomous and self-regulating, lingered on, almost as carefully guarded under Conservative as under Liberal management. The *per capita* expenditure of central government in 1851 was £2.00; by 1891 it had only increased to £2.50 (by 1913 it was to be £4.00). In the 1880s and 1890s this situation came under increasing criticism, much of which the Boer War seemed to confirm and popularize.

Slow military progress in the Crimean War of the 1850s led to criticism of the competence of the ruling élite; military ineffectiveness and the poor quality of recruits in the South African war led to a public cry among the propertied classes for a reappraisal of the economic, social, and even political arrangements of the nation as a whole.

Before considering the various schools of criticism of traditional Liberalism, a general influence should be noted, that of 'social Darwinism'. We saw earlier that positivists were strong supporters of *laissez-faire*. In the 1880s and 1890s the influence of social Darwinism began to take a different form. The struggle for 'the survival of the fittest' began to be seen less in terms of individuals in the market-place and more in terms of competition between nations. This dramatically reduced the number of units under discussion, and raised the question, prompted also by the imperialism which was related to this national competition, of whether individual 'races' were not better subjects for inquiry than a myriad of individuals, and whether 'advanced races' could control their destinies by governmental, social, or perhaps even genetic organization. This concept—a marrying of the British science of evolution and the German concept of the organic state—powerfully affected contemporary thought: the language of 'race' became the common coin of reformers right across the political spectrum, from Rudyard Kipling, ostensibly the poet of the right, through J. A. Hobson and L. T. Hobhouse, the philosophers of the new liberals, to G. B. Shaw, regarded as the playwright of the left. The popular form of social Darwinism readily became a facile assumption of racial superiority, linked to imperialism, as the popular press reported the successes of the many small-scale colonial military expeditions. Popular reporting of these emphasized the importance of individual daring, character, and initiative, 'deeds that won the Empire', rather than the enormous technical disparity between a disciplined European army armed with rifles and from the 1890s the occasional machine-gun, and local forces relying on massed use of spears or, at best, sporadic musket fire.

Criticism of the liberal state in its classic Victorian form came from three chief political directions: from discontented Conservatives and Unionists who believed their political leadership was excessively hidebound by the canons of Peel–Gladstone fiscal policy, from Liberals who believed Liberalism must move on to meet new challenges, and from socialists who, at least at first glance, challenged the whole order of the state. Elements from each of these came together to demand 'national efficiency', a slogan intended to suggest a willingness to use government power to organize and legislate for an 'Imperial race' fit to meet the challenges of the world.

The free-trade state had always had its critics. The most influential of these in the second half of the nineteenth century was John Ruskin, art critic and social commentator. Politically impossible to categorize, Ruskin's powerful prose in works such as *Unto this Last* (1862) attacked the aesthetics of industrial society, but he offered no very systematic critique. His aesthetic criticisms were taken up by the Pre-Raphaelite Brotherhood, a group of painters, writers, and craftsmen who emphasized, especially through the writings and designs of William Morris, the values of pre-industrial England, a mythical land of craftsmen, contented peasants, and romance. From such influences sprang wide-ranging changes in design and architecture, epitomized by the 'English style' of domestic architecture of Norman Shaw and, at the turn of the century, Lutyens, which characterized the best of the building of the new suburbs. From Morris also sprang a socialist rhetoric of enduring potency: the image of a rural, self-sufficient, egalitarian society of sturdy yeomen. Morris did not confront industrialization, he by-passed it.

The aestheticism of the Pre-Raphaelites, and their general critique of middle-class morality, was given fresh impetus by the aesthetes of the 1880s and 1890s, the most notable of whom was the wit and playwright Oscar Wilde, ruined, like his fellow Irishman Parnell, by the public exposure of his sexual habits. Wilde's remarkable essay, 'The Soul of Man under Socialism', exemplified the links between aestheticism and individualist rather than collective socialism.

From 1884 these leanings towards socialism were supplemented by the London-based Fabian Society whose members included Sidney and Beatrice Webb, George Bernard Shaw, H. G. Wells, and, later, the young Ramsay MacDonald, all strong social evolutionists. The Fabians' criticism of the Liberal economic order was not so much that it was unjust, but that it was inefficient and wasteful: a centrally-planned economy and labour market, administered by an élite of trained professionals, would eliminate inefficiency, the trade cycle, and its by-products such as unemployment and poverty. It would attain this end gradually through legislation and not by revolution (hence the name Fabian, after the Roman general whose tactics the society emulated). Perhaps the chief contribution of the Fabians was to assist in the development of a fresh concept of 'progress' on the British left which in the 1880s was becoming limited in its horizons by the persistent wrangles over Home Rule. For the Fabians addressed themselves to the existing intelligentsia: they were not a popular movement. But popular discontent with the limitations of Gladstonian Liberalism was also developing; Keir Hardie, a coal-miner from the Ayrshire coalfield, represented the view that the increasingly unionized working class must have its own representatives in the House of Commons (where MPs were still not paid). Hardie, elected for West Ham in 1892, helped form the Scottish Parliamentary Labour Party in 1888 and, in 1893, founded the Independent Labour Party in Bradford. The ILP saw itself as a socialist party, but it had difficulty in establishing a popularly-supported organization. It shared with the Liberals an anti-imperialist rhetoric, supported 'Home Rule All Round', but called also for nationalization. H. M. Hyndman's Social Democratic Federation was more vigorous in its quasi-Marxist ideology, but gained very little popular foothold.

Old Liberalism, New Liberalism, Labourism, and Tariff Reform

All these movements were limited in their impact; the Liberals remained overwhelmingly the dominant party of the 'left' (the use of the word became common in British political discussion for the first time in the 1880s). None the less, the ideas being put forward, and the threat of their organizational success, concentrated Liberal minds. Liberals made their own contribution to the intellectual debates of the last two decades of the century. Always the party of land reform, their enthusiasm for it was rekindled by works such as the American Henry George's

Joseph Chamberlain's tariff reform campaign assaulting the free-trade tradition as caricatured by F. Carruthers Gould in the *Westminster Gazette*, 12 November 1903.

Progress and Poverty (1880). Posing the question, 'what *does* produce poverty amid advancing wealth?', George's answer was, crudely stated, the rents of the landed proprietor and the exclusion of workmen from free access to land, both rural and urban. The solution was a thoroughgoing and efficient land tax, known as 'the single tax'. The land campaign was a major theme of radicalism until the First World War, and beyond.

'Why do we sit and quietly behold degradation worse than that from which we have rescued women and children in mines and factories?' asked Arnold Toynbee, the liberal Christian historian and radical and, with T. H. Green, a great radical influence in the Oxford of the 1870s and early 1880s. Toynbee's followers (such as Canon Barnett, founder of Toynbee Hall in East London in 1884) encouraged, first, personal (often religious) commitment on the part of the intelligentsia to on-the-spot observation of working-class problems, and, second and later, an acceptance that voluntary effort would not be sufficient by itself to solve those problems. 'Advanced radicals' came to anticipate much greater government involvement in the economy, and much more 'positive liberalism' to see that each individual had the means by which he or she could make the most of his or her individual abilities. This was bound to cost money, and Liberals believed this money should be raised by increasing direct taxation, in particular death duties and a graduated income tax, to achieve a measure of redistribution at the same time as raising revenue. An important step in this direction was taken by the 1892–5 minority Liberal government which paid for increased social reform and naval expenditure by imposing for the first time an effective death duty. 'New Liberalism', as this movement came to be called, was an attempt to justify the free-market system by making it work 'fairly'; it attempted a rationalization of capitalism, not its replacement. The movement, whose most effective author was J. A. Hobson, also a strong critic of 'immoral' imperialism, hoped to convert the Liberal Party to 'New Liberalism' and thus to allow the continuation of the Liberals as a broadly-based party, capable of continuing to assimilate and integrate the urban working class. This would avoid the German situation, where the working class had formed its own class-based Marxist party which rejected the legitimacy of the German State. This view was reinforced by political expediency on the Liberals' part. Following a series of adverse legal decisions which questioned their legal right to picket and their freedom from damages culminating in the famous Taff Vale case (1900–1), some trade unions, now in the late 1890s growing fast, joined with the ILP to form the Labour Representation Committee in 1900. The Liberals, split three ways by the Boer War, were at their weakest, and seemed to be able to offer the trade unionists, hitherto Liberal, little chance of redress. The secretary of the LRC, Ramsay MacDonald, negotiated an electoral agreement with the Liberals in February 1903, by which Liberal and Labour constituency parties would not split the progressive vote to let in a Unionist, but would reach local agreements by which a number of Labour candidates would have a good chance of being elected.

This accommodation between the two parties of the left showed the considerable area of agreement that existed between them: the Labour Party (as the LRC became in 1906) was part of the 'party of progress', at least for the time being, sharing many of its reforming aspirations, and its commitment to free trade.

The Unionists (as the coalition of Tories and Liberal-Unionists should be called after 1895 when Joseph Chamberlain and Lord Hartington, the Liberal-Unionist leaders, entered Salisbury's Cabinet) wished to conserve the British constitution as it then stood. But most of them also conserved its fiscal arrangements and remained free traders. Lord Salisbury gave no effective support to protection despite his large majority in both Houses.

The imperialist faction within his party, however, increasingly came to see some form of imperial protection as essential. Their reasons for this were threefold. First, they believed that the growing success of the American and German economies was due to the protection of young industries, and that in the new era of technically sophisticated industry—chemicals, electricals, automobiles—Britain would lose out unless there was protection, a degree of planning, and much more co-operation between industry and education, all things that only government could supervise. Second, they believed that an Imperial Customs Union (analogous to the German *Zollverein* of the early nineteenth century) could integrate the empire's economy, Britain producing manufactured goods, the colonies raw materials. Third, they saw tariffs, including duties on food, as the only alternative to direct taxation to pay for the social reforms necessary to make the imperial race fit for the increasingly harsh competition between nations which they believed the future would bring. This programme was embodied in the Tariff Reform campaign launched by Joseph Chamberlain in 1903 while still Colonial Secretary, much to the embarrassment of the Prime Minister, Arthur Balfour, who had succeeded his uncle, Lord Salisbury, the previous year. Well financed, sophisticatedly organized and presented, Tariff Reform divided the Unionist Party (though the young Winston Churchill was one of the few MPs who actually left it). It was renounced by the electorate in a series of by-elections and then in the general election of 1906, when the Liberals together with 29 Labour MPs returned with a huge overall majority. England had turned from Home Rule in the 1880s and 1890s, but not from free trade. The Peel–Gladstone tradition of open markets and cheap food still carried great weight: 'the big loaf and the little loaf' was the Liberals' effective catch-phrase.

But although the 1906 Liberal success was the result mainly of negative factors—hostility to Tariff Reform, the dislike of Balfour's 1902 Education Act by nonconformists (their ranks swollen by a great religious revival), general criticism of the Unionists' handling of imperial affairs—the atmosphere had changed. There was much 'old Liberalism' (and 'old Toryism') still around, but the critiques of the Victorian liberal state made from the left, the right, and by Liberals themselves, bit deep.

The opening years of the twentieth century (there was much debate as to whether it began on 1 January 1900 or 1901) brought the widespread use by the better-off of its characteristic appliances, available in the 1890s but slow to find markets because of technical inadequacies—electric light in the houses, telephones, typewriters, gramophones, automobiles—and, soon, wireless and aeroplanes. The first building in the world specially designed as a cinema was opened in Colne, Lancashire, in 1907. Quite suddenly, the Victorian years and their preoccupations began to seem worlds away. The deaths of the three most notable public figures of those years—Gladstone in 1898, Victoria herself in 1901, Salisbury in 1903—emphasized the change.

Edwardian Years: a Crisis of the State Contained

Reappraisals of the nineteenth-century state were reinforced by a series of social enquiries in the 1890s and early 1900s into the working of the labour market and into social conditions—investigations such as Charles Booth's *Life and Labour of the People in London* (which appeared in four editions of thirty-three volumes in all, 1889–1903) and Seebohm Rowntree's *Poverty: a study of town life* (1901). Booth and Rowntree for the first time attempted to define 'poverty' as a social phenomenon (as opposed to the Poor Law's definition of pauperism which was a legal category). Rowntree found over 27 per cent of the population of York living in what he called 'primary or secondary poverty'. Standards of living might have risen for employed working people since the 1880s, but a significant proportion of the population was shown still to live in 'poverty' (a relative term) and on the brink of economic disaster. This contrasted markedly with the flamboyant 'plutocratic' living, noted earlier, of some members of the court and aristocracy.

Almost 30 per cent living in poverty was shocking, and it shocked contemporaries. But it also meant that 70 per cent were living in relative affluence, a proportion inconceivable in the days of the 'iron law of wages' of the mid-century. In the 1860s, Gladstone as Chancellor had admitted that the economy necessarily functioned with an 'enormous mass of paupers', and Victorians had been aware, in an ill-defined and helpless way, of the waste and suffering around them. Matthew Arnold's *Culture and Anarchy* (1869) described London's East End as containing 'those vast, miserable, unmanageable masses of sunken people'. Their reactions to it had been consequently local and personal, in the form of personal, charitable endeavour to alleviate the lot of those actually known to them or of particular categories of the so-called 'deserving poor', for example, distressed gentlefolk. Now, at the turn of the century, systematic investigation not only

The residuum. A mother and child in Glasgow, *c.*1910, an unusual early flash photograph of one of Rowntree's 10 per cent living in primary poverty.

raised alarm that an 'imperial race' could be so impoverished, but, by providing figures, suggested manageability and means of redress: until the scale of the problem was known, it could not be tackled. 'While the problem of 1834 was the problem of pauperism, the problem of 1893 is the problem of poverty' remarked Alfred Marshall, the leading free-trade economist; he implied that the problem of poverty had become both definable and solvable.

The Liberal governments of 1905–14, especially after Asquith became Prime Minister in 1908 on Campbell-Bannerman's death, made a considerable attempt to begin to come to terms with these questions. Free school meals (1907); old age pensions (a scheme drawn up in 1908 by Asquith before becoming Prime Minister, though seen through the Commons by David Lloyd George, his successor as Chancellor of the Exchequer); the Development Act (1909) anticipating Keynesian deficit financing; Winston Churchill's labour exchanges (1909); and Lloyd George's National Insurance Bill (1911) giving compulsory insurance to certain workers for benefits in times of sickness and unemployment, paid for by the State, the employer, and the employee—these and a host of smaller measures constituted the first legislative milestones of the modern welfare state. They were based on the rejection of the Victorian principle that individual probity and diligence would ensure modest prosperity: the reforms accepted that capitalism was wasteful, inefficient, and punishing to individuals regardless of personal merit, and that 'voluntaryism' was not enough. But they were none the less the reforms of free-traders who believed that marginal adjustments to the system could phase out the injustices of capitalism and make it 'fair'.

These reforms were expensive but based on a wide measure of consensus; it was the raising of revenue to pay for them which caused particular controversy, a controversy compounded by the need to raise large sums to pay for a fleet of 'Dreadnought' ships to match German naval expansion. The Tariff Reformers advocated protective indirect taxes to raise such revenues: the Liberals legislated for expanded direct taxes. Lloyd George's budget of 1909 brought a long-festering issue to a head by introducing a 'super-tax' on the incomes of the very rich and an attempt at an effective tax on land. Balfour and the Unionists used the House of Lords to throw out the budget.

This was the culmination of increasing use of the Lords to frustrate Liberal legislation: the Home Rule Bill of 1893 and a series of measures in 1906–8 had been either mutilated or destroyed. The rejection of the budget, traditionally the prerogative of the Commons, struck at a central tenet of British representative government. The Unionists argued that the conventional exemption of financial legislation meant that Liberals were using it to 'tack' on what was really social legislation—but all taxation was, and always had been, ultimately social in its consequences. Two general elections in 1910 left the Liberals dependent on Labour and Irish support, but none the less with a clear majority against the Lords: the Unionist leadership—though not all its followers—eventually conceded the point and the Parliament Act of 1911 limited the Lords' veto to two years.

This great institutional battle had begun with a basic question about social organization: where would the extra tax burden fall—on the rich through the super-tax or on the poor through food taxes? Its progress raised another, about constitutional organization. For the Liberals, as required by their Irish supporters, now introduced the third Home Rule Bill which, together with disestablishment of the Anglican Church in Wales, became law under the provisions of the Parliament Act in 1914, though suspended in practice for the duration of the war.

The Unionists reluctantly swallowed the budget, but Home Rule they would not stomach. With implicit encouragement from their new leader, Andrew Bonar Law (who replaced Balfour in 1911), they took literally the slogan coined by Lord Randolph Churchill in 1886: 'Ulster will fight and Ulster will be right.' Guns, many of them German, were shipped to Northern Ireland. There was doubt about the loyalty of the army to the State. Three times denied possession of power by the electorate of the United Kingdom as a whole, the Unionists brought Ireland to the edge of civil war in 1914 despite substantial Liberal concessions on the Ulster question, which might have been introduced rather earlier. The outbreak of the First World War prevented posterity from knowing whether they would have gone over the edge.

Edwardian Britain was thus a turbulent time for politics and politicians. The resurgence of Liberalism and the Liberals' willingness to come to terms with many problems long delayed or frustrated was a painful business for the Unionists, who continue to regard themselves, in or out of power, as the natural rulers of the nation.

But if an old élite's decline caused the greatest trouble, new, rising forces were also very active. The movement for women's suffrage went back to J. S. Mill's attempt to amend the 1867 Reform Bill to give women the vote. Some progress was made, for some women gained the vote for local elections, and for the synod of the Church of England, and could stand as candidates for local councils, school boards, and the poor law board. But the marginal public role given to middle-class women in the 1870s and 1880s—helping the priest, the doctor, or the MP; being secretary to the charity whose chairman was almost always a man; taking university examinations but not degrees—was no longer enough. Exclusion from voting for elections of the imperial Parliament exemplified what had come to be seen as deprivation; the campaign for women's votes was a campaign for a new concept of citizenship. Mrs Fawcett's National Union of Women's Suffrage Societies, uniting in 1897 a number of well-established organizations, was a broadly-based movement of impeccably liberal credentials which made considerable headway. It was, however, outflanked and outshone by the Pankhursts' Women's Social and Political Union (1903). The WSPU increasingly advocated violence against both property and individual politicians, as well as inflicting through imprisonment and hunger strikes considerable hardship and even occasionally death upon its members. Whether the WSPU helped or hindered the cause is hard to say: on the one hand, it dramatized it; on the other, its support for violence alienated many potential supporters among MPs and in particular Asquith, the Prime Minister, and made its legislative success less likely. Despite committed support within the Liberal and Labour Parties, and from a few Unionists, no legislation had been passed by 1914.

The Edwardian years also saw a very considerable expansion of the trade union movement, from 2.0 million members in 1901 to 4.1 million in 1913. In the years after 1908, price inflation and stationary wages encouraged this burgeoning movement to exert its strength; and there was a series of major strikes in 1910–12, culminating in the first general railway strike in 1911, which Lloyd George, as Chancellor, defused—also something of a precedent. Since Labour Party membership could only be held through being a trade union member, and since most trade unions came to be affiliated to the Labour Party (the affiliation in 1909 of the coal-miners, the chief union still hitherto supporting the Liberals, was a particular triumph), the Labour Party grew considerably in strength. A wide network of constituency parties was established with a ferment of ideological discussion, much of it necessarily Utopian in character (much of it inspired by William Morris), for the means of implementation was as yet very limited. The party had a secure base in the Commons, but of a limited size, and considerably dependent on its pact with the Liberals which brought it some thirty seats at the 1906 election. Its limited success at elections was not surprising, given that in the sort of industrial seats in which it would expect to succeed, about 60 per cent of adult men were not enfranchised. As yet, the party in the Commons saw itself largely as a pressure group for trade union interests, successfully amending the original Liberal bill so as to prevent the legal incorporation of the unions through the 1906 Trade Disputes Act, the consequence of the Taff Vale case. The Labour Party also intervened on social questions and on foreign policy. This slow progress at Westminster led some

HMS Dreadnought, launched 10 February 1906, the ship that inspired the slogan 'We want eight and we won't wait'.

trade unionists (notably some of the Welsh miners) to turn to syndicalism, that is, 'direct action' by trade unions to promote workers' control, circumventing MPs, Parliament, and the mechanisms of representative government.

The Labour Party's existence and success, closely linked to the expansion and difficulties of trade unionism, reflected a social, as much as an intellectual, difference from the Liberals. The solidarity of the Labour movement was based on cultural and social affinities, the shared experiences of working people in work and leisure, as much as any articulated perception of themselves as a separate class. Working people did not feel themselves to be alienated from the propertied classes, but they did feel themselves to be different. The Liberals reinforced this by their failure to adopt working men as candidates: however broad the agreement on policy matters, the middle-class members of the Liberal Associations—the people who called the tune in the constituencies—would not adopt as candidates men whom they would expect to enter their houses by the servants' door.

'Your English summer's done'

The refurbished Liberalism of the Edwardian years thus faced many difficulties. Legislatively, it met these dynamically and imaginatively with the first of the two great reforming governments of the century. It successfully contained and in large measure resolved the crisis over fiscal policy, welfare policy, socialism, and militarism which had brought many Continental nations to a political impasse by 1914 (though Ireland remained potentially an exception to this). It was not domestic divisions which were to bring Liberal governments in Britain to an end, but foreign affairs. We noted earlier the ambivalent consequences of the *Entente* policy pursued by Lord Lansdowne, Balfour's Foreign Secretary, and between 1905 and 1914 by Sir Edward Grey for the Liberals. Britain was committed implicitly and emotionally, but not in terms spelt out, to the French–Russian side of the European equation. Secret military conversations after 1905 between the British and the French increased this commitment. Although the greatest imperial power, Britain could bring little direct influence to bear on Continental affairs. R. B. Haldane's army reforms developed an Expeditionary Force intended for Europe, but, though efficient, it was tiny compared to the vast, conscript armies of the Continental powers. Indeed, the Germans simply discounted it, to their cost. As the concept of the 'Concert of Europe' gave way to overtly nationalistic self-assertion, the British contribution waned. Though personally strongly anti-German, Grey continued to avoid formal alliances, but by 1910 it was clear that Germany would be Britain's adversary, if she were to have one.

In a series of incidents in North Africa, the Balkans, and Turkey, and in the continuing escalation of the navy building programme (despite British attempts, especially in 1911–12, to negotiate a limitation agreement) Anglo-German hostility became confirmed. It began to take on a cultural as well as a diplomatic and military aspect. The respect mixed with concern characteristic of British views of German achievements in the 1890s began to change to alarm and fear.

When events in the Balkans and Central Europe in June and July 1914 led rapidly to war, as Germany estimated that the moment for her bid for mastery had come, the British could bring little influence to bear. Britain had less to gain from war than any of the other major European powers except perhaps Russia. Whether the Liberal Cabinet would have entered the war at all had the Germans not invaded Belgium is open to doubt. But the Germans ignored both the traditional British concern for the strategic importance of the Low Countries, and the implications of guarantee of Belgian independence which they as well as the British had signed in 1870 to last during the Franco-Prussian War. The attack on Belgium decided the matter, and Asquith led his Cabinet into war with only two resignations—John Morley and John Burns. He did so with a heavy heart: the blithe spirit which infused the enthusiastic rush to the colours to join the war that was to be 'over by Christmas' was not shared by Britain's political leadership.

Britain was remarkably unprepared psychologically and, on the whole, physically for a Continental land war. War on land, even in the Crimea and South Africa, had been seen as a marginal matter, to be fought by professionals and a few volunteers. Military values were influential amongst the aristocracy and gentry and increasingly in the public schools, but elsewhere made little impact. Attempts by groups on the right to militarize society—from the Militia of the 1850s, through the Riflemen and the Volunteers, to Lord Roberts's National Service League in the 1900s—had conspicuously failed. 'Trafalgar Day' was the annual martial celebration, reflecting the essentially naval and defensive cast of the public mind—the 'blue water' policy, as it was called. Except in certain rural areas, 'to go for a sodger', 'to take the King's shilling', had for ordinary people been an act of desperation in a time of unemployment or personal catastrophe. The British public liked bands and bright uniforms because they were entertainments, the exact opposite of harbingers of war. Pomp and domesticity was the British style.

Government contracts for guns and ships were by the Edwardian years considerable in value and an important part of the economy of the north-east of England, but, in general, military matters seldom impinged on the thinking of government and society. Certainly, they had not penetrated the very fabric of the political, social, and economic order as they had in virtually every Continental state. The first industrial nation had offered the world a remarkable public experiment in liberal, capitalist democracy whose success was premised upon free trade and world peace. Tuesday, 4 August 1914 brought that experiment to an abrupt halt.

> There's a whisper down the field where the year has shot her yield,
> And the ricks stand grey to the sun,
> Singing:—'Over then, come over, for the bee has quit the clover,
> And your English summer's done.'
>
> Rudyard Kipling, 'The Long Trail'

KENNETH O. MORGAN

10. *The Twentieth Century*

(1914–1983)

The First World War

AT the Lord Mayor of London's annual banquet at the Mansion House on 17 July 1914, the Chancellor of the Exchequer, David Lloyd George, issued stern warnings about the ominous condition of British society. At home, the 'triple alliance' of miners, railwaymen, and transport workers was threatening a mass united strike to back up the railwaymen's claim for union recognition and a 48-hour week. Alongside this prospect of nation-wide industrial paralysis, there was across the Irish Sea a state of near civil war in Ireland, with 200,000 or more men under arms in Protestant Ulster and the Catholic south, and the likelihood of the age-long saga of Irish nationalism being brought to a grim and bloody resolution. Abroad, there were nationalist troubles in India and in Egypt. Nearer home in south-east Europe, the ethnic nationalities of the Balkans were in renewed turmoil following the assassination of the Austrian Archduke, Franz Ferdinand, at Sarajevo in Bosnia on 28 June.

On the eve of world war, therefore, Britain seemed to present a classic picture of a civilized liberal democracy on the verge of dissolution, racked by tensions and strains with which its sanctions and institutions were unable to cope. And yet, as so often in the past, once the supreme crisis of war erupted, these elements of conflict subsided with remarkable speed. An underlying mood of united purpose gripped the nation. The first few weeks of hostilities, after Britain declared war on 4 August, were, inevitably, a time of some panic. Only dramatic measures by the Treasury and the Bank of England preserved the national currency and credit. Manufacturing and commerce tried desperately to adjust to the challenges of war against the background of an ethic that proclaimed that it was 'business as usual'. The early experiences of actual fighting were almost disastrous as the British Expeditionary Force, cobbled together in much haste and dispatched to Flanders and France, met with a severe reverse at Ypres, and had to retreat from Mons, in disarray and suffering heavy losses. Reduced to only three corps in strength, its fighting force was gravely diminished almost from the start. Only a stern resistance by the French forces on the river Marne prevented a rapid German advance on Paris and an early victory for Germany and its Austrian allies.

After the initial disasters, however, the nation and its leaders settled down for a long war. Vital domestic issues such as Irish home rule were suspended for the duration of hostilities. The political parties declared an indefinite truce. The industrial disturbances of the summer of 1914 petered out, with the TUC outdoing the employers in voicing the conventional patriotism of the time. A curious kind of calm descended, founded on a broad—though very far from universal—consensus about the justice of the war. The one element required to make it acceptable to a liberal society was some kind of broad, humane justification to explain what the war was really about. This was provided by Lloyd George, once a bitter opponent of the Boer War in South Africa in 1899, and for many years the most outspokenly left-wing member of the Asquith Liberal government. Lloyd George remained suspiciously silent during the early weeks. But in an eloquent address to a massed audience of his Welsh fellow-countrymen at the Queen's Hall, London, on 19 September 1914, he committed himself without reserve to a fight to the finish. He occupied, or claimed to occupy, the highest moral ground. It was, he declared, a war on behalf of liberal principles, a crusade on behalf of the 'little five-foot-five nations', like Belgium, flagrantly invaded by the Germans, or Serbia and Montenegro, now threatened by Austria-Hungary. It was not surprising that a claim that the war was a holy cause, backed up not only by the leaders of all the Christian churches but by all the Liberal pantheon of heroes from Fox to Gladstone, met with instant response, not least in the smaller nations of Scotland and Wales within Britain itself.

This broad consensus about the rightness of the war was not fundamentally eroded over the next four terrible years. Of course, it went through many changes, especially after the unpopular decision to impose conscription for the armed services was instituted in May 1916. Eventually, by 1917, sheer war-weariness was taking its toll, quite apart from other factors such as the growing militancy from organized labour and the Messianic appeal of the Bolshevik revolution in Russia. Of course, too, this consensus was sustained by subtle or crude

Recruits to the army under the 'Derby scheme', Southwark Town Hall, autumn 1915. In October 1915, Lord Derby introduced a scheme designed to preserve the voluntary recruitment system by allowing men to register to 'attest' their willingness to serve. Popular enthusiasm remained extremely high: 235,000 men volunteered under the Derby scheme in October–November 1915. But universal male conscription duly followed in early 1916.

manipulation of the news services, censorship of the press, government-sponsored legends of atrocities allegedly committed by 'the Huns'. There was much persecution of radical or anti-war critics. In spite of government pressures, bodies such as the Christian pacifist 'No-Conscription Fellowship' and the Union of Democratic Control (which sought a negotiated peace) were by 1917 making some impact on public opinion. Lord Lansdowne's appeal for peace (29 November 1917) caused a great stir. Nevertheless, the available evidence for the war years suggests that the broad mass of the population retained its faith that the war was just and necessary, and that it must be fought until the total surrender of the German enemy, whatever the cost. Recruitment to the armed services from volunteers was heavy and enthusiastic: indeed voluntary recruitment proved more successful in swelling the ranks of the army in France in 1914–16 than was the compulsory method of conscription thereafter. The long years of military and naval conflict that dragged on from the initial stalemate on the western front in the autumn of 1914, until the final Allied breakthrough in August–September 1918 were accepted with resignation and a kind of grim endurance.

The psychological and moral impact of those appalling years sank deep into the memory and the outlook of the British people. They profoundly coloured the literary sensibilities of a whole generation. They helped shape responses to the threat of foreign war for twenty years after the Great War came to an end. The war on the western front took the unfamiliar form of a prolonged slogging match between heavily-defended forces on either side, dug into slit trenches, and unable to exploit the new techniques of mobile striking power so dramatically tested in the Franco-Prussian war of 1870. For almost four years, the war in France showed little movement. There were occasional British attempts to seize the initiative. Always they ended in huge casualties on a scale scarcely comprehensible to a nation which lived on the luxurious memories of a century of almost unbroken peace. The British offensive at Loos was beaten back in September 1915. More damaging still, in June 1916 a new British advance on the Somme proved a calamitous failure with 60,000 men falling on the first day. British casualties here alone amounted to 420,000. The most terrible of these experiences came at Passchendaele in August–September 1917, when over 300,000 British troops were recorded as dead or wounded, many of them drowned in the mud of Flanders amidst torrential rain. Both the cavalry and mechanical inventions such as the 'tanks' made no impact in so immobile a campaign. The new fighter aircraft had little effect. As on other occasions, the class divide that cut off commanding officers from the rank-and-file infantrymen and hindered communication between them was fatal throughout. In effect, the British ceased to be a viable offensive force for the next few months. March and April 1918 saw the British army desperately striving to ward off a new German advance in the Amiens sector. Not until the ultimate dramatic breakthrough by Haig that August did the war show signs of coming to a resolution. Meanwhile attempts, advocated by Lloyd George and Churchill amongst others, to circumvent the stalemate on the western front by a more peripheral 'eastern' strategy also led to successive débâcles. The Dardanelles expedition in the summer of 1915 was a colossal exercise in military mismanagement and led to further huge losses; so did the expedition to Salonika a year later. The Dardanelles in particular did immense harm to Churchill's

War casualty, Beaumont Hamel, the Somme. Dead German soldier. In the First World War, 750,000 Britains were killed, many of them in trench warfare on the western front in France.

reputation as a rational politician, from which he took years to recover. Even on the high seas, Britain's traditional area of supremacy, the one major battle, the encounter off Jutland in June 1916, was at best a draw between the British and German high fleets. The British Grand Fleet lost three battle cruisers, three other cruisers, and eight destroyers in an ill-conducted engagement.

Later anti-war propaganda depicted an angry populace displaying fierce hostility towards the military and naval commanders responsible for this terrible catalogue of disaster in almost every theatre. 'War poets' such as Wilfred Owen and Isaac Rosenberg (who fell in battle) and Siegfried Sassoon and Robert Graves (who survived), stirred particularly by the carnage of Passchendaele, all encouraged the view that a mass renunciation took place of the very idea of war itself, of the carnage that could result in half an entire generation of young men being wiped out.

The bare statistics of the war—750,000 killed, another 2,500,000 wounded, many permanently disabled—reinforced this belief in a mass rejection of militarism. That was not, however, how it appeared to most people at the time, even if it should have done so. While the British commander-in-chief on the western front, Sir John French, was indeed removed from command at the end of 1915, his successor, Sir Douglas Haig, a grim, taciturn Lowland Scot, steadily built up a massive public reputation for courage and integrity, a reputation matched by Sir Edwin Lutyens's towering war memorial to commemorate the British dead at Thiepval. Other naval and military leaders, such as Admiral Beatty and General Allenby (who conducted a brilliant campaign from Egypt, through Palestine into Syria in 1917–18, to eliminate the Turks as significant allies for the Germans), became almost popular heroes. The trenches became the symbol of stern, but inescapable, resolution. Bruce Bairnsfather's famous cartoon of 'Old Bill', urging his comrade that if he knew of 'a better 'ole' he should go to it, symbolized a popular mood of almost humorous tolerance of the terrors of trench warfare. When, after desperate military crises and with the immense military and financial aid of the United States, the British and French armies forced their way through the German lines to reach the borders of Germany itself by the time of the armistice on 11 November 1918, mass enthusiasm for the war appeared at its zenith. Britain seemed in danger of inventing a new military cult unknown in these islands since the days of Marlborough.

A major factor in the widespread popularity of the war—and also in its subsequent bitter unpopularity—was the involvement of the whole population and the entire social and economic fabric in total war. After a leisurely start, in 1915–16 the war brought about a massive industrial and social transformation; it erected a leviathan of state power and collectivist control without precedent. The forces of production and distribution in industry and agriculture were all harnessed to fuel the needs of a mighty war machine. The model was set by the new Ministry of Munitions of which Lloyd George assumed control in May 1915. Created to deal with bottle-necks in the supply of arms and ammunition, the Ministry became the engine of a massive central machine which invigorated the entire industrial structure through its 'men of push and go'. It achieved an immense impact as well on such different areas as social welfare, housing policy, and the status of women. The coal mines, the railways, merchant and other shipping were all taken under state control. The old pre-war shibboleths of *laissez-faire*, including the hallowed principle of free trade itself, were bypassed or ignored. Equally, the traditional system of industrial relations was wrenched into totally new patterns. The Treasury Agreement of March 1915, negotiated between the government and the trade unions (except for the miners), forbade strikes but also guaranteed collective bargaining and, indirectly, a new access to government for trade union leaders. The Treasury Agreement certainly did not achieve its aim of universal industrial peace during the war years. There were major disputes in the coal industry, notably a successful official strike by the South Wales Miners in July 1915. The work of the Ministry of Munitions in trying to 'dilute' the work-force by introducing unskilled workers (especially women) into engineering factories, and in trying to control the movements of labour in the armaments industry brought much trouble, notably on Clydeside. The unofficial activities of shop stewards in Scotland and also in Sheffield in 1916–17 remind us that the consensus of the war years was a shallow one and very far from unanimous. Nevertheless, the war did ensure a continuing corporate status for the unions—and also for employers, newly combined in the Federation of British Industry. A new organic, planned system of industrial relations appeared to be possible. It was significant that powerful businessmen such as Sir Eric Geddes and Sir Joseph Maclay, Lord Devonport and Lord Rhondda, appeared in key departments of central government. This symbolized the transformation in the relationship of industrial and political leadership that was taking place. Edward VII's Liberal England was being turned into a corporate state, almost what a later generation would term 'Great Britain Limited'.

Over a vast range of social and cultural activities, the collective impact of the Great War was profound indeed. Left-wing opponents of the war such as Ramsay MacDonald of the Labour Party noted ironically that the imperatives of war were achieving far more for social reform than had all the campaigns of the trade unions and of progressive humanitarians in half a century past. New vistas of governmental activity were being opened up. Fresh layers were being added to the technocratic, professional, and civil service élite that had governed Britain in the years of peace. The administrative and managerial class expanded massively. Social reformers such as William Beveridge or Seebohm Rowntree, even the socialist Beatrice Webb, became influential and even honoured figures in the recesses of central government, especially after Lloyd George succeeded Asquith as Prime Minister in December 1916. Wages went up; working conditions

Women workers in a munitions factory, January 1917. Over 700,000 women worked in arms production (including shipbuilding) during the First World War: the trade unions were persuaded to accept the 'dilution' of skilled labour involved. The new status of women (with 4,814,600 in employment by January 1918) led to their being granted the vote in 1918.

improved. The 1917 Corn Production Act revitalized British agriculture and gave a fresh lease of life to tenant farmers and their labourers. Attention was also paid to technical and other education, notably through H. A. L. Fisher's Act of 1918 which made free elementary education general and sought to create a ladder of opportunity from the elementary to the secondary and higher levels of education. Governmental inquiries, one of them headed by as conservative a figure as Lord Salisbury, opened up new vistas for state housing schemes, an area almost totally neglected by the New Liberalism before 1914. The principle was laid down for a system of subsidized local-authority houses, to provide the hundreds of thousands of working-class dwellings for rent that were required, and to remove the blight of slums in city centres and older industrial areas. Concern was voiced, too, for public health. The supreme irony was that a war which brought the loss of human life on such a colossal scale also saw the preservation of life at home through improved medical arrangements, better conditions for children and old people and nursing mothers, and such innovations as the Medical Research Council. By the end of 1918, the government was committed to the idea of a new Ministry of Health to co-ordinate the services for health and national insurance, and to take over the duties of the Local Government Board.

One important element of British society above all other gained from the wartime experience—indeed for them (a majority of the population, in fact) this was an era of emancipation. Women in Britain were supreme beneficiaries of the war years. Thousands of them served at the front, often in medical field hospitals. The spectacle of Nurse Edith Cavell martyred by the Germans for assisting in the escape of British and French prisoners of war in Belgium added powerfully to the public esteem of women in general. At home, suffragette leaders such as Mrs Pankhurst and her elder daughter Christabel (though not her socialist younger daughter, Sylvia) aided in recruiting campaigns for the government. More widely, women found vast new opportunities in clerical and administrative work, in munitions and other engineering factories, and in many other unfamiliar tasks previously reserved for men only. The very dissolution wrought by total war exerted powerful pressures in eroding the sex barriers which had restricted British women over the decades. It was hardly possible to argue now that women were incapable of exercising the rights of citizenship to the full; in the 1918 Representation of the People Act, therefore, women thirty and over were given the vote. It was almost anti-climactic. A long, bitter saga of persecution and prejudice ended with a whimper. Here as elsewhere, by emphasizing the positive, progressive consequences of the war, with the full panoply of 'reconstruction' (ill-defined) which was supposed to be launched when peace returned, the government contrived, perhaps unintentionally, to extend and fortify the consensus of the time.

For British politics, the Great War produced massive and tumultuous changes. At the outbreak of war, the House of Commons was still largely dominated by the Gilbertian rivalry of Liberals and Conservatives (or Unionists). However, for the Liberal Party the war brought disaster. Partly this was because of the serious inroads into individual and civil liberties that war entailed. Partly it was due to a deep-seated ambiguity about the very merits of the war that many Liberals harboured. The turning

Lloyd George talking to Indian soldiers near Fricourt, on the Somme, September 1916. Both as Secretary of State for War (July–December 1916) and as Prime Minister (from December 1916) Lloyd George projected his personal leadership by visits to soldiers on the front in France.

of Asquith's Liberal administration into a three-party coalition in May 1915 marked a new stage in the downfall of Liberalism. Thereafter, Asquith's own apparently lethargic and fumbling leadership was accompanied by severe internal party divisions over the fundamental issue of military conscription. Lloyd George and Churchill both endorsed conscription as the symbol of whole-hearted commitment to 'a fight to the finish'. More traditional Liberals such as Simon and McKenna were hesitant. Asquith himself dithered unhappily. In the end, conscription came for all adult males aged between eighteen and forty-five, but criticism of Asquith and the Liberal ethic generally continued to mount.

In December 1916 the final crisis came. There had been complaints for months over government failures, not only in the field, but also over the inability to resolve the Irish question and to settle labour disputes at home. Between 1 and 9 December

1916 there followed political manoeuvres of Byzantine complexity over which historians continue to dispute like so many medieval schoolmen. Lloyd George joined with two leading Unionists, Bonar Law and the Irishman Sir Edward Carson, in proposing to Asquith a new supreme War Committee to run the war. After days of uncertainty, Asquith refused. Lloyd George then resigned and, in a crucial trial of strength between 4 and 9 December, emerged as Prime Minister of something like an all-party coalition. It included not only all the Unionists but also (by a majority of one vote on the National Executive) the Labour Party as well, in addition to roughly half the Liberals in the House of Commons. Henceforth, between December 1916 and November 1918, Lloyd George built himself up into a semi-presidential position of near-impregnability. He was the Prime Minister of a supreme War Cabinet, backed up by a new Cabinet office and a 'garden suburb' or kitchen cabinet of private secretaries. Beneath this apex extended a mighty machine of centralized power. Lloyd George's triumph helped to win the war—but for his own Liberal Party it meant a débâcle. The party remained split, weakened at the grass roots, ineffective and divided in Parliament, shorn of much of its morale and impetus in the press and in intellectual circles. The New Liberalism, which had animated so much social reform before 1914, just spluttered out. When the war ended in November 1918, the Liberals were a divided, much weakened rump, a supreme casualty of total war.

Their place was taken, quite unexpectedly, by the Labour Party. This party had also been much divided by the outbreak of war. In contrast to the patriotism of trade union leaders, Ramsay MacDonald and many on the socialist left had been opponents of entering the war. MacDonald had to resign his leadership of the parliamentary Labour Party in consequence. Issues during the war such as the impact of conscription (military and possibly industrial), and the decision over whether or not to serve under Lloyd George also plagued the Labour Party. Nevertheless, the long-term consequences of the war for the party were wholly beneficial. The trade unions on which Labour depended were much strengthened by the war experience. Their membership roughly doubled to reach over eight million by the start of 1919. The party was also given new stimulus by the revolution in Russia, and by the wider anti-war radicalism in the last two years of the war. In effect, Labour was serving in government and acting as the formal opposition at one and the same time. It was ideally placed to exploit the internal difficulties of the Liberals.

Finally, the 1918 franchise reforms extended the electorate from about 8 million to over 21 million. This meant a huge increase in the working-class vote and an encouragement of the tendency to polarize politics on grounds of class. The 1918 party constitution gave the party a new socialist commitment and, more important, a reorganized structure in the constituencies and in Head Office, dominated throughout by the trade unions. The advance of Labour was a powerful political consequence of the war, though quite unforeseen at the time.

The real beneficiaries were the Conservatives. The war encouraged a process by which they became the natural majority party. Apart from being united by the call of war, as the patriots they claimed to be, after being divided over tariffs and other questions before 1914, the Conservatives became increasingly dominated by business and manufacturing interests. They were now largely urban or suburban in their base, not a party of squires. At the end of the war, with new business-orientated figures such as Stanley Baldwin and Neville Chamberlain coming through, the Conservatives were poised, like the Labour Party, to destroy the Edwardian political system. When the war ended on 11 November 1918, Lloyd George assumed total command. His rump of coalition Liberals were in electoral alliance with the Conservatives, in opposition to the 'pacifists' of the anti-government Liberals and the 'Bolsheviks' of the Labour Party. A new era of right-wing domination was in the making.

Externally, the war years encouraged further changes. It was, in all senses, a profoundly imperial war, fought for empire as well as for king and country. Much was owed to military and other assistance from Australia, New Zealand, Canada, South Africa, and India. Anzac Day (with memories of Suvla Bay, Gallipoli) became a tragic, symbolic event in the Australian calendar. In 1917 Lloyd George actually convened an Imperial War Cabinet of Prime Ministers to assist the Cabinet of the mother country. A powerful empire statesman like Smuts of South Africa was even called upon to participate in the deliberations of the British Cabinet. In commerce, imperial preference was becoming a reality. The imperial mystique was a powerful one at this time. The main architect of the day, Edwin Lutyens, had been in his younger days a disciple of the arts and crafts movement inspired by William Morris. Now he and Herbert Baker were turning their talents to pomp and circumstance by rebuilding the city of Delhi. It was to be dominated by a massive Viceroy's residence and Secretariat buildings as symbols of classical authority. During the war years, the imperial idea was taken further then ever before. Indeed, the secret treaties of the war years ensured that at the peace the mandate system or other stratagems would leave Britain with an imperial domain larger than ever, with vast new territories in the Middle East and up from the Persian Gulf. Buoyed up by the eccentric operations of individualists such as 'Lawrence of Arabia' and fired by the heady prospects of vast oil riches in Mesopotamia and elsewhere in the Middle East, the bounds of the British Empire extended ever wider.

Yet in reality it was all becoming increasingly impractical to maintain. Long before 1914, the financial and military constraints upon an effective imperial policy were becoming clear, especially in India with its growing Congress movement. There was something else now—new and increasingly effective nationalist uprisings against British rule. Unlike Wales, which was almost mindlessly patriotic with Lloyd George at the helm, Ireland offered a disturbing spectacle of colonial revolt. The Easter rising of April 1916, conducted by a few republicans and Sinn Fein partisans, seemed to be a fiasco. But, aided by the brutal reaction of Asquith's government, by mid-1918 Sinn Fein and its republican creed had won over almost all the twenty-six southern Irish counties. A veteran home ruler such as John Dillon was being swept aside by new nationalist radicals like Michael Collins and Éamon de Valera. By the end of the war, southern Ireland was virtually under martial law, resistant to conscription, in a state of near rebellion against the Crown and the Protestant ascendancy, or what was left of it. The long march of Irish nationalism, constitutional and largely peaceful in the decades from O'Connell to Parnell and Redmond, seemed on the verge of producing a new and violent explosion. One clear moral of the war years, therefore, was that the political and social consensus, fragile enough for Clydeside and the Welsh mining valleys, did not extend at all to southern Ireland. With the powerful thrust of Irish republicanism, a new kind of nationalist revolt against the constraints of imperial rule was well under way. Indians and Egyptians, among others, were likely to pay careful heed. The war left a legacy of a more integrated but also a more isolated Britain, whose grandiose imperial role was already being swamped by wider transformations in the post-war world.

The Twenties

When peace returned, it seemed that little had changed. The continuity between war and peace was confirmed by Lloyd

George's overwhelming electoral triumph at the 'coupon election' of December 1918, a ratification of the patriotism and unity of the war years. The Prime Minister was acclaimed, almost universally, as 'the man who won the war', the most dominant political leader since Cromwell. The electoral verdict was indeed an overpowering one. The supporters of the coalition government numbered no less than 526 (of whom 136 were Liberals and almost all the rest Unionist), against a mere 57 Labour MPs and 26 Independent Liberals. The results were not so conclusive under closer examination. The Labour Party's tally of 57 MPs concealed the fact that the party had polled two and a half million votes, and was on the verge of a massive electoral breakthrough. In Ireland, Sinn Fein captured 73 seats out of 81 in the south; its representatives withdrew from Westminster and set up their own unofficial parliament or 'Dáil' in Dublin. Even so, the mandate on behalf of the Prime Minister and his wartime associates seemed quite irrefutable. The election seemed to confirm, too, that socio-economic normality in many respects was being rapidly restored. Many of the wartime controls and the apparatus of state collectivism disappeared as if they had never been. Major industries were returned to private hands—the railways, shipping, even the coal mines whose owners were perhaps the most hated group in the entire capitalist world. The government also began a consistent financial policy to ensure an eventual return to the gold standard; this would entail a deflationary approach, with a steady contraction of the note issue expanded so rapidly during the war. The City of London, the class system, private capitalism appeared destined to continue their unchallenged reign. To indicate that this was capitalism with a human face, the government also began with a flurry of reforming activity in 1919–20. Indeed, Lloyd George had campaigned far more vigorously at the election as a social reformer anxious to build a 'land fit for heroes', than as a chauvinist determined to hang the Kaiser or 'squeeze Germany till the pips squeaked'. So there followed a vigorous, if short-lived, programme to extend health and educational services, to raise pensions, and spread universal unemployment insurance. Most spectacular of all was the subsidized housing programme launched by the Liberal minister Dr Christopher Addison which, with reluctant treasury support, achieved a total of over 200,000 publicly-built houses in the 1919–22 period, a limited but valuable start in dealing with one of the major social scandals in the land.

But it soon became disturbingly clear that life was not normal and that the comforting framework of pre-1914 could not easily be restored. There were new and disruptive economic problems that resulted from the loss of foreign markets and the sale of overseas investments to pay for the war. The most ominous aspect of this, on which newspaper headlines focused attention, was the huge increase in the national debt. The unredeemed capital of the debt stood at £706 million in 1914. Six years later it had soared to £7,875 million. This resulted in a passionate cry for 'economy', the ending of 'waste' in public expenditure, and a return to a balanced budget and a firm currency after the rapid inflation of 1918–19. Politically, too, things were very far from normal. Lloyd George's coalition had come to power in unhappy circumstances, with a background of conspiracy surrounding the calling of the 1918 'coupon' general election. Its moral title to power was in doubt. Furthermore, as a coalition it was prey to internal disputes, and constant tension between the Liberal Prime Minister and his Conservative colleagues over domestic, foreign, and imperial affairs. Lloyd George himself, a remote, Olympian figure, preoccupied with international peace conferences, aloof from the House of Commons, a Prime Minister without a party, an adventurer careless in his financial and sexual activities, was not one who inspired universal trust or affection. So the consensus of the armistice period soon evaporated and new conflicts took its place.

A series of challenges were launched which gradually undermined the coalition's claim to govern. New patterns were being formed which would shape the course of British history for the next twenty years. On the left, Lloyd George was bitterly attacked by many Liberals over his casualness towards old and hallowed principles such as free trade. His policy in Ireland appeared even more shocking since the British government pursued war against the IRA in 1919–21 with an unrestrained policy of retaliation which led to bloody atrocities being committed by the auxiliary forces that were maintained by the Crown to back up the army and the constabulary. In December 1921, Lloyd George, always by instinct a negotiator, eventually made peace with the Sinn Fein leaders, Arthur Griffith and Michael Collins. From January 1922, an Irish Free State, consisting of the twenty-six Catholic counties of southern Ireland, was created, with just the six Protestant counties of Ulster in the north-east left within the United Kingdom. But this volte-face was too late to repair Lloyd George's tarnished image amongst liberal opinion. In the Labour Party and trade union world, the Prime Minister totally lost the reputation he had long enjoyed as a patron of labour. His

John Maynard Keynes, drawn here by David Low in a cartoon in the *New Statesman and Nation,* 28 October 1933, was the most influential economist of the twentieth century. His *General Theory* (1936) revolutionized ideas about economic theory and policy, while *Economic Consequences of the Peace* (1919) helped spread disillusion with the results of the First World War.

government used tough methods, including emergency powers and the use of troops as strike-breakers, in dealing with national strikes by miners, railwaymen, and many other workers (including even the police) in 1919–21. Thereafter, the government failed to prevent massive unemployment (soon rising to over a million workers) from growing up and casting a blight over the older industrial areas. Episodes like the apparent deceiving of the coal-miners over the Sankey report and the proposed nationalization of the mines in 1919, and the further undermining of the 'Triple Alliance' to frustrate the miners again on 'Black Friday' (15 April 1921) sank deep into the consciousness of the working class. A government elected to promote national solidarity and social unity had made the class divide wider than ever before. If the coalition was attacked on the left, it was increasingly under fire on the right as well. Conservatives longed for the return of a healthy system of independent party politics, freed from the buccaneering methods of an autocratic Prime Minister and his retainers. Although the coalition hung on for almost four years, it was in dire straits and Lloyd George himself a Prime Minister at bay.

Above and beyond all this, there was a wider mood of disillusion with the peace treaties and the 'system of Versailles'. The peace settlement was increasingly unpopular. It was linked with covert secret treaties concluded during the war between Britain and its allies, and with unjust terms, for financial reparation and frontier arrangements, imposed on the defeated Germans. No book more effectively expressed this mood than did the economist J. M. Keynes's *Economic Consequences of the Peace* (1919). The work of a financial adviser to the Treasury who had resigned in protest during the Paris peace conference, it rapidly became a best seller on both sides of the Atlantic. It seemed to show conclusively that the reparations imposed on Germany would lead to its financial ruin and thereby to the permanent weakening of the European economy. Keynes also evoked, in memorable and picturesque language, the frenzied, corrupt atmosphere in which the various covert bargains were struck by the peacemakers in Versailles. Lloyd George was condemned as a man 'rooted in nothing'. The premier's efforts to act as the peacemaker of Europe in successive international conferences became unpopular. Britain refused any longer to act, in Bonar Law's striking phrase, as 'the policeman of the world'. The empire might be larger than ever, but it must be accompanied by a withdrawal from commitments in Europe. Otherwise another tragedy would afflict the land as it had done in August 1914. The final blow for Lloyd George's coalition came in October 1922 when it seemed that Britain was on the verge of war with Turkey over the defence of the Greek position in Asia

Minor and protection of the Straits. Conservatives as well as the British left revolted against this rekindling of jingoism. The right-wing basis of the government collapsed. Lloyd George fell from power on 19 October 1922, a political pariah for the rest of his life.

Two kinds of reaction against Lloyd George's government followed. They were symbolized respectively by Ramsay MacDonald and Stanley Baldwin, both prominent in the movements that led to the downfall of the coalition in October 1922. MacDonald, with his heady Utopian internationalism and 'Brave New World' idealism, was the perfect voice for the growing Labour Party, whose tally of seats rose rapidly in the 1922 and 1923 general elections. He could straddle both the socialism of Clydeside and the social conventions of the London establishment. Alternatively, and more influential still, Stanley Baldwin led the Conservative forces of suburban middle-class respectability and of orthodox patriotism, all alarmed at Lloyd George's political experiments and the international adventurism of British foreign policy after the war. Baldwin, Prime Minister in 1923–4, 1924–9, and 1935–7, was an appropriate leader for a Britain desperate for a return to tranquillity and social peace.

There was constant flux and upheaval in other spheres of public life as well. Many of the settled patterns of pre-war now seemed under assault. In Wales and Scotland there were small movements of intellectuals, which suggested that the very unity of the kingdom could itself be threatened. Two small nationalist parties were formed on the Irish model, Plaid Cymru in Wales in 1925 and the National Party of Scotland in 1928. However, their significance was to lie in a distant future. In the arts, in literature, music, painting, and architecture, the surviving presence of pre-war giants such as Kipling and Hardy, Elgar and Lutyens masked the underlying challenge of avant-garde movements expressive of 'modernism' and revolt. Amongst the novelists, the main work of Joyce and of D. H. Lawrence had already been written; indeed after *Women in Love* appeared in 1920, with its echoes of the *malaise* of the war years, Lawrence's later work seemed relatively unimpressive. More innovative were the writings of the coterie of intellectuals and artists linked with the 'Bloomsbury group'. In particular, the remarkable series of 'stream of consciousness' novels produced by Virginia Woolf, with their subtle delineation of human character and strangely fluid form, testified to the vitality of 'modernism' in the novel. More orthodox was E. M. Forster's *Passage to India* (1924), the work of a novelist indirectly associated with Bloomsbury, which, in its treatment of the interaction of Western and Eastern cultures, portrays the declining self-confidence of Western liberal humanism. The most notable pioneering development in poetry was T. S. Eliot's 'The Waste Land' (1922) with its disturbing rhythms and imagery; its pervading tone of Christian resignation and private melancholy captures one powerful aspect of the culture of the twenties. It was not a creative time for the theatre other than Shaw's *St. Joan*, his most powerful philosophic affirmation. Nor was it an age of great imagination in art, design, and architecture either; painters like Ben Nicholson were still seeking a new style, while others such as Paul Nash were apparently marking time. In the world of art, the Bloomsbury group again provided a few notable rebels, Roger Fry, the art critic and patron, painters such as Duncan Grant and Vanessa Bell, trying to break out of the mould of realism in pictorial representation. Bloomsbury, indeed, with its writers and artists, and associated figures like the economist J. M. Keynes, the essayist Lytton Strachey, and its philosopher-mentor G. E. Moore, embodied many of the strengths and limitations of the

The May rowing races at Cambridge University, in the summer of 1922. The twenties saw a great release of upper-class gaiety amongst the so-called 'bright young things' of Oxford and Cambridge.

British cultural scene in the twenties. It genuinely attempted to infuse British art with the inspiration of the modernist poets and surrealist artists of continental Europe. It combined the cult of the new with an effective iconoclasm, most popularly conveyed in Lytton Strachey's satirical studies of the feet of clay of leading Victorian personalities, from the queen downwards. More negatively, Bloomsbury encouraged an inbred, almost tribal, view of artistic communication; it became in time a sheltered enclave with dynastic overtones. Writers in the thirties were to criticize the Bloomsbury group as a new cultural establishment. They attacked them for laying insufficient emphasis on moral (rather than purely aesthetic) sensibility and for their supposed lack of political or public concern. Probably the Bloomsbury ethos encouraged a tendency for the art of the classes and masses to grow further and further apart.

Developments in the arts, however, with their expressions of revolt and emancipation, chimed in with wider social movements of the time. The women who gained the vote, partially in 1918 and then (conclusively) in 1928, were able to enjoy other freedoms as well, the right to smoke, to enjoy new leisure interests such as the films, to pursue a more open and less constrained 'sex life', and to wear clothes that were spectacularly far less drab or puritanical. The 'bright young things' extolled in memoirs of the twenties, for whom the satires and plays of Noël Coward appeared to have been specifically written, were limited enough in their outlook. They were usually of middle- to upper-class background. They, or their friends, were strongly associated with the public schools, with Oxford and Cambridge. Oxford, in particular, became linked with a kind of free cultural self-expression, tending to decadence, nihilism, or both, just as it was to be identified (equally wrongly) in the thirties with anti-war protest. The older universities were probably far less influential in society at large than later myth-mongers alleged, but they merged into the experimental climate of a more formless, rootless world.

Certainly, the older arbiters of moral standards seemed to be suffering a crisis of authority after the war. Nowhere was this more apparent than amongst the churches, manifestly among the casualties of total war, with the possible exception of the Roman Catholics with their strongly Irish membership. The nonconformist chapels, moral beacons to many in the Victorian heyday, were now suffering from falling membership, declining funds, diminished authority. Even in their strongholds in Wales and Scotland, the chapels were in steady retreat. Not least, the challenges to Puritanism and Sabbatarianism that the war had produced severely undermined what sanctions the chapels could muster. The Church of England, too, maintained its established, national role with much difficulty after the war. Archbishops such as Randall Davidson and Cosmo Lang spoke in terms of the old cohesion and disciplines, but their message appeared increasingly ineffective. In a formal sense, Britain was still a recognizably Christian country. Its Church leaders were still honoured and respected, indissolubly bound to Crown and landed aristocracy. Sunday was still a day of tranquillity and gloom when the trains did not run, and shops and theatres were closed, as also were public houses in Wales and Scotland. The revision of the Anglican Prayer Book in 1927–8 produced furious public debate; the old battles between Anglo-Catholic and evangelical wings of the established Church were vigorously resumed. The identification of religion with middle-class values, with the family, the community, and a safe form of patriotism was still maintained. So, too, was the link of religion with the empire, notably through youth movements such as the Boy Scouts and the Church Brigade. The war itself encouraged a kind of secular religiosity, symbolized in the Cenotaph erected by Lutyens in Whitehall as a memorial to the war dead. And yet, for all the formal trappings to remind the people of their religious inheritance through the centuries, the impact and mystique of Christianity was clearly on the wane, especially among the post-war generation and ex-servicemen.

The inability of the churches significantly to influence the course of events was dramatically shown during the 1926 general strike. In that year, the terrible cycle of industrial decline, unemployment, and social bitterness led to the worst explosion of class conflict that Britain had yet known. The great strikes of 1919–21 had now passed away. The Prime Minister, Baldwin, called for 'Peace in our Time, O Lord'. But in the greatest industry in the land, coal-mining, tension remained high, with a background of wage cuts, dismissals, and falling living stand-ards for mining families. In April 1926 the government refused to renew a subsidy to the mining industry. On 2 May Baldwin broke off negotiations with the TUC delegation. Almost by accident, the unions lurched into a general strike. For nine days (3–12 May) Britain was at a virtual standstill. Never before had the potential economic strength of the unions in challenging the government and the constitutional order been shown with more powerful effect. The Church leaders, with their call for concili-ation, were impotent in the wings.

THE
BRITISH WORKER
OFFICIAL STRIKE NEWS BULLETIN
Published by The General Council of the Trades Union Congress

No. 1.	WEDNESDAY EVENING, MAY 5, 1926.	PRICE ONE PENNY

IN LONDON AND THE SOUTH

Splendid Loyalty of Transport Workers

EVERY DOCKER OUT

" London dock workers are absolutely splendid," said an official of the Transport and General Workers' Union.

" So far as they are concerned, it is a 100 per cent. strike. There is no trouble and everything is going smoothly."

POLICE HELP REFUSED

At Swindon the railwaymen are keying Mr. Cramp's injunction to remain steady and to preserve order. The Great Western works re, of course, closed, and no trains re running.

It was stated at a mass meeting of the N.U.R. that Mr. Collett (the

The General Council suggests that in all districts where large numbers of workers are idle sports should be organised and entertainments arranged.

This will both keep a number of people busy and provide amusement for many more.

chief mechanical engineer) had declined the oer of the police and the military to guard the railway works, saying he could rely on the strikers to preserve law and order. Railway workshops at Wolverton, Crewe, and elsewhere are closed.

CHANNEL SERVICES

At Dover the whole of the tramways staff are out. The cross-Channel boat service is greatly curtailed, and a large number of passengers are awaiting the opportunity to cross.

NOT ENOUGH !

From 2½ to 3 million workers have ceased work.

The Government announced yesterday's wireless that 30,000 volunteers had registered, expressing willingness to take the strikers' places. It doesn't seem enough !

Published for the General Council of the Trades Union Congress by Victoria House Printing Company, 2, Carmelite-street, London, E.C.4. Telephone (8 lines) : 8210 City.

WONDERFUL RESPONSE TO THE CALL

General Council's Message : Stand Firm and Keep Order

The workers' response has exceeded all expectations. The first day of the great General Strike is over. They have manifested their determination and unity to the whole world. They have resolved that the attempt of the mineowners to starve three million men, women and children into submission shall not succeed.

All the essential industries and all the transport services have been brought to a standstill. The only exception is that the distribution of milk and food has been permitted to continue. The Trades Union General Council is not making war on the people. It is anxious that the ordinary members of the public shall not be penalised for the unpatriotic conduct of the mineowners and the Government.

Never have the workers responded with greater enthusiasm to the call of their leaders. The only difficulty that the General Council is experiencing, in fact, is in persuading those workers in the second line of defence to continue at work until the withdrawal of their labour may be needed.

WORKERS' QUIET DIGNITY

The conduct of the trade unionists, too, constitutes a credit to the whole movement. Despite the presence of armed police and the military, the workers have preserved a quiet orderliness and dignity, which the General Council urges them to maintain, even in the face of the temptation and provocation which the Government is placing in their path.

To the unemployed, also, the General Council would address an earnest appeal. In the present fight there are two sides only—the workers on the one hand and those who are against them on the other.

Every unemployed man or woman who " blacklegs " on any job offered by employers or the authorities is merely helping to bring down the standard of living for the workers as a whole, and to create a resultant situation in which the number of unemployed must be greater than ever.

The General Council is confident that the unemployed will realise how closely their interests are involved in a successful issue to the greatest battle ever fought by the workers of the country in the defence of the right to live by work.

MESSAGE TO ALL WORKERS.

The General Council of the Trades Union Congress wishes to emphasise the fact that this is an industrial dispute. It expects every member taking part to be exemplary in his conduct and not to give any opportunity for police interference. The outbreak of any disturbances would be very damaging to the prospects of a successful termination to the dispute.

The Council asks pickets especially to avoid obstruction and to confine themselves strictly to their legitimate duties.

SOUTH WALES IS SOLID !

Not a Wheel Turning in Allied Industries

' MEN ARE SPLENDID ! '

Throughout South Wales the stoppage is complete, and everywhere the men are loyally obeying the orders of the T.U.C. to refrain from any conduct likely to lead to disturbance.

So unanimous has been the response to the call of the leaders, that not a wheel is turning in the industries affiliated to the T.U.C.

MONMOUTHSHIRE

Complete standstill of industries in the eastern valleys. Absolute unanimity prevails among the rank and file of the affiliated unions, and not a single wheel is turning in the allied industries.

Monmouth Education Authority—which has a majority of Labour representatives—has arranged to feed the school-children where required.

ABERDARE VALLEY

All railway and bus services are at a standstill. The miners' attitude indicates that they are absolutely loyal to the advice of their leaders to refrain from anything in the nature of riotous behaviour.

NEATH

The workers have unanimously responded to the call in support of the miners, and the stoppage is complete.

With one exception, safety men are remaining at their posts. The behaviour, of the men is splendid.

AMMAN VALLEY

Every industry and almost the entire transport services are at a standstill at Ammanford and throughout the populous Amman Valley.

GLAMORGANSHIRE

The men are obeying implicitly the instructions of their leaders not to create any disturbance. Crowded meetings of miners have registered their unanimous intention to stand by the T.U.C.

ABERTRIDWR

At the Windsor Colliery, Abertridwr, a deputation of the men and the management met and agreed to safety men being allowed to work.

A Trades Council, composed solely of branches affiliated to the T.U.C., has been formed to act as a Lock-out Committee for Abertridwr and Senghenydd.

PORT TALBOT

Perfect order is being maintained at Port Talbot, where all the industries are shut down.

The front page of 'the British Worker', published by the TUC General Council, 5 May 1926, to counter the British Gazette, directed by Churchill on behalf of the government. In the nine days that it lasted, the general strike had a massive impact upon the economic life of the country, but in the end the TUC surrendered tamely enough on 12 May to Baldwin's government.

In practice, the general strike was peaceful enough. There was no violence directed against the many blacklegs (including many Oxford and Cambridge students who forsook their studies for the purpose) who drove buses and engaged in other strike-breaking activities. There was no violence either from, or directed against, the police or the armed forces. In the end the TUC suddenly called the strike off on 12 May, with industrial areas in Yorkshire, Cumbria, Tyneside, South Wales, and Scotland as solid as ever, and with several groups of key workers (such as power engineers) never called out at all. It was a complete defeat for the unions, and especially for the miners, who remained out on strike for several more bitter months. Britain's class war had been a brief, bloodless skirmish. For middle-class bystanders it had even been painless, and almost great fun.

Still, it is obvious that the divisiveness revealed and reinforced by the general strike was one powerful factor that survived to plague the unity of the nation over the next twenty years or more. In mining and other areas, it was still a living factor in the early eighties. The general strike may have been shown to be ineffective in the circumstances of 1926, with the unions half-hearted and the government well prepared and (in the case of such ministers as Winston Churchill, the Chancellor) even belligerent. Nevertheless, 1926—'Year One' in the later recollection of one Welsh miner—did demonstrate the extraordinary loyalty and class solidarity within the working-class communities of Britain, not only in older mining, steel, and shipbuilding areas but also among the newer service workers of a 'semi-skilled' category in road or rail transport and distribution. The class divisions of the country were starkly revealed, even if they did not spill over into physical violence. A deep suspicion also was displayed about the alleged neutrality of the police and the civil service, even perhaps of the newly-formed BBC, which had in fact fought hard to perserve its independence in the face of governmental pressure. In mining districts, the general strike brought a legacy of victimization by mine-owners, swingeing wage cuts, and attempts to undermine the basic role of the Miners' Federation as voices of the workers. If demagogic miners' leaders such as Arthur Cook moved on to the sidelines, their successors in the unions and the Labour Party were no more accommodating towards a social system so manifestly distorted in its rewards and opportunities, and which made such a mockery of the supposed social unity of the war years. As Britain continued to limp through the depression years, memories of the

Mass production at Morris Motors, Cowley, Oxford, 1929.
Here the body foundation is being rubbed down after the first coat of paint.
The car industry, pioneered by William Morris at Cowley and Herbert Austin
at Longbridge, made a dramatic impact on British economic life and leisure
patterns in the twenties.

general strike endured, and a heritage of class protest along with
it.

In the later twenties, the land settled down into a pattern that
endured until the 1940s. The population continued to grow, if
more slowly; it rose from 40,831,000 in 1911 to 42,769,000 in 1921,
and to 44,795,000 by the 1931 Census. But within it there were
deep and growing contrasts, as younger writers such as George
Orwell were later to emphasize. For much of southern England
and the Midlands, the twenties were a time of growing contentment and prosperity. There were many housing developments in
the form of suburban middle-class estates, stemming from the
abortive Addison housing programme of 1919–21 and later
schemes by Neville Chamberlain which gave a direct subsidy to
private house-builders. A larger proportion of the population

emerged from the war with middle-class aspirations—home ownership; a quiet family environment; more leisure pursuits (there were, for instance, over a million cars in private hands by 1930 of which the most celebrated was the 'Baby' Austin); domestic comforts and mechanical aids such as Hoovers. The power of broadcasting through the BBC brought entertainment and instruction into the privacy of the home. For the junior managers, civil servants, schoolteachers, skilled workers, and others, members of the white-collar administrative and professional groups that had expanded so dramatically between 1880 and 1918, the twenties were not such a bad time, with prices starting to fall, houses more freely available on easy terms, and more leisure interests to pursue. Newer technologically-advanced industries were mushrooming, notably the modern car plants of Herbert Austin at Longbridge and William Morris at Cowley, both in the Midlands. New patterns of suburban residential life flourished around them. For such people, the humdrum, reassuring values symbolized by the nature-loving Prime Minister, Stanley Baldwin, embodying in his own person the message of 'safety first', seemed attractive after all the unwanted excitements of the war and the general strike.

Yet for many other areas, it was a time of growing despair and disillusion. The countryside, for instance, was sunk in depression in the twenties after the brief, heady revival of the war years. The rural population steadily declined, especially in the more mechanized agricultural sector of the wheat-growing areas of southern England. Prices of farm products fell; the level of rural incomes declined; the vitality of small country towns, from the Highlands to Cornwall, became impoverished. British country life preserved its traditional unchanging appearance on the surface; the 'green revolution' vastly enlarged the number of small landowners in the 1918–26 period, the greatest transformation in landholding since the Norman Conquest. But beneath the surface was a pattern of indebtedness, burdens of mortgages and bank loans, and visible decay which saw the gap in the quality of life between town and country growing wider. Since much of British literature took the countryside as its basic point of reference, this could have serious cultural, as well as social, implications.

In the older industrial communities, especially in the north and north-east of England, industrial South Wales, and the Clydeside belt of mid-Scotland, and in the slums of Belfast across the Irish Sea, it was a time of mounting despair. The inadequacy and squalor of working-class housing and living conditions became increasingly well documented in the twenties, as did the environmental decay that cast a pall over older areas such as Jarrow or Wigan or Merthyr Tydfil. Along with damp, insanitary housing and poor schools and public services went appalling figures of child illness and mortality, tuberculosis for the middle-aged, lung disease for miners, physical deformity for the old. There was a markedly lower life expectancy in the older industrial regions of the north, Wales, and Scotland, contrasted with the county towns and spas of the English south-east and the West Midlands. The social gulf grew ever wider in the twenties, made more severe still by the endless unemployment which afflicted older industries such as steel-making, shipbuilding, and coal-mining, all of them starved of capital investment. The decision to return to the gold standard at the pre-war parity in 1925 was one taken by Churchill as Chancellor, in the face of biting criticism (after the event) from Keynes but with the broad endorsement of most orthodox economists and businessmen. It meant a serious overvaluing of British coal and steel exports, and a still higher rate of unemployment for the working men producing them. In terms of the quality of educational and medical facilities, of amenities such as libraries, swimming baths, or public parks, the social divisions were ever more apparent in the land over which Baldwin serenely presided. The era of 'safety first', with all its secularization, meant (according to some famous lectures by the socialist economic historian R. H. Tawney, published in 1929) the establishment of a new 'religion of inequality'. Among its features, two-thirds of the aggregate national wealth was owned by 400,000 people (less than one per cent of the population), along with immense disparities in the quality of life throughout British society.

Yet this growing social division occasioned surprisingly little revolt or protest at the time. In part, this was because of the warm solidarity of the working-class world which generated its own values, culture, and entertainment, even during the depression years. The relics of that period—the working-men's clubs and libraries; the vibrant world of the miners' lodge, the choir and brass band; the credit base provided by the 'co-op' in working-class communities—seem remote from the Britain of the 1980s. But they do testify to the strength and optimism of working-class life even in these gloomy years. The anodyne of mass entertainment was also encouraged by the rulers of the people to help promote patriotic loyalty. This 'bread and circuses' tradition dated from the Victorian music-hall. Many of its heroes such as George Robey (who had refused a knighthood) still flourished.

But it was an art-form rapidly being outstripped by the new silent and talking pictures: Charlie Chaplin was now the darling of the halls. Beyond the innate resilience and dignity of working-class Britain, there were still qualities that kept the land relatively peaceful and integrated. These may have owed some-

Jack Hobbs and Herbert Sutcliffe opening the innings for England against Australia in the second test match at Melbourne, February 1925, in which they put on a century stand. Between 1905 and 1934 Hobbs scored a record number of centuries (197), including 11 against Australia, and had a career total of 61,221 runs in first-class matches.

thing to the much-maligned governments of the time. Neville Chamberlain's active and creative period as Minister of Health, 1924–9, which effectively saw the end of the old Poor Law, was one notable milestone in this process. The football crowds of the cloth-capped workers and the aspiring life-styles of the new middle class in the suburban housing developments were bound together by some semblance of common values. Familiar symbols could unite them all—perhaps the ever-popular figure of George V, perhaps the passive reassurance offered by Baldwin. The sporting hero of the decade was Jack Hobbs, opening batsman for Surrey and England, who in 1925 overtook the record number of centuries (125) scored by the legendary W. G. Grace. Modest, unprotesting, a devoted church-goer and tee-totaller, a model family man, Jack Hobbs was the prototype of the loyal artisan dedicated to Crown and country. He was a professional 'player' content to be led by amateur public-school 'gentlemen' (who entered the Oval playing arena by a different gate). He always played a straight bat and always accepted the umpire's verdict, however disappointing or unfair, without complaint. Jack Hobbs's placid, kindly personality provided an acceptable touchstone for a society struggling to preserve a traditional order in the swirling tides of the post-war transformation.

The Thirties

The twenties ended in a confused haze of nostalgia and innovation. The pomp and affluence of 'high society' and court life were as resplendent as ever. Cigarette cards and magazines acclaimed the personal appeal of social celebrities such as the aged tea magnate 'Tommy' Lipton or hostesses such as Lady Londonderry. Familiar giants still bestrode the land elsewhere. Elgar survived as Master of the King's Musick until 1934; Kipling remained as Poet Laureate until 1936; Thomas Hardy died, full of years and honour, in 1928. The mood of 'safety first' permitted only the most guarded forms of innovation. Its political figurehead in the late twenties was the Labour leader, Ramsay MacDonald, called upon to form a second Labour government in 1929. MacDonald had a background of anti-war protest in 1914–18, but as a reassuring figure in the general strike, the hammer of socialist extremists, and intimate of salons in high society, he seemed to be comfortingly locked within the aristocratic embrace. A licensed rebel, he was a safe enough symbol for a society committed to modest, but controlled, change. With Lloyd George now an isolated veteran and Churchill actively excluding himself from the Tory mainstream because of his 'die-hard' views on Indian self-government, MacDonald appeared to be a reliable guide in taking a few measured steps towards the apocalypse.

In fact, the second Labour government proved to be a disaster. In large part, this was because of forces far removed from political control. The crash in the American stock exchange in October 1929, followed by a downward spiral of trade and employment, was beyond the reach of any government to correct. For all that, it was all too apparent that the British Labour government had little to offer as a socialist or any other kind of palliative to unemployment that rose with alarming rapidity to reach nearly three million of the insured population at its peak in late 1932. Although unemployment gradually declined later in the thirties, in fact industrial stagnation and social decay continued. Beyond the world-wide forces of over-production and a slump in demand, there were factors peculiar to Britain alone. There was here an industrial structure unduly geared to a declining range of traditional industries, coal, steel, textiles, shipbuilding. There was a history of low investment, overmanning, and inefficient work practices, intensified by a culture that for decades had elevated humane disciplines and gentlemanly virtues in place of business education or entrepreneurial skills. The entire industrial and manufacturing base contracted with extreme violence. There was no sign of recovery visible until 1935. Long before then, the spectacle of hopelessness and despair in mining and other areas, of hunger marches and demonstrations by the unemployed, of the rigours of 'life on the dole' with all the helplessness and hopelessness that were implied had become one to which the great British public had become resigned or immune.

There were those who argued that a new kind of political initiative was required to regenerate and revitalize the nation and its economy, and to propel them in new directions. In the left centre, Lloyd George remained throughout the thirties an ageing, largely disregarded prophet, urging the need for a New Deal on the American model. On the far left, there were a variety of nostrums proposed, from the collectivism of the Socialist League, and later the Left Book Club, to the pure sectarianism of the tiny Communist Party. Sidney and Beatrice Webb claimed to see the future working in Soviet Russia. On the radical right, Sir Oswald Mosley left first the Conservative then the Labour

Ribbon private housing development at Stanmore, Middlesex, in the thirties.
The development of suburban housing at this time was spectacular on the
outskirts of London and other major cities. Stanmore, at the terminus of the
Bakerloo, was one of many areas boosted by the underground railway to assist
commuters to work.

Parties, and tried to create a British variant of Fascism with an
admixture of corporate planning and anti-Semitism. Meanwhile
the veteran socialist writers, Bernard Shaw and H. G. Wells, in
their different ways promoted the cause of a planned, antiseptic,
scientific Utopia. But the most popular solutions were sought
within the traditional mix of British politics. By August 1931 it
was obvious that MacDonald's Labour government was in
desperate straits. The climacteric arrived with a massive run on
the pound accompanied by the publication of the May report
which alleged that high government spending and an unbal-
anced budget were the root causes of industrial collapse. The
government was urged to cut social spending, including the

social benefit which was all that the unemployed had in order to subsist at all. The Cabinet was hopelessly divided, buffeted between the bankers and the TUC. On 23 August MacDonald resigned.

The next morning, however, instead of a Conservative–Liberal administration taking his place, it emerged that MacDonald was to stay on as Prime Minister of a new 'National' government from which almost all his own Labour Party colleagues would be excluded. At a subsequent general election in October, this government (which had latterly taken Britain off the gold standard and devalued the pound) was returned with a huge majority, with 556 supporters, and the Labour Party reduced to a mere 51, with almost all its leading former ministers defeated at the polls. This 'National Government' was to set the tone for Britain in the thirties. MacDonald, its figurehead, gradually faded from the scene, an increasingly pathetic personality. Baldwin lingered on until 1937. He was still able to summon up immense reserves of political and tactical skill, as when he pushed through a bill to grant more self-government to India in 1935, or in his total outmanoeuvring of Edward VIII in 1936 when that uncrowned monarch flouted popular convention by seeking in vain to retain his crown and also to marry a divorced American woman, Mrs Simpson. But the main energy within the government came from a new technocratic style of Conservative, freed from the rural stereotypes of Victorian days. Dominant among them was Neville Chamberlain, heir to a famous Birmingham dynasty, the outstanding figure in political life in the thirties, at home and (later) abroad. Chamberlain it was who led a half-recovery of the economy in the earlier part of the decade, with much investment in housing and in consumer durables, and new affluence for advanced industrial zones of the East Midlands and southern England. Emigration from older regions such as South Wales, Durham, Cumberland, and Scotland was balanced by new growth in the suburbs and the centres of light industry. There was a distinctive managerial regulatory style in government, Britain's 'middle way' in economic policy. There were benefits for farmers in the form of milk and other marketing schemes and production quotas, and advantages for urban and suburban residents such as improved transportation (the London 'tube' being a notable example), extended gas and electricity services, and cheap housing. A century of free trade was buried at the Ottawa conference in 1932 when a new commercial system of tariffs and imperial preference, due to last until the 1970s, was inaugurated. The effect of tariffs upon the British economy was deeply controversial, but the cartelized steel industry was one industrial giant that appeared to show some benefit. The voters were duly grateful. They returned the National Government—now almost wholly Conservative—with a comfortable majority in the 1935 general election, and gave Chamberlainite managerial Conservatism a broad support until new divisions emerged over foreign policy at the end of the decade.

The politics of the National Government were based, unequivocally and unapologetically, on class and regional division. The older industrial areas were placed under the aegis of the 'special areas' schemes. In popular parlance, industrial Scotland, the north-east, Cumbria, much of Yorkshire and Lancashire, and South Wales were the 'depressed areas', self-contained societies only visible to the outside world when their refugees appeared in London and Birmingham to take part in hunger marches or to beg for coppers from theatre queues. There was an ironic, self-sustaining pattern about life in these so-called 'depressed' communities. There, industry was contracting, which meant that their rateable income fell further; this meant that amenities decayed still more, industrial decline was accelerated, and the entire, repetitive cycle became ever more severe. Some of the most powerful literature of the time—George Orwell's somewhat ambiguous saga of *The Road to Wigan Pier*, Walter Greenwood's pathetic account of *Love on the Dole*, Lewis Jones's moving treatment of life in Welsh mining villages in *Cwmardy* and *We Live*—evokes poignantly the consequences of this structural poverty upon the social and cultural sensibilities of the time. But little was done to remedy the causes. There were local philanthropic gestures by the Quakers and other idealists. There was some assistance from the government through the special areas commissions, although virtually nothing was done to diversify or overhaul the industrial base of these areas by a new regional policy. Thomas Jones ironically proposed that they might be turned into open-air archaeological museums, while trains carried off their inhabitants to the delights of employment at Dagenham or Hounslow. There were also novelties such as trading estates which offered inducements to industralists to group together and move into older industrial areas by offering cheap rates or investment grants. The town of Slough in Buckinghamshire, for instance, became a focus for much industrial activity in the thirties—while its architectural horrors became the target for the unwontedly bitter satire of John Betjeman. But, in general, a combination of the constraints imposed by the Treasury and the Bank of England, and of a lack of urgency by government kept the areas of staple industry effectively without support. Not until the impact of rearmament in the period that followed the 1935 Defence White Paper, with its emphasis on engineering and aircraft production, was there a significant rise in employment.

But the main reason why so little stimulus was provided for the industrial regions crucified by depression was that they were self-contained and limited in extent. The majority of the population in other parts of Britain found that life after the holocaust was acceptable and in many ways agreeable. The thirties were a time of very low inflation, cheap private housing, and of a growing choice for consumers. An average of 345,000 houses was built annually between 1933 and 1937. The motor car industries, electrical, chemical, and textile concerns continued to thrive. In the Midlands, towns like Leicester and Coventry experienced unprecedented growth and affluence. The rewards of life were ever more apparent. Professional footballers for Herbert Chapman's Arsenal, though poorly paid, enjoyed a diet which included steak and champagne. In outer London, the spread of the 'tube', north towards Cockfosters on the edge of Hertfordshire, or west towards Uxbridge on the borders of Buckinghamshire, illustrated the expansion of the service and professional sectors of the white-collar population. In growing suburban communities such as Hendon, Harrow, or Kingsbury, there were smart shopping precincts, many new cinemas and football grounds. The untidy ribbon of semi-detached middle-class housing stretched far along arterial roads and bit deep into the surrounding countryside, relatively unhampered by environmental controls designed to preserve the 'green belts' around cities. The Western Avenue out of London became a byword for uncontrolled industrial and residential development, with a miscellany of factories in debased historicist styles (which a later generation, incongruously enough, often regarded as monuments of modern art). If one explanation for the lack of social change in Britain amidst the unemployment and depression of the thirties lies in the lack of political and economic power vested in the older industrial areas, another lies in the growing commitment to a pleasing and acceptable form of suburban life by larger and larger sections of the population left relatively unscathed by the bleak years.

Britain in the thirties, then, displayed a surprising degree of stability in a European continent which saw totalitarianism engulf Germany, Italy, and Austria, and the French and Spanish republics cast into disarray. The social and cultural hierarchy changed very little. The prestige of Parliament, of the law courts, of a highly stratified educational system headed by Oxford and Cambridge that remained almost totally a public-school pre- serve, all remained as high as ever. The monarchy retained its esteem by responding subtly to marginal changes in the outlook of the mass democracy: George V's attendance at the annual working-class festival of the Wembley Cup Final was one instance. The king's silver jubilee in 1935 provoked widespread national rejoicing. Even the brief crisis associated with the abdication of Edward VIII left the monarchy as an institution essentially unimpaired. The nation remained comfortably iso- lated from a strife-torn Continent, inhabited by faraway peoples of whom the British knew little.

In the arts, the thirties were in many ways a remarkably flourishing and creative period. In poetry, the most important figure remained T. S. Eliot, a conservative Anglo-Catholic of American birth, whose 'Four Quartets' appeared from 1930 onwards. Eliot, in fact, increasingly found the drama a more congenial art form, starting with *Murder in the Cathedral* (1935), a powerful commentary on the martyrdom of Thomas Becket. The most influential writers of the period, however, reacted strongly against what appeared to them to be the withdrawal and detachment of the Bloomsbury ethos in the twenties. In the maelstrom of the time, younger poets such as W. H. Auden, Stephen Spender, Cecil Day Lewis, and Louis MacNeice reflected the political excitements of the time. Auden's cele- brated poem 'Spain' (1937), inspired by his brief period of service in the Civil War, epitomized the current literary mood. It is significant that all these young poets flirted with a kind of neo-Marxism, if they did not actually become Communists. Conversely, two of the abler young novelists of the time, Evelyn Waugh and Graham Greene, were converts to Roman Catholi- cism, albeit with very different political and other outlooks. British music was less volatile, though the romantic strains of Holst and Delius had to contend with the experimental endeavours, atonal, even unstructural, of the followers of Stra- vinsky and Schoenberg. Vaughan Williams, a contemporary enough figure in his diatonic compositional techniques, yet deeply English in his reliance on traditional airs and themes, demonstrated how modernity could be safely reconciled with the native musical tradition. In the visual arts, the thirties was a period of great excitement and innovation, both in sculpture and in painting. A new vitality for British sculpture was heralded by the work of Henry Moore, son of a Yorkshire miner, and the disciple of Epstein; another pioneer was Barbara Hepworth, the wife of the painter Ben Nicholson. British painting was also unusually vigorous at this period, ranging from the rustic Christian symbolism of Stanley Spencer to Paul Nash's successful engagements with French surrealism. Britain was generally a better country to look at in the thirties, with a much-needed innovation in architecture and design, without precedent since the heyday of Norman Shaw, Voysey, and Mackintosh before 1914. From dramatic set-piece public buildings which manifested the influence of Gropius and the German Bauhaus, through industrial factories and cinemas with *art nouveau* or art deco overtones, down to mundane but important landmarks such as Pick and Holden's attractive new underground railway stations for London Transport, British architecture offered many departures and a real sense of liberation. At a more accessible level, the new life shown by the Royal Academy and by such accepted popular arts festivals as Sir Henry Wood's London 'proms' suggested some qualified cultural advance, if hardly a cultural revolution.

In a variety of ways, then, Britain in the thirties showed distinct signs, outside the older industrial areas, of being a land at peace with itself, and enlivened by some cultural imagination. But the mood began to change abruptly in 1937, not through any immediate domestic disunity or reappraisal, but through the external impact of foreign affairs. Much of Britain's internal harmony in the twenties and thirties had been founded on a quiescent foreign policy. The mood dictated by Keynes in 1919, the mood that had dislodged Lloyd George in 1922, had permeated the whole society. Right-wing reluctance to engage in overseas military adventures was countered by a profound belief on the left that the 1919 peace settlement was in any case vindictive and morally indefensible, the product of national and imperial rivalries rather than of a yearning for a more harmonious world. In the twenties, Britain's defences were gradually run down, with little public protest, based on the 'ten year' premiss that no major war would be fought within the next decade. The battle fleet was especially cut back in this period, most enthusiastically by Churchill himself while at the Treasury. The giant new naval base at Singapore, recently completed, already seemed an anachronism. The main military commitment was to the Raj in India, but a gradual, partial accommodation with Gandhi and the Congress movement enabled the British garrison in the subcontinent to be reduced slowly from 57,000 in 1925 to 51,000 in 1938. Equally, the increasingly harmonious relations with the

A 'Peace' demonstration during the Czech–German crisis over the Sudetenland, held at Trafalgar Square on 18 September 1938 immediately after Neville Chamberlain's first meeting with Hitler at Berchtesgaden. The speaker shown here is Lord Meston, president of the Liberal Party.

Irish Free State, culminating in the 'agreements' of 1936 and the virtual wiping out of all debts owed to Britain by Ireland minimized another potential source of military or naval difficulty. The public mood in the early thirties remained a passive one, even after the advent of Hitler in Germany in January 1933. The British labour movement was pacifist-inclined, with a few exceptions such as Ernest Bevin of the Transport Workers. It opposed voting arms estimates on behalf of a right-wing National government. On the socialist left, there were advocates of a Popular Front such as Sir Stafford Cripps who urged the need for an alliance with the Soviet Union and argued that socialism alone was the true remedy for international discord. Conversely, most Conservatives had no wish for an adventurous foreign policy, especially since Baldwin had assured the people that there was no real defence possible in a future war which would be determined largely by air power. The bomber would always get through. There was scant Conservative enthusiasm for upholding the authority of the League of Nations in crises in Manchuria in 1931 or Abyssinia in 1935. There were those on the right, notably some press lords, who declared that there was common ground between Great Britain and Hitler's Germany, bound together by Teutonic racial origins and anti-Communism. A miscellaneous group of politicians and journalists found a haven in Lord and Lady Astor's mansion at Cliveden, by the Thames, near Marlow. It was widely believed to be turning the mind of the Foreign Office in these fellow-travelling directions.

When the opportunity for action came, public opinion was resistant. Hitler marched into the Rhineland in early 1936, in direct contravention of the Versailles settlement. But only a few voices, like the isolated and unpopular Winston Churchill, called for a military response from Great Britain. Earlier, the British public had generally endorsed, though with much embarrassment, the appeasement policy of the Foreign Office following the Italian invasion of Abyssinia. In effect, the Italians were allowed to occupy this ancient empire in the Horn of Africa with the minimum of British involvement, economic or military. Formal commitments were made to the League and to the spirit of collective security, but they added up to little enough. Sir Samuel Hoare, the Foreign Secretary, was offered up as a public sacrifice during the Abyssinian crisis, but it was clear that the appeasement of Mussolini's Italy was a collective government decision. Cabinet records now available confirm the point. In any event, Hoare re-entered the government a few months later with little controversy. Again, in Spain where a left-wing, democratically-elected Republican government was subjected to invasion by a right-wing Nationalist force led by General Franco, with later armed assistance from Italy and Germany, the British government adhered rigidly to 'non-intervention', even if this meant the eventual downfall of democracy in Spain. The advent of the powerful figure of Neville Chamberlain in October 1937, a confident man committed to an active, positive pursuit of a working accommodation with the Fascist dictators, as opposed to Baldwin's passive style of appeasement, confirmed a growing mood of non-involvement in Europe. Key figures in the civil service such as Sir Horace Wilson and Sir Nevile Henderson (ambassador to Berlin) pushed this policy forward.

At various levels, however, the public mood suddenly began to change. Even the government began to turn its mind to the need to overhaul the national defences, especially in the air.

From 1935 onwards, a new fighter-based air force was in the making, backed up by the latest technology invested in 'radar' and other anti-aircraft and defence systems. Through men like Tizard and his rival Lindemann, the voice of scientific innovation was again sporadically heard in the corridors of power. By 1937 the rearmament programme was visibly under way, despite pressure from the Treasury which voiced concern at the effect on the balance of payments. Privately, it is now known that a wider range of financial relationships was entered into with the United States which alone could underwrite the arms programmes capable of being launched by a Britain still in economic difficulties. More widely, the public psychology was deeply stirred by events in the Spanish Civil War. Not only poets such as Auden or prose writers like George Orwell, but many scores of British working-class volunteers who fought with the International Brigade were being propelled towards a new commitment to internationalism. Jewish refugees from Germany brought the reality of Hitler's regime and of anti-Semitism home to British opinion. Even on the Labour left, trade union leaders such as Bevin and Citrine turned vigorously against neo-pacifist Labour politicians who denied armed assistance to trade union and labour groups crushed in Fascist Germany and Austria. Chamberlain's equilibrism was harder to sustain, especially for a Prime Minister so lacking in the skills of flexibility.

The German advance in 1938, the seizure of Austria and the subsequent threat to Czechoslovakia, ostensibly on behalf of the Sudeten Germans in the western fringe of Bohemia, produced a national crisis of conscience. Chamberlain responded with managerial decisiveness. At Berchtesgaden, Bad Godesberg, and finally at Munich in September 1938, he came to terms with Hitler. In effect, he allowed the Germans to annex Sudetenland on the basis of any timetable they chose, without British or French armed retaliation. For a brief moment, it seemed that this policy of surrender had mirrored the public's response. Chamberlain returned in triumph, announcing, in an ominous phrase, that it was to be peace in our time. But this abdication of responsibility could no longer adequately be justified. Those who have claimed that Chamberlain was seeking a breathing-space, in order for Britain to challenge Germany more effectively in military terms later on, do not find support from the records of Cabinet deliberations. The criticisms of Churchill and his associates, and even of Anthony Eden who had recently resigned from the Foreign Office in protest at Chamberlain's conduct of foreign affairs, now accorded far more precisely with popular sentiment. By the end of 1938, as it became clear that Munich had really meant the sacrifice of Czechoslovak democracy to armed aggression, nation-wide anger was overwhelming. Chamberlain, so impregnable a figure a few months earlier, the most powerful Prime Minister since Lloyd George in 1916, suddenly looked like a man on the run. Rearmament was stepped up and new negotiations begun with the engineering trade unions to try to build up munitions and aircraft production. When Hitler finally invaded Prague in March 1939, public anger exploded. Chamberlain was forced by outside pressure to enter into a military commitment to defend Poland, a land in Eastern Europe far away from British shores, with no guarantee that the Soviet Union would assist in protection of Poland's eastern frontiers. A century of almost unbroken British non-involvement in continental Europe, dating from the winding up of the Peninsular War in 1812, was abruptly reversed. The government was stampeded by a horrified public opinion. There was even a formal attempt to conclude an alliance with the Soviet Union, although things went so slowly that in the end Russia formed a pact with Germany instead in August. During the summer, there was evident a new mood of determination to resist German aggression with the full combined resources of the nation and the empire. On 1 September 1939 Hitler took the fateful step of invading Poland. After a few desperate attempts to patch up a last-minute compromise, Chamberlain announced in a broadcast on 3 September that Britain had declared war on Germany. There was scarcely any dissent, even from the tiny Communist Party, many of whose leading figures opposed the official Moscow line and took up the anti-Fascist cause. In the House of Commons, it was a Labour member, Arthur Greenwood, who 'spoke for England', and, as events showed, for virtually all of Wales, Scotland, Northern Ireland, and the dominions as well.

In the later stages of the appeasement controversy, the climate of public debate became unprecedentedly bitter. The complacency of the early thirties was set aside. There was the continuing hostility between the National government and the Labour Party over the unending tragedy of unemployment, and the scandals of the 'dole' and the operation of the 'means test'. Added to this was a powerful rift on the right between the 'men of Munich', Chamberlain, Simon, Hoare, and their followers, and the nationalist critics headed by Churchill who denounced the policy of craven appeasement as dishonourable. Episodes such as the distant impact of events in Czechoslovakia brought left- and right-wing protest together, as Spain or Abyssinia could never have done. Domestic and international conflicts merged into one passionate, turbulent whole. Chamberlain, the architect of much of the prosperity of the thirties, the titan of the suburban middle class, the dominant leader of the decade, suddenly became the hated symbol of a fraudulent, decadent political order. He became foremost among the 'guilty men' so brilliantly denounced by two young radical journalists, Michael Foot and Frank Owen, in a fierce polemic in 1940, perhaps the greatest feat of political pamphleteering since the days of Wilkes.

Any society ruled by Neville Chamberlain at such a time should have found it hard to unite behind a common cause. Yet, as in August 1914, Britain did so. Indeed, when war broke out in 1939 there was a unanimity that pervaded all regions and classes. As in 1914, the war was represented publicly as a crusade on behalf of oppressed nationalities and persecuted races—which, indeed, it largely was, and far more plausibly so than in 1914. Middle and working class, capitalist and worker, socialist and conservative entered the war for different motives, or perhaps for different priorities along the political spectrum. But broad imperatives survived to create a new consensus. As twenty years earlier, Britain regained its sense of unity and national purpose amidst the challenge and turmoil of total war.

The Second World War

The public mood after the outbreak of the Second World War was notably less passionate or strident than after August 1914. Neither the militarism nor the pacifism of that earlier conflict was echoed now. In large measure, this was because of the curious features of the early months of the war. During the so-called 'phoney war' period down to April 1940, the fighting seemed remote, almost academic. It is a curious, twilight phase well portrayed in Evelyn Waugh's novel, *Put Out More Flags*. There were massive air-raid precautions, trenches in public parks, barrage balloons aloft, anti-aircraft weaponry deployed on public buildings. Thirty-eight million gas masks were distributed to men, women, and children; hundreds of thousands of schoolchildren were evacuated from major cities to distant, and presumably safer, rural areas (though many later drifted back home). Rationing of food, clothing, petrol, and other commodities suddenly became commonplace. The war itself was uneventful, with traditional pleasures such as the long-range enjoyment of a British naval victory, when the German battleship *Graf Spee* was fatally cornered by three smaller British vessels in the

Children in the war. Evacuees arriving at Eastbourne, Sussex, at the outbreak of war in 1939. In all, 827,000 schoolchildren were evacuated from major cities to seaside towns and rural areas in the autumn of 1939 to escape from German bombing raids, though many later returned home.

estuary of the River Plate off Montevideo harbour in late 1939. The uncertainty of the public mood was mirrored by the ambiguous nature of the government. Although the Cabinet had been reconstructed, to include Churchill himself, back at the Admiralty as in 1914, it was still the regime of the old gang, the National government of 1931 writ large. The trade unions in particular looked with deep suspicion at an administration still headed by their old adversary and class enemy, Chamberlain. Then in April 1940 the cold war hotted up. The Germans invaded Norway, scattering before them the British naval and military forces at Narvik. Soon afterwards, the Netherlands and Belgium were overrun, and the French army broke up in disorderly retreat. The security of the British Isles themselves was now under clear and pressing threat.

The old regime of the thirties could survive no longer. In a fateful division in the Commons on 7–8 May 1940, eighty Conservatives rebelled against the leadership of Chamberlain. Two days later he resigned, and Winston Churchill now emerged as wartime Prime Minister, with Labour and Liberals both joining the government. The change of premier was generally free of the apparent conspiratorial intrigue of December 1916. Indeed, Churchill had a vastly broader base of support in press and Parliament, and distinctly more loyalty from the military, naval, and air high command than Lloyd George had ever experienced. Churchill embodied a traditional sense of patriotic unity as no one else amongst his contemporaries could ever do. War gave his career a new impetus and relevance. His inspiring oratory over the radio and in the Commons conjured up new reserves of national will-power in this 'finest hour' for his country. He was able to exploit a humiliating military disaster in the retreat from Dunkirk as a kind of triumph for British ingenuity and determination. With France surrendering to the German forces by mid-June, British territorial security was threatened as never before since the days of Napoleon I in 1804.

The extent to which Britain was prepared to defend itself in military and naval terms is debatable. On the home front, apart from mobilized reserves, the 'home guard' of civilians was later to be effectively parodied as a 'dad's army' of amateurs muddling through with good humour. Its military effectiveness was, perhaps fortunately, never put to the test. But the real battle lay in the air, where the reserves of Spitfire and Hurricane fighter aircraft were rapidly built up by the press lord, Beaverbrook, now the Minister of Aircraft Production. From mid-August onwards, the German *Luftwaffe* launched wave after wave of blitz attacks, first on British airfields and aircraft factories, later on London, Coventry, Plymouth, Liverpool, Hull, Swansea, and other ports and major cities. Almost miraculously, civilian morale and national defences stood firm against this terrifying bombardment. In the air, the 'few', the legendary pilots of the Spitfires and Hurricanes, took heavy toll of the *Luftwaffe* in August–October. By Christmas, the threat of imminent invasion had effectively passed, though the 'blitz' on London and else-where continued. Churchill's personal reputation soared; the united spirit of his people grew with it. Dunkirk and the Battle of Britain in the air launched a thousand myths. They helped to encourage a latent isolationism and an unjustified feeling of national self-sufficiency, which led to a coolness towards Western European unity after the war. The British were aware that they alone of the belligerent Western democracies had escaped enemy occupation, as they had done consistently since 1066. For all that, the rhetoric of the 'finest hour' of 1940 captured the pride and the passion of what was felt to be a supreme moment of historic achievement.

The later course of the war on land, and more especially on sea and in the air, had a major long-term effect on the international and imperial status of Great Britain. It had begun by being a traditional European conflict to preserve national security and the balance of power in the West, to keep control of the Channel by extensive deployment of the British navy in the North Sea and in the northern Atlantic, along the western approaches. In effect, this aspect of the war reached a successful outcome by the summer of 1941, with the frustration of German threats to invade Britain (about which Hitler was always in any case hesitant) and the beating off of the *Luftwaffe* attacks. With the operations of the British merchant navy and (from early 1941) American lease-lend ensuring tolerable supplies of food and raw materials for the rest of the war, there was no imminent danger to the British Isles themselves, even though sinkings by German U-boats continued

Winston Churchill talking to Australian troops in the western desert at El Alamein, August 1942. One result of Churchill's visit was that Auchinleck was replaced by Montgomery as commander of the Eighth Army. Montgomery won a decisive victory over Rommel's Axis forces at El Alamein in October–November 1942.

apace. Churchill kept a close eye on the ports of neutralist Eire and its anti-British premier, de Valera. The further hazards of guided missile attack by V1 and V2 machines, launched from bases in Holland in the summer and autumn of 1944, while deeply alarming and the source of much damage to life and property in south-east England, did not seriously imperil the security of the nation either.

However, from late 1940, the war soon demonstrated wider, imperial themes. From being initially a conflict to preserve Western and Central Europe from the aggressive menace of German Fascism, the war rapidly turned into a broader effort to sustain the Commonwealth and empire as they had endured over the decades. The white dominions—Australia, New Zealand, Canada, and, far more hesitantly, South Africa—lent immediate support in terms of raw materials and armed naval and other assistance. In addition, the credits run up with India and Egypt in particular, the so-called 'sterling balances' which gave much trouble after the war, were vital in assisting with British payments for supplies, and in partially redressing the loss of overseas assets and the fall in 'invisible' income. The entry of the Soviet Union into the war in June 1941, and even more that of the United States in December 1941, following the Japanese assault on the US fleet at Pearl Harbor, ensured that the war would remain a worldwide one, fought in every continent and every ocean, and that the cosmic structure of the British Empire would come under acute threat.

Much British military, naval, and air-force effort was put into preserving the traditional lines of communication in the Middle East, centred on the Suez Canal, and the bases of the Persian Gulf and its hinterland, with their huge oil reserves. British forces fought with much success to put pressure on the Italians in Abyssinia and Somaliland, after Italy entered the war in August 1940. Even more endeavour went into preserving Egypt and the north African littoral. In 1941 the British forces under Wavell captured the whole of Cyrenaica and advanced towards Tripoli, but were later forced to retreat back towards Egypt. The fall of Tobruk in early 1942 led to a major political crisis at home, in which Churchill's own position appeared under threat. The most important military engagement of later 1942 concerned the struggles of the British Eighth Army, under first Auchinleck then Montgomery, to resist a German advance towards Cairo and Suez. However, the final breakthrough by Montgomery at El Alamein in November 1942 resulted in a successful and sustained British drive across modern Libya, through Tripoli, and into Tunisia. Here, Montgomery linked up with the American armies under Bradley which had moved eastwards from the initial landing near Algiers. Subsequent Allied campaigns, including the capture of Sicily and a prolonged drive through Italy, from the Anzio beach-head to the Alps, again had a strong concern with the imperial lines of strategic communication, and with control of the eastern Mediterranean. Those who argued that a second front should be launched in France in 1943, to relieve pressure on the Red Army in Russia, viewed this concentration in the Mediterranean with much frustration and anger. However, Churchill's Mediterranean commitment prevailed. In 1944, British forces again landed in Greece both to drive out the Germans and to beat down a native left-wing movement, ELAS.

In the Far East also, the war involved desperate efforts to shore up the empire at its base. The invasion of the Japanese through China into Indo-China and the Dutch East Indies, including the capture of all the American bases in the Philippines, led Churchill to place the Far East, with the approaches to the Indian subcontinent, even higher than the Middle East in the military priorities. There were dreadful losses. The most fateful of all involved the sinking of the battleships *Prince of Wales* and *Repulse* by Japanese bombs and torpedoes on 10 December 1941. There followed a rapid Japanese advance through Malaya and on 15 February 1942 the surrender of over 30,000 British and empire troops on Singapore. This disaster, the result of grave miscalculations by the commanding officer, General Percival, and by Churchill himself (who underestimated Japanese fighting power), was described by the Prime Minister in the House as 'the worst capitulation in British history'. It was a landmark in the fall of empire. Henceforth, for instance, Australia and New Zealand were to look to the USA for protection in the Pacific rather than to the imperial mother country. However, the disasters went no further. Japanese advances into Burma were held off, with such forces as Orde Wingate's 'Chindits' gaining immense acclaim. British rule in India, threatened by disaffection by the Congress movement within the subcontinent as well as by Japanese assault from Burma, was sustained. By late 1944, the British position in eastern Asia and the Pacific, even with the loss of Malaya, Singapore, and Hong Kong, was still a powerful one, even if dependent on American land and naval assistance.

At last in June 1944, with the final invasion of France from the Normandy beach-heads by Allied forces under the command of Eisenhower and Alexander, the war again assumed a European aspect. British military tactics in this last phase has led to some controversy amongst military historians, especially the delays in pushing through northern France and the Low Countries. The airborne landing at Arnhem was a débâcle. Even so, in the end it was a rapid and triumphant campaign. It was General Montgomery who formally received the unconditional surrender of the German forces at Lüneburg Heath on 9 May 1945. Hitler himself had committed suicide a few days earlier. Japan also surrendered on 15 August after two atomic bombs had wrought huge devastation at Hiroshima and Nagasaki, killing over 110,000 people.

Throughout, the war etched deep into the national psychology, without raising either the doubts or the euphoric jingoism of the Great War of 1914–18. The most satisfying fact of all was that casualties were so much lighter in the six years of the Second World War than in the four years of slogging trench warfare in 1914–18. This time a total of 270,000 servicemen were lost in six years, as well as over 60,000 civilians killed on the home front in German air raids. The campaigns had been more peripheral, more episodic, and in the end far more effectively conducted on a technical basis. Even veterans of the peace movement such as the philosopher Bertrand Russell felt that here was almost a good war. At the same time, all the vital questions surrounding Britain's external role remained unanswered. In the Middle and Far East, supreme strains had been put on the imperial system, even if Britain assumed control again of territories such as Hong Kong, Sarawak, Malaya, and Singapore in Asia, and British Somaliland in Africa. The Americans were concerned, at wartime conferences and at the Potsdam peace conference of July–August 1945, to speed up the process of decolonization. Churchill was led to observe anxiously that he had not become the king's minister, or fought a bloody war for six years, in order to achieve the dissolution of the British Empire. But already his outlook was being overtaken by events.

On the home front, the impact of total war was scarcely less momentous. As in the earlier war, there was a vast upheaval in the pattern and structure of the population, and a new juggernaut of centralization and state control to regulate social and economic life. Unlike 1914–18, however, the apparatus this time seemed to operate with far more justice—and more likelihood of the momentum being continued into the post-war world. The war clearly expressed a profound spirit of egalitarianism, of a type previously unknown in British history at any period. George Orwell felt that a social revolution was taking place. The ration books, gas masks, identity cards, and other wartime controls afflicted the people equally and implied a mood of 'fair shares'. So did the communal sufferings during the blitz. A notable impact was achieved by the 'evacuees', the schoolchildren removed from London, Birmingham, Liverpool, and other cities to take refuge in rural communities in England and Wales. For the first time, large sections of the nation got to know each

'Tube shelter perspective' by Henry Moore: one of a series of 'shelter drawings', based on Liverpool Street extension underground railway station 1941. One symbol of common suffering during the war years was the use of tube stations as refuges during the London blitz. By September 1940, 177,000 people were sleeping in the underground system. The incomplete extension running from Liverpool Street held about 12,000, many of whom stayed underground for weeks on end.

other. The medical and food provision for the evacuated children of the urban slums meant a great improvement in their physical and mental well-being. For their parents, war miraculously meant that full employment was restored, after the terrible decay of the thirties. Egalitarianism also encouraged a new faith in social planning, even if the links between shop floor and pit-head and the drawing-board deliberations of London-based bureaucrats were not necessarily obvious or automatic. The result, however, was that, in the wartime mood of unity and equality of sacrifice, novel questions began to be asked about public policy. A profound conviction arose, equally amongst the armed forces, that this time the 'land fit for heroes' would not be so wantonly set aside as it was widely felt to have been in the years after 1918. This mood was captured with much precision by the wartime illustrated magazine, *Picture Post*, edited by Tom Hopkinson, by the newspaper the *Daily Mirror*, and by the popular radio talks of the Yorkshire author J. B. Priestley, whose Cobbett-like style of native radicalism achieved widespread appeal.

The most celebrated document of this mood was the Beveridge report of November 1942. The work of an austere academic economist, it outlined an exciting scheme of comprehensive social security, financed from central taxation, including maternity benefits and child allowances, universal health and unemployment insurance, old age pension and death benefits. It was, in the phrase of the time, provision 'from the cradle to the grave'. An ecstatic public response gave the uncharismatic Beveridge a new celebrity as another 'People's William'; it ensured that social policy would remain high on the public agenda after the war, along with other priorities such as a free national health service.The Barlow report (actually issued in 1940) visualized a complete overhaul of the stagnant 'depressed areas'. Subsequently the 1945 Distribution of Industry Act began a long-overdue process of reversing the economic decline of areas such as north-east England and South Wales by diversifying and modernizing their economic infrastructure. The Uthwatt report of 1942 outlined a new dynamic approach to town planning with 'green belt' provision around major conurbations, new controls over land use, and 'new towns' to cater for the overspill of older cities. Underlying all these wartime blueprints was a commitment to full employment, spelt out in the 1943 budget and a government White Paper of 1944.The tragedy of stagnation and economic and human waste that had crucified many communities in the thirties would not be repeated. Spokesmen for the unemployed marchers then, people like 'Red Ellen' Wilkinson, MP for Jarrow and leader of the 1936 Hunger March, were now active in government. Underpinning this vogue for social innovation was the transformation of fiscal policy, with a commitment to counter-cyclical policies, a manpower budget, and the management of demand. These were taken up even by such traditionalist wartime Chancellors as Kingsley Wood and Sir John Anderson. Keynes himself served at the Treasury and greatly influenced the powerful Economic Section of the Cabinet. The leading critic of the post-war settlement of 1919, he was now a key figure, not only in domestic budgetary policies, but also in external financial arrangements including the attempt to ration- alize international trade and currency through the Bretton Woods agreement. The most radical nostrums were now pro- posed in the most staid of circles: nationalization of major industries and the Bank of England; a levy on inherited capital; a salaried state-directed medical profession. They all provoked growing arguments between Conservative and Labour Cabinet ministers, with angry sniping from the back-benches by free- booters such as Emanuel Shinwell, a forthright Glasgow Jew, and Aneurin Bevan, a brilliant Welsh ex-miner. But such a flowering of social and intellectual debate, far more precisely conceived and of far wider appeal than the 'reconstruction' discussions of 1917–18, under the aegis of such a traditional wartime leader as Churchill, was indeed a sign of a new climate.

In culture and the arts, the war gave some new life to old values. Literature, significantly enough, was not stimulated to anything like the same degree as in 1914–18; there was nothing remotely resembling the generation of 'war poets' of that earlier period. Some encouragement was given to war artists, officially sponsored to depict experiences in the blitz and elsewhere: Henry Moore, John Piper, and Graham Sutherland are three notable examples. Interestingly, music was one art form given a powerful stimulus, especially through the patronage of the wartime creation of CEMA (Council for the Encouragement of Music and the Arts). Lunchtime piano concerts in London during the blitz by Dame Myra Hess suggested a new popular enthusiasm for music. The composers' response came in powerful creations by Michael Tippett (a pacifist who produced a moving and humane work, *A Child of Our Time*) and the work of Benjamin Britten. The latter's *Peter Grimes*, first performed in June 1945, gave a remarkable new vitality to English opera, still largely derived from the light concoctions of Gilbert and Sullivan fifty years earlier. During the war also, the cinema became more recognizable as an innovative art form. Films such as *In Which we Serve* and *Brief Encounter* drew effectively upon wartime themes—separation, loss, sacrifice—to imbue a commercially-inclined industry with some creative realism. Of all the media for cultural communication, however, it was BBC radio which loomed largest in the public mind. Comedians like Tommy Handley, popular singers like Vera Lynn, war reporters like Richard Dimbleby and Wynford Vaughan Thomas, became the great mass entertainers and communicators of their time. In a world convulsed by unfamiliar social and intellectual ideas, the BBC remained a basically conservative, reassuring institution, committed to God, the king, and the family, to the continuities of life and the permanence of the national heritage. In the holocaust of six years of war, that appeared to be what the mass populace required and demanded.

It was, in any case, an increasingly aware and educated populace. British education had not undergone any major overhaul since 1918; its expansion had been cruelly cut back by

The Festival of Britain was launched on London's South Bank on 1 May 1951 to commemorate the centenary of the Great Exhibition. The centre-piece was Robert Matthew's new Festival Hall. The Festival exhibition stands are visible behind it.

the Geddes economies of 1922. Large sections of the working-class community had virtually no secondary schooling at all, while the proportion attending university or other higher education down to 1939 was extraordinarily small by international standards, and almost entirely of wealthy or middle-class background, save only in Wales. Hence the Butler Education Act of 1944, another social landmark of the war years, laid the framework of a new comprehensive secondary system for all, divided like Gaul into three parts, secondary modern, grammar, and technical. At the same time by giving new life to the grammar schools, and outlining a vast future investment in school building and equipment, it helped ensure a far greater degree of literacy and of social and occupational mobility. In the post-war world, the age of the grammar-bred boy and girl would surely dawn, whatever doubts surrounded the standards of the 'modern' schools which the unsuccessful majority would attend.

The First World War had produced an official commitment to the restitution of traditional values and ideas, whatever the mass popular enthusiasm for social change, or even revolution, both in working-class circles and intellectual coteries. The Second World War saw far less division between aspiration and reality. Indeed, the congruence between a public commitment to change and a private administrative recognition that pre-war society was dangerously unjust and divisive was the most important legacy of the Second World War for the British people. One major aspect of this was that the trade unions were now very far from being the outsiders that they had been after 1918. The most powerful union leader of the day, Ernest Bevin of the Transport and General Workers, was the dominant government minister on the home front, after Churchill appointed him Minister of Labour in May 1940. Under his aegis, the unions worked with government in regulating working practices, in improving industrial conditions, and in the strategy of economic planning with an intimacy never before achieved. Walter Citrine, secretary of the TUC, became virtually an ancillary member of the government. There were indeed strikes during the war, notably among miners in Kent in 1942 and among boy apprentices on the Clyde in 1941 and in South Wales in 1942–3 But they were relatively minor events contrasted with the wider consensus that was emerging. By the end of the war in 1945, the TUC had drafted a revised list of public priorities, including the nationalization of major industries and public services, the maintenance of full employment, a welfare state on the lines of the Beveridge report, and a more egalitarian policy based on the wartime ethos of 'fair shares'.

At all levels, this feeling chimed in with a noticeable mood of political radicalism. Indeed, in the years 1940–5, Britain may be said to have moved more rapidly to the left than at any other period of its history. In government, Labour ministers of the Churchill administration loomed large on the home front. Ernest Bevin; Clement Attlee, the deputy Prime Minister; Herbert Morrison, the Home Secretary; Greenwood, Dalton, and others became familiar and trusted figures. They were talismans of the faith that post-war reconstruction would indeed be carried into effect. So, too, were reformist Conservative ministers such as R. A. Butler, author of the Education Act. Their outlook harmonized with the new orthodoxies of the planners, many of them Liberal theoreticians such as Keynes or Beveridge, or simply apolitical technocrats. Beyond the confines of Westminster and Whitehall, it was clear that the public was becoming more radical—at least, it should have been clear, since this was documented in Gallup polls in the newspapers, though little attention was paid by contemporaries to these unfamiliar forms of sociological evidence, of transatlantic origin. In by-elections, there were several successes for the vaguely Christian socialist Common Wealth Party. There was the widespread public enthusiasm for the Red Army, newly popular after Stalingrad and the advance towards Berlin. Even in the armed forces, so it was murmured, left-wing or novel ideas were being bandied about in current affairs groups and discussion circles. Letters homne from servicemen in the western desert or the Far East voiced the angry determination for a better deal in the post-war world.

Reconstruction, then, was a far more coherent and deep-rooted concept as the war came to its close. In 1918, many of the blueprints had been poorly-conceived and destined for rapid oblivion at the hands of the Treasury. This time it had been more plausibly a people's war. The ideas were more precise and had both more democratic impetus and more intellectual ballast behind them. The outcome was revealed with dramatic effect as soon as the war ended. The Churchill coalition broke up with unexpected suddenness in May 1945, a few days after the German surrender and with hostilities still continuing in the Far East against the Japanese. To Churchill's dismay, the Labour Party's national executive, voicing the wishes of the rank and file, insisted that Labour's ministers leave the government. A general election was called for July. The 'coupon election' of 1918 had been an unreal exercise throughout. Even if not polluted by the hysterical 'hang the Kaiser' jingoism to the extent that Keynes had suggested, that element was undoubtedly present. A general patriotic exaltation made the campaign of November–December 1918 a poor guide to the public mood. In June–July 1945, however, the spirit was more sober and focused more precisely on housing and health, full employment, and industrial regeneration, on post-war social imperatives rather than on external or imperial themes. In this sense, the power and prestige of Winston Churchill, the revered war leader, were an irrelevance, even an embarrassment to the Conservative Party. The result, to the general astonishment, was a political landslide without precedent since 1906. Labour made 203 gains and won, in all, 394 seats to the Conservatives' 210. Clement Attlee, the prosaic, reticent leader of the Labour Party, found himself propelled into 10 Downing Street, at the head of a government elected with a massive majority. Alongside were such experienced figures as Ernest Bevin as Foreign Secretary, Herbert Morrison as deputy Prime Minister, Hugh Dalton at the Treasury, and Sir Stafford Cripps at the Board of Trade. It was a striking comment on the changed atmosphere of the war years, and no doubt a delayed verdict on the bitterness of the thirties, with its memories of Munich and Spain, Jarrow and the hunger marches. For a rare moment in its history, Britain appeared to present a spectacle of discontinuity and disjunction. It left ministers and the mass electorate at the same time exhilarated and bewildered. As James Griffiths, one new Labour minister, exclaimed in genuine bewilderment at the deluge, 'After this—what?'

The Post-War World

In fact, one phase of continuity was to be followed by another. The Labour government of 1945–51, while productive of much domestic partisanship and occasional bitterness during its six years of office, launched a new kind of consensus, a social democracy based on a mixed economy and a welfare state which took Britain well enough through the difficult post-war transformations and endured in its essence for another generation or more. Not until the very different political and economic climate of the later 1970s did the Attlee-based consensus which emerged from the post-war period come to be challenged. Until then, the balance between innovation and stability that the post-1945 regime introduced seemed to conform to the general will.

At one level, the Attlee government certainly brought about a remarkable programme of sustained reformist activity. Major industries and institutions were brought into public ownership—coal, railways, road transport, civil aviation, gas, electricity, cable and wireless, even the Bank of England. In all, 20 per cent of the nation's industry was taken into the 'public sector'. Remote groups of corporate private capitalists were replaced by remote boards of corporate public bureaucrats. Not until the nationalization of iron and steel in 1948–9 brought differences within the government to the surface did the main premisses of public ownership, as spelt out in the 1945 Labour manifesto, come to be challenged. There was also the great extension of publicly-financed social welfare, popularly dubbed 'the welfare state'. The most spectacular and controversial feature of this was the National Health Service introduced by Aneurin Bevan in 1946, and coming into effect in July 1948. The Health Service generated much debate at the time, and much resistance by the doctors who viewed with alarm attempts to implement a salaried system to make them state employees, and to abolish the sale of private practices. However, the public consensus after the war was sufficiently powerful to force the bill through, and to enable free medical attention for all citizens to come into effect. Other notable measures included the national insurance system introduced in 1946, very much on the lines of Beveridge's wartime proposals; a new drive for state-subsidized 'council' houses which yielded well over a million new and temporary dwellings up to 1952; increased old age pensions; a raising of the school-leaving age; and child allowances. These measures were by no means greeted with such unanimous acclaim at the time as is sometimes alleged. The government made many concessions to its critics. Bevan himself had to allow the retention of private practice by the medical profession, and 'pay beds' within the nationalized hospitals, a typically British compromise. In secondary education, the public schools flourished side by side with the state grammar schools. Indeed, the years of socialist rule after 1945 saw Eton and other privately-endowed educational institutions never more thriving, with their charitable status protected by the Inland Revenue. Public housing schemes were whittled down by pressures to encourage homes for sale and the principle of a 'property-owning democracy'. With all its limitations, however, the welfare state gained a broad measure of support, and was accepted as a vital attribute of the balanced, compassionate society over the next twenty years. Despite a ministerial fracas in April 1951, which led to the resignation of Aneurin Bevan and two other ministers over charges on dentures and spectacles, the underlying principles of a publicly-supported, comprehensive welfare state survived largely unscathed. So, too, did the commitment to full employment and new regional policies that gave renewed life to once derelict areas such as the Welsh valleys, Durham, Cumberland, and the central industrial belt of Scotland. In the light of these benefits, trade unionists were prepared to accept wage freezes, devaluation, and disagreeable hardships. Their loyalty to their own government survived all rebuffs.

Later legend made this era one of austerity and general gloom. So in some ways it was. From the outset, Britain faced a huge post-war debt. There were continuous shortages of raw materials and of basic food supplies, made worse by the lack of dollars which led to a severe imbalance of trade with North America. There were moments of near-panic like the run on sterling, following convertibility of the exchanges, in July 1947; the decision to impose devaluation of the pound against the dollar in September 1949; the balance of payments difficulties during the Korean War in July–August 1951. Rationing for food, clothing, petrol, and many domestic commodities survived until 1954. Planning and controls, administered by faceless bureaucrats in Whitehall (and circumvented by 'spivs' and the 'black market'), became part of the conventional stereotypes of the time. For all that, most working-class people, the vast majority of the population, viewed the years since 1945 as much the best that had been generally known since the late-Victorian heyday. Wages rose to 30 per cent above their 1938 level. There were higher living standards, guaranteed employment, most satisfying environmental and educational facilities. In a world, too, where popular sport such as football and cricket, and also the cinema and the dance-hall, were readily accessible, the leisure aspects of the good life were catered for as well. Football stadiums such as Highbury, Villa Park, or Old Trafford attracted each week over 60,000 enthusiastic (and entirely peaceable) spectators. In 1951, in its last few months in office, the Labour government launched a Festival of Britain, to commemorate the centenary of the Great Exhibition of 1851. At a time of economic shortages and much gloom in overseas affairs, it seemed to some jaundiced critics hardly the right time for a festival of national rejoicing. But the Festival proved a triumphant occasion. It led, amongst other benefits, to a dramatic cleaning-up of the derelict south bank of the Thames, focusing on a superb new Festival Hall for music and other arts. It released new powers of creativity for architects, sculptors, and designers. At the same time, it suggested also some of the technological and manufacturing skills latent in the

British people. Along the Thames at Battersea, the fun fair was a riot of gaiety and invention. The Festival was testimony to a people still vital and vigorous in its culture, still at peace with itself and secure in its heritage.

In fact, the buoyancy implied by the Festival of Britain was more than sustained by the Conservatives after 1951. Churchill, Eden, Macmillan, and Douglas-Home, the Prime Ministers during the period of unbroken Tory rule from 1951 to 1964, pursued a policy of social peace. The trade unions were generally permitted to develop their freedoms and collective bargaining powers that they had strengthened during the war. There were few major strikes, and no domestic violence, even in Northern Ireland. The welfare state was reinforced, with relatively few incursions into its provisions. Full employment remained a broad priority; indeed, it was thought to be ensured in perpetuity by the Keynesian methods of demand management symbolized in the financial creed of 'Mr Butskell' (a hybrid of the Tory Butler and the Labour leader, Gaitskell, which suggested the centrist policies of the time). When unemployment again reared its head in 1959–60, the Conservatives were as vigorous in promoting interventionist regional policies as their Labour predecessors had been. The Prime Minister of this period, Harold Macmillan, was dubbed 'Supermac' by the (half-admiring) left-wing newspaper cartoonist, 'Vicky'. There was, therefore, no major departure from Attlee-style consensus between 1951 and 1964. The return of another Labour government under Harold Wilson by a narrow majority in 1964—confirmed by a much larger majority in 1966—suggested no great deviation from the broadly-accepted political and social framework of the past twenty years.

Political harmony at home gave scope to experiment and innovation in the arts. After a barren decade in the 1940s, the fifties saw major works from many novelists of distinction, several of whom had begun writing before the war: Joyce Cary, Lawrence Durrell, Angus Wilson, and Iris Murdoch were among the most significant. British drama also experienced a renaissance at this period, from the avant-garde work of the Irishman Samuel Beckett, and of Harold Pinter, to the social realism of committed figures such as John Osborne. The latter's *Look Back in Anger* (1955), performed at the radical stronghold of the Royal Court theatre in Sloane Square, created a stir with its contemptuous rejection of social change in Britain since 1945. The ambiguous, romantic phenomenon of the 'angry young man' was born. In *The Outsider*, Colin Wilson captured the dilemma of the alienated intellectual. Poetry also showed much vitality, notably through the Welsh poet Dylan Thomas, until he drank himself to death in New York in 1953 while on a trip to the United States. There was also the 'Ulster Renaissance' in Northern Ireland. Beyond the shores of Britain, British visitors to the United States noted the near-monopoly of British dramatists and actors on Broadway. The illusion was nourished that Britain, for all its acknowledged economic weakness and technical backwardness, could still, through its cultural attainments, play Greece to America's Rome.

British music was also unusually lively, with Britten in particular active both in composition and in opera, and older figures like Walton also vigorous. What was perhaps more encouraging was that music-making showed clear signs of being a less esoteric or middle-class activity. School orchestras and amateur music groups flourished. Local festivals were springing up apace, with the one launched at Edinburgh in 1947 the most distinguished. A major factor in all this was state patronage through the Arts Council, however much controversy its presence and influence aroused. One area where there was less evidence of advance, unfortunately, was architecture and town planning. The 'new towns' were mostly bywords for grim, Stalinist uniformity, while opportunities to rebuild older cities ravaged in the blitz were too often cast aside, notably in Manchester and the City of London around St. Paul's. Ugly, high-rise flats pierced the skyline. New civic buildings and universities were often severe and unattractive. 'Plate glass' was not a concept that commanded enthusiasm, and the design of major urban centres and older cathedral cities suffered accordingly.

Elsewhere in the arts world, the BBC, in both radio and, to a much lesser degree, television, showed signs of being cultural pioneers. The Third Programme became from 1946 a powerful stimulus to music and drama. Television became a nation-wide phenomenon after 1950, and, with all its admitted limitations, served a useful social role in introducing the nation to itself. The BBC was also valuable in catering for the interests of minorities, including intellectuals, speakers of Welsh, and Asian and other coloured immigrants. The cinema also gradually became a medium for renewed artistic experimentation. It was fortified by the mass audiences that its low prices and informal atmosphere were able to attract, and its immediate freedom from the rival challenge of television. The most notable film events of the late 1940s were the Ealing Studios comedies, distinctive for their reinterpretation of traditional British themes with restrained humour and gentle tolerance. *Passport to Pimlico, Kind Hearts and Coronets* and others of this genre were testimony to the continuities and coherence of British society. Far less interesting were endless films produced in the shadow of the British class system, which depicted the working class in the affectionate, patronizing, uncomprehending terms familiar to West-End theatre-goers over the generations. Foreigners were usually suspect or simply comic (as they were in the children's books of Enid Blyton which poured forth at this time). Enduring symbols such as the friendly village 'bobby' were given sentimental currency in the film *The Blue Lamp* or in television serials. More positively, in the later fifties, some of the new tides sweeping through the French, Italian, and (to some degree) the American cinema had some real impact on Britain also. A wave of socially realistic films, often with sharp social comment to offer, suggested a shift in cultural attitudes. The popularity of *A Taste of Honey* or *Saturday Night and Sunday Morning*, with their searching penetration of working-class values and the human relationships moulded by them, implied a new depth and sensitivity in the British cinema industry. At a wider level, it suggested the security and stability of Britain at this transitional period in its history.

Margaret Rutherford, Stanley Holloway, and Paul Dupuis in a scene from Passport to Pimlico (1949), one of the most successful of the post-war Ealing Studios comedy films, produced by Michael Balcon.

The stability of the domestic scene was much assisted by the general quietude of external policy. Britain in 1945 was still a great power, one of the 'Big Three' at the international peace conferences. It demonstrated the fact by manufacturing its own atomic and hydrogen bombs. Until the cumulative effect of economic decline took its inevitable toll, this façade was preserved up to the Moscow Test-Ban Treaty of 1963. Britain had its own powerful defence systems, its own supposedly independent nuclear weaponry, its own sterling area, its private strategic, trading, and financial ties with a mighty, if dissolving, empire. In medical, physical, and chemical science, Britain was still pre-eminent, as the international acclaim for such Nobel prize-winning pioneers as Fleming and Florey, Crick and Watson suggested.

However, Britain's international position was qualified by the gradual, but necessary, retreat from empire that the post-war period witnessed. It was a relentless process, even during the regime of such a veteran imperialist as Sir Winston Churchill. The granting of self-government to India, Pakistan, Burma, and Ceylon (Sri Lanka) by the Attlee government in 1947–9 was the key moment in the transfer of power. It was an unambiguous statement of Britain's military and financial inability, and above all lack of will, to retain possession of distant lands by force. The process of decolonization gained in momentum in the fifties, with territories in West and East Africa and elsewhere receiving their independence, even Kenya and Cyprus, where there were bloody engagements against native nationalist forces. In southern Africa, the eventual break-up of the Central African Federation in 1963 meant independence for Northern Rhodesia (Zambia) and Nyasaland (Malawi) also. By the early 1960s, only a scattered handful of miscellaneous territories—British Honduras, the barren wastes of the Falkland Islands, Gibraltar, Hong Kong, Aden, Fiji, and a few other outposts—were still under direct British rule. There was little enough nostalgic hankering for the mystique of empire now. Empire Day disappeared from the calendar of state schools; Indian civil servants anonymously returned home; the king ceased to be Emperor of India. Then in October 1956, the Prime Minister of the time, Anthony Eden, astonishingly engaged in covert moves with the French and the Israelis to occupy the Suez Canal Zone, after the Egyptians had declared that that crucial waterway was henceforth to be nationalized. World opinion turned against Britain, even in the United States. Sterling was threatened; oil supplies dired up; the British troops withdrew ignominiously, censured

*The retreat from
Empire 1947–1980*

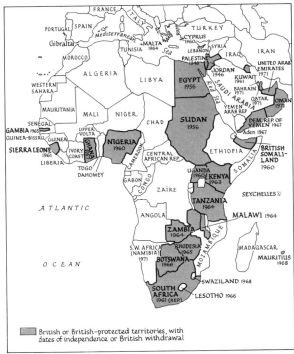

British or British–protected territories, with
dates of independence or British withdrawal

by the United Nations. There were few signs of prolonged public
anger; the voices of the older imperialism were relatively muted.
In the 1959 general election, the Conservatives fought, and
comfortably won, on the basis of domestic prosperity—'You've
never had it so good', in the argot of Macmillan. On the other
hand, the American politician Daniel Moynihan could write of
the new prestige of Britain in the Afro-Asian Third World for
having liberated so large a proportion of the world's population
without the bitterness of the French in Algeria, the Dutch in
Indonesia, or the Belgians in the Congo. A world that had once
listened to the liberal nostrums of Bentham and Ricardo, Mill
and Gladstone, now hearkened to the social democratic creed
proclaimed by Laski and Tawney of the London School of
Economics, the *New Statesman*, and (even in opposition) the
Labour Party.

In its post-imperial phase, Britain became a more introspec-
tive power, one whose role in world affairs was uncertain. As the

Commonwealth connection became more ceremonial—though with important practical aspects like the imperial preferences for Commonwealth products such as butter and meat—the relationship with America, bitter-sweet in many ways, loomed ever larger. From 1949 the United States and Britain were bound together, strategically and geopolitically, in NATO. Another organization SEATO, for South-East Asia, followed on shortly. Thereafter, British and American policies marched closely together, whether a Conservative or a Labour government was in power. The British prided themselves that this meant an equal 'special relationship' between the English-speaking peoples. It is clear, however, that in practice this relationship involved Britain striving desperately to maintain an illusory posture of independence. In the Korean War, in dealings with Communist China (other than its formal recognition), in the Middle East, above all in Europe in the face of Russian threats, British and American policies were similar, if not identical. A rare attempt at rebellion such as the British involvement in the Suez operation in 1956 was quickly snuffed out. The Nassau agreements led to defence and economic dependence on the United States being more pronounced than ever.

Nearer home, there were attempts from 1947 onwards to form a political and economic union of Western Europe. From the dawn of this idea just after the war, British governments were suspicious, if not openly hostile. They cited the Commonwealth connection, the special relationship with the United States, the distinctiveness of the British constitutional and legal system, the autonomy of British socialist planning. More powerfully, most British people regarded other Western Europeans as incomprehensible aliens, with few natural ties linking them across the English Channel. The first British attempt to join the European Common Market was rebuffed by President de Gaulle of France in 1963; years passed before another effort was made. It cannot be said that the British showed any overwhelming sense of grief at this failure to be admitted to an alien institution which would mean dearer food and a threat to national sovereignty. The Euro-enthusiasts were swimming against the clear tide of public opinion.

In this self-contained, somewhat insular, society, the general pattern was set by consumer-led affluence. Beneath the surface, economists, the new soothsayers of the age, detected slow rates of growth and falling productivity. Sociologists unearthed deep inequalities and class divisions which prevented the modernizing of a 'stagnant society'. Attitudes to British institutions and conventions were marked by an overpowering complacency. For the British, life seemed now distinctly better. A falling birth-rate meant smaller and more affluent households. Homes were better furnished. Families increasingly had cars; they could buy their homes on cheap mortgages; they managed each summer a decent holiday abroad in Spain, France, or Italy. Nor were these growing delights confined to the semi-detached middle class in the suburbs. Working-class people also enjoyed airlifted package holidays to the sunny Mediterranean coast, and revelled, in pubs, clubs, and elsewhere, in the freedom of choice afforded by higher wages and shorter working hours. The working-class young became a favourite target for sociological analysis and conventional head-shaking, with their more eccentric life-styles and a more expansive pop culture. A sporting hero such as the long-haired Northern Ireland and Manchester United footballer, George Best, suggested very different values from those of Jack Hobbs in the twenties. The musical breakthrough effected in the early 1960s by the Beatles, a group of Liverpudlian youths, made

Britain the harbinger of the supposedly 'permissive' society, in which drink and drugs were freely available, skirts spectacularly shorter, sexual restraint much less in evidence. England's football World Cup victory in 1966 added an aura of patriotism to the new aggressiveness of the young.

In addition, middle-class reformers pioneered other social changes, assisted by the hedonistic outlook of a Prime Minister such as Harold Macmillan, and the civilized tolerance of a Labour Home Secretary, Roy Jenkins. Sexual offences, homosexual and otherwise, were less liable to the rigours of the law. Abortion, along with the Pill and other easily obtainable contraceptives, offered scope for endless sexual indulgence; there were far more divorces, and one-parent families. The youth cult seemed for a time to be sweeping the land, allegedly fostered by President Kennedy's 'New Frontier' in America. In particular, a variety of cultures mingled in British universities. Here a growing number of uprooted working-class students merged with more aggressive middle-class contemporaries to fortify the appeal to youth with the protection of mere numbers. Many new universities sprang up in the ten years after 1963, while older universities were much expanded. 'More meant worse' complained some critics. Others countered that British potential was scarcely being exploited when only 5 per cent of the relevant age-group went on to higher education of any kind. Since the basic problems of subsistence were apparently being resolved by the economics of abundance, the articulate university young could turn their energies to new crusades.

The Campaign for Nuclear Disarmament in the later fifties owed much to the idealism of the middle-class young. For a time, it threatened to undermine the Labour Party as a potential party of government. Later in the sixties, the same kind of passion flowed into protest against the American war in Vietnam. Student rebellion, familiar abroad in Berkeley or the Sorbonne, briefly flared up in British campuses, and then, equally mysteriously, petered out.

These movements had wider implications. Beneath the veneer of public contentment, there was in reality a variety of divisive forces that were deeply entrenched. A wide range of different groups were, in the period of Harold Wilson's first premiership (1964–70), exploding into revolt. The young, as has been seen, were finding the values of consumerism and conformism unappealing in a world whose ecology was being disturbed and whose very existence was threatened by weapons of unimaginable horror. Elsewhere, young people in Wales and Scotland

A defaced road sign in north Wales in the late 1960s. The Welsh Language Society, formed in 1962, aroused much enthusiasm among the young with its campaign to protect the Welsh language, including the obliteration of English words and place-names on road signs in Wales.

generated a tide of nationalist protest, more familiar in the Basque regions of Spain or in French Quebec. Wales and Scotland had not fully enjoyed the economic growth of the 1950s. Their national aspirations were hardly fulfilled by such formal institutions as the Secretaries of State created for Scotland and much later (in 1964) for Wales. Scottish nationalists complained, with justice, that the very title of Elizabeth II was a misnomer in their country. In Wales, there was the added theme of an ancient language and culture threatened with extinction in the unequal battle against anglicized 'admass' culture. Victory for a Welsh Nationalist at Carmarthen in a by-election in 1966 was followed by renewed civil disobedience (and a few bombing attempts) on behalf of the Welsh language. In Scotland, the Nationalists captured the Hamilton seat, and several local authorities; a new anti-English mood seemed to be sweeping Highlands and Lowlands alike. Less constitutional or placid were the demands of the black or brown minorities, over a million of whom had migrated to Britain from India, Pakistan, West Africa, and the West Indies since 1950. In addition to dilapidated housing and racial discrimination in employment and (sometimes) at the hands of the police, there was the added hazard of racial bigotry in older urban areas. This was fanned by the inflammatory rhetoric of a maverick right-wing Cassandra, Enoch Powell. 'Rivers of blood' were forecast in British cities on the lines of the race riots of the United States.

More disturbing still, in Northern Ireland, an artificial state kept in being by the control of the Protestant majority from 1920 onwards was in disarray. A powerful civil rights movement arose on behalf of the Roman Catholic (and usually nationalist) minority. But, in practice, attempts to maintain religious and racial harmony clearly broke down. Troops were moved into Belfast and Londonderry to preserve order. An alarming wave of bombing attacks in English cities signified that the IRA and Sinn Fein were taking the age-old struggle of Irish nationalism into a new and sinister phase. In the later sixties, with minorities on the march from Brixton to Belfast, liberal consensual Britain seemed to be breaking down, as it had almost done in 1910–14.

Hitherto the social fabric had been kept intact, at least in part, because of high and advancing living standards for the population as a whole. But clear evidence mounted up in the 1960s that increasing economic pressures were adding to the new social tensions. Britain lurched in that miserable decade from one financial expedient to another, with frequent balance of payments crises and many runs on sterling. Devaluation of the pound in 1967 did not produce any lasting remedy. Inflation began to rise significantly, especially in the early 1970s when a Conservative government under Edward Heath recklessly expanded the money supply, a misguided version of Keynesianism. All the predictions of Keynesian economists were now overturned as rising inflation was accompanied by a growing toll of unemployment as well. At first this was confined to the older industrial regions of the north-east, Scotland, and South Wales. The rise of nationalism in the last two was much associated with the closure of collieries and factories and the laying off of labour. But by 1973 it was clear that the economic problems of Britain were having far more general consequences. The nation's capacity to generate wealth, along with its share of world trade and production, were in serious, perhaps terminal, decline. Britain seemed to have replaced Turkey as the legendary 'sick man of Europe'. In retaliation for declining living standards the unions replied with collective industrial power. Strikes mounted up, most acutely in the case of the coal mines. A national miners' strike was called in February 1972 and was wholly successful. The Heath government experienced the full extent of the miners' ability to disrupt national production and energy supplies, despite all the contraction of the coal industry since the 1950s. Another miners' strike in February 1974 saw the government call an election on the theme of 'Who governs Britain?' The answer was a small swing to Labour and the government duly fell. The miners again won all their demands and their rightful place high in the wages table. This background of a widening mood of protest, a reluctance to accept traditional sanctions and disciplines, institutional power from the unions thrust against a declining productive base—these formed the ominous backcloth as Britain emerged from its brief, heady acquaintance with 'affluence' to confront the unfamiliar challenges of a new international order.

The Seventies and Beyond

In its most recent phase, Britain has offered a permanent, painful case for macro-economic and sociological treatment. Its economic decline has continued, comparatively in relation to almost all other developed nations, and even in absolute terms compared with earlier production levels. It was much aggravated by the dramatic change in the energy situation in 1973–4 as a result of which Britain and other Western nations suffered a fourfold increase in the price of Middle East oil. This gave new impetus to Britain's own major development in this decade, the exploitation of the oil reserves in the North Sea, and of North Sea natural gas also. With nuclear power stations and hydro-electric schemes, as well as abundant supplies of coal, Britain was in many ways far better prepared to confront these new difficulties than many of its competitors. But the huge rise in the price of oil inevitably fuelled inflation on a scale unknown since 1919. It was reinforced by trade union pressure for enormous wage increases of anything up to 30 per cent until late 1975. British inflation continued to run at a historically high level, reaching over 20 per cent for a time in 1980, before it sank in 1982–3 to a more manageable figure of less than half that amount. With surging price rises and pressure from wage and other unit costs, unemployment re-emerged as the major domestic scourge. By 1980 it was over two million, a total unknown since the thirties. With government investment and the money supply curtailed, unemployment had advanced to well over three million by the spring of 1983. There seemed to be a deep rot at the heart of the economy, with hundreds of thousands, many of them teenagers or other young people, doomed to perhaps years on national assistance, while public welfare services were steadily curtailed. There was evidence of decline elsewhere as well. Although the population continued to increase, from over 50 million in 1951 to over 56 million in 1981, it was noted that there was actually a fall in the period of 1975–8. The birth-rate fell sharply during the recession, while a large proportion of the population were elderly, placing strains on the social services and necessarily reliant on the wealth created by the able-bodied still in employment.

The outcome was most disruptive for the social fabric. An initial period of runaway inflation in 1974–5 was stemmed by a period of an uneasy so-called 'social contract' with the unions, negotiated by the Labour governments of Wilson and then Callaghan in 1975–8. Unions agreed to moderate their wage demands in return for specified government policies geared to their needs, and especially to job protection. There were no serious strikes thereafter, until the so-called 'winter of dis-content' in 1978–9, when a rash of strikes by public service workers, including even council grave-diggers, helped to ensure a Conservative election victory. Thereafter, the unions continued to be assertive in 'right-to-work' demonstrations in protest at cuts in public spending and the high rate of unemployment. Not only traditionally vulnerable areas such as Scotland, Merseyside, and the north-east but once thriving regions such as the West Midlands showed rates of joblessness amounting to over 15 per cent. In the steel industry, mighty plants like Consett, Shotton, and Corby were closed down for ever. More indirectly, the quality of life was impoverished by declining investment in health and educational services (including the universities) and by reduced expenditure on art and the environment. Britain now provided a classic example of the post-Keynesian phenomenon of 'stagflation', with industrial recession and high inflation at one and the same time.

These economic pressures led to severe strains being placed on the stability of society in the seventies. They fuelled other social, communal, or ethnic tensions already much in evidence. The most disturbing case was still Northern Ireland where deep-seated racial and religious animosities between Protestants and Roman Catholics were aggravated by the most acute rate of unemployment in the United Kingdom. Throughout the seven-ties, the state of Northern Ireland became more and more alarming. The success of the civil rights movement dislodged the old Unionist ascendancy; the Stormont assembly was wound up in 1973 in favour of direct rule by Westminster. But renewed violence by the IRA was paralleled by the aggressive anti-Papist demagogy of the Reverend Ian Paisley. The end of Stormont certainly brought communal peace no nearer. Troops continued to patrol the Bogside and the Falls Road. There were tense border incidents between Ulster and the Irish Republic to the south, from where the IRA derived funds and weapons. On occasion, the endemic violence of Northern Ireland stretched across the sea in the form of terrifying bomb attacks on English cities, and even assassinations of politicians. The age-old racial feuds of Ireland were no nearer pacification in 1983 after six centuries.

Other tensions of the period were less violent but equally disturbing. Scottish and Welsh nationalism continued to express themselves, though usually in constitutional form. After the failure of 'devolution' measures in 1979, Celtic nationalism seemed to be in retreat, but in Wales especially there continued to be much political and cultural conflict. The defence of the Welsh language still attracted much passionate loyalty, and even threats of fasts unto death by angry patriots. Englishmen who owned a 'second home' in the Welsh countryside sometimes found it burned down by local incendiarists. Wales and Scotland, however, remained, on balance, peaceful societies, less torn apart by nationalist anguish than their Celtic neighbour across the sea. More alarming were the troubles afflicting the large black community, much of it resident in poor, dilapidated ghetto areas in large cities. There were sporadic troubles in the Notting Hill area of London and the St. Paul's district of Bristol. In the summer of 1981 it seemed for a time that Britain was experiencing the full horrors of race riots on the American pattern, as black youths in the Toxteth area of Liverpool and the Brixton district of south London engaged in prolonged rioting, all faithfully recorded (and perhaps whipped up) by television reporting. A lack of trust between the immigrant community and the police force was one notable aspect of these events. But, with unemployment especially serious for young blacks, and a pervasive background of discrimination in jobs, housing, and social opportunity, the relations between the races was a mounting cause for concern and alarm.

Other troubles piled up. Some examples of trade union protest, for instance the demonstrations against the Grunwick works in north London, seemed to go far beyond the usual limits of industrial protest in the intimidation that characterized them.

The North Sea oil rig 'Sea Quest'. Britain discovered oil reserves in the North Sea in 1969. The first oil was extracted in 1975 and by mid–1978 nine fields in the British sector were in production. By 1980 Britain was self-sufficient in oil and had become an oil exporter, with powerful beneficial results for the balance of payments. North Sea gas was another major new source of energy.

Football matches and other sporting occasions were scarred by mindless violence by teenage spectators. Britain's traditional stability appeared, therefore, increasingly under fire from many sources. An American congressman gloomily observed that Britain was becoming as 'ungovernable as Chile', an alarming parallel for Americans. This proved to be an absurd exaggeration. Few societies would have survived high unemployment, rising inflation, and public retrenchment with as much equanimity as did the British. Despite evidence of hallowed institutions being treated with less than their historic respect—Oxford university being subjected to 'sit-ins'; police, judges, Church leaders (and football referees) failing to sustain their former authority; even members of the royal family being subjected to public criticism or harassment—the broad fabric of institutional and civic life held firm. But, without doubt, the points of friction and potential dissolution were so numerous that age-old sanctions and restraints would have to be re-examined and re-defined for British civilization to survive at all.

During this period of some turmoil, Britain's view of the outside world underwent a phase of introspection. In practice, a deep psychology of insularity dictated popular attitudes, as it had frequently done since 1918. The formal alliance with the Americans in NATO continued, but attracted little passionate commitment. Indeed, the revival in the late 1970s of the Campaign for Nuclear Disarmament, a singularly peaceful form of protest, suggested that the dependence of this alliance on a mounting arsenal of nuclear weapons of a quite horrific kind aroused much public disquiet. The proposed Cruise missiles aroused still more. After much diplomatic infighting, Britain entered the European Common Market in 1973. A unique referendum in 1975 saw a large majority, almost two-thirds in all, recording its support for British membership. But 'Europe' attracted affection largely in non-political contexts. Continental package holidays, the popularity of Continental cars and food products, European football matches did not make the British love their neighbours across the Channel any more fervently. British attitudes towards the Common Market continued after 1975 to be governed by sullen hostility; opinion polls recorded consistent opposition to membership of the EEC. In any case, an organization which consisted largely of a massive, anonymous, bureaucratic juggernaut, with scant democratic constraint, located far away in Brussels and Strasbourg, could hardly win public love in as independent a nation as Britain. The linking of the Common Market with higher food prices, butter mountains, wine lakes, and the like, was widely condemned, inevitably so by a people which had known a policy of cheap food since the repeal of the Corn Laws in 1846. The British were reluctant Europeans as they were reluctant Atlanticists. Yet the Commonwealth ties were becoming more and more intangible, too. Whether in the form of coloured immigrants into British cities or test matches in the Antipodes, they could produce friction rather than goodwill.

The withdrawal from empire continued apace with little public resentment. Economic and military weakness dictated a policy of controlled retreat. The most difficult surviving problem was that of Southern Rhodesia, where a racial holocaust was threatened in a land adjacent to South Africa with its apartheid system. In a dramatic reversal, Mrs Thatcher's Conservative government granted total self-government to Rhodesia (re-named Zimbabwe) in December 1979; the protests of white settlers were ignored. Parliament and public greeted this imperial retreat with a fanfare of acclamation. The spirit of Kipling and Rhodes had finally been exorcized. It seemed unlikely that empire would disturb the British psyche any further. Then, quite unexpectedly, the distant barren outpost of the Falkland Islands was invaded by the Argentines in late March 1982. The British government responded vigorously in the face of a huge public outcry. The two remaining aircraft-carriers and dozens of other war vessels, many fighter planes, and 10,000 troops were assembled in a task force and dispatched 8,000 miles away to the stormy seas of the South Atlantic. In a swift and successful campaign, the islands were soon recaptured; the Union Jack again flew in Port Stanley on 14 June. The Falklands War was immensely popular; dissidents, CND or otherwise, were unable to gain a fair hearing. At the same time, it seemed most improbable that a war to retain these distant and almost valueless outposts, scarcely known to British people before the fighting began other than from postage stamps, would encourage a revived mystique of imperial grandeur. There was no more popular anxiety to commit naval strength or financial resources to the South Atlantic after the war than there had been before. What the Falklands episode possibly did was to confirm a rising tide of impatient insularity amongst the British people. In the face of international scepticism, Britain could still display great-power status, and demonstrate its military, naval, and technological superiority over a Fascist dictatorship such as the Argentine republic. National pride was refurbished. But the jingoism of the Falklands petered out almost as soon as it began. Britain returned to the familiar domestic scene of strikes, economic decline, and social discontent.

The problems of the early eighties were intensified by a Conservative government under Mrs Thatcher which seemed to be the most right-wing that Britain had known in the twentieth century. At the same time, the Labour Party, with Tony Benn spearheading a grass-roots movement towards fundamentalist socialism, appeared to be moving equally far to the left. Consensus seemed to have disappeared. Pedants quoted W. B. Yeats to the effect that 'the best lacked all conviction and the worst were full of passionate intensity'. Some found solace in a new political party formed by dissident right-wing members of the Labour Party; this was the 'Social Democratic Party', committed to Keynes-style economic centrism, to an incomes policy, Europeanism, and the Atlantic alliance. Remarkably, despite much fatalism about the economy, the June 1983 general election provided an immense triumph for Mrs Thatcher and the Conservatives. They captured 397 seats, as against 209 for a visibly declining Labour Party, 17 for the Liberals, and only 6 for the SDP. But renewed fears for moderate middle-ground opinion being swept away in the maelstrom were somewhat assuaged by other, more hopeful developments. The economic changes in the country were not without compensation. In part, they were the result of a beneficial change in the national economy, with Britain becoming self-sufficient in North Sea oil, and thus in a unique position of strength in its energy base. The balance of payments suddenly moved (until 1983) into a large and continuing surplus. This also meant that the dominance of manufacturing industry in the British economy would be far less paramount henceforth. Certainly the technological wonders of oil, electronics, and aerospace, of Concorde, the Humber Bridge, the High-Speed Train, and the computerized microchip age suggested that the native reserves of innovation and scientific ingenuity had not run dry.

Nor was the land proving to be culturally barren or intellectually unadventurous at this time of economic and social difficulty. British poets and novelists remained remarkably creative. The British musical scene was never more flourishing than in the early 1980s, with London plausibly claimed to be the musical capital of the world, and important orchestral and operatic developments in Leeds, Cardiff, and elsewhere. British weekly literary periodicals remained of unique intellectual quality. The BBC was still the most distinguished communica-

The police carry out an arrest during the disturbances in the Railton Road area, Brixton, South London, in the summer of 1981. There was much violence against property but Lord Scarman's report laid some of the blame on poor relations between the police and the black community, many of whom consisted of unemployed young people.

tions agency in the world. Universities, for all their financial problems, maintained a steady flow of creative achievement in the arts and pure and applied science. One American commentator, Bernard Nossiter, even claimed that the apparent rundown and unemployment in Britain masked something far more hopeful—a deliberately creative use of leisure in which the British middle and working class opted for greater freedom from the drudgery of mass automated work and rebelled against the norms of ever-increasing production. This view was probably too optimistic, and ignored long-held traditions in antique working practices and managerial inertia, which held the economy, and to some extent the society, in thrall. But it confirmed a belief that British talents were not necessarily unequipped to cope with the new stresses of sociological upheaval and financial decline any more than with the burdens of commercial leadership and international power in earlier centuries.

Britain in the 1980s manifested a remarkable skein of elements of dissolution and stability, in fragile coexistence. The forces of disruption were evident enough. There were physical reminders in the troubles in Northern Ireland, in the industrial world, and in the black ghettos in the cities. There was the new challenge to the political consensus posed in their various guises by the neo-Marxist Labour left headed by Benn, by the racialist perversities of the quasi-Fascist National Front, perhaps by the patrician élitism displayed at times by some Social Democrats. Traditional relationships—the young towards their parents, 'feminist' wives towards their husbands, workers towards their employers and union leaders, students towards their teachers, citizens towards the custodians of law and order—seemed to be in flux. *Is Britain Dying?* was one evocative book title of the period. British stability was too often expressed, by contrast, in an almost religious preference for ancient forms and ancestor worship, as in the veneration of the royal family, as devout in 1983 as at any time in British history.

The turbulence, however, seemed not incapable of control. Comparatively, in a violent century, Britain still remained a peaceful country, in which ancient institutions and norms commanded respect and adherence. Indeed, in some ways, the experimentalism of the 'permissive' years of the sixties was being followed by a new passion for traditional standards and values, commitment to a job, to more conventional forms of sexual experience, to family life, to a kind of patriotism. Even religious life showed some renewed vitality. In the turmoil of the eighties, Britain remained far from ungovernable. There was striking evidence from opinion polls which recorded, in the face of all the evidence and the processed gloom of the news media, a popular commitment to British life and an enthusiasm for one's country, rare in the Western world. Divisions were capable of being bridged in the light of a prevailing attachment to places, traditions, and myths. The more ceremonial aspects, such as the enthusiasm for the Crown, masked a more fundamental kind of commitment, to which West Indian and other newer immigrant citizens could also respond.

The truth was, perhaps, that Britain in the years from 1914 to 1983 had not changed all that fundamentally. Despite two world wars, the mass unemployment of the thirties, and the social turmoil of the seventies, the face of Great Britain, like Snowdonia or Thomas Hardy's Egdon Heath, might show surface changes of light or pattern; but the underlying geology remained the same. In 1983, as in 1914, the British retained a profound, non-exclusive sense of place. A loyalty to London or 'the north' or East Anglia or Cornwall, to the separate nationalities of Wales and Scotland, was still a living reality. The population remained intensely various, distinct, individual.

More parochially, there was the rich, voluntary involvement in village or small-town life, often translated in surprising forms into larger conurbations as well. Britain in the 1980s remained a profoundly neighbourly society. Most powerfully of all, the British constantly expressed a deep sense of their history. Even in the turbulence of the later twentieth century, an awareness of the past came through as variously as in old cathedral cities, or in the Durham Miners' Gala or the Welsh national *Eisteddfod* or the Highland games. The monarchy and Parliament embodied this sense of history; so, too, more painfully, did the sense of resolve generated by the crisis of war or external threat. In the mass media, historical or other documentary productions on television or film revived the mystique of ancient identity, just as the broadcasting services were powerful in the self-awareness of the Scots, Welsh, and Northern Irish. In spite of decades of almost unbearable upheaval, Britain remained an organic, closely-knit society, capable of self-renewal. Its very forms of native protest—CND itself—often testified to an innate tolerance and gentleness, a respect for individuality and eccentricity, a rejection of coercion and uniformity. the 'Liberty Tree' was being nurtured in 1983, as with the Levellers or Tom Paine. In the later twentieth century, as in times of greater pomp, power, and prosperity in the past, the values of being British could still be affirmed and sustained. So might they be again, in centuries yet to unfold.

FURTHER READING

8. REVOLUTION AND THE RULE OF LAW

GENERAL

Elie Halévy, *England in 1815* (Paris, 1913, London, 1924), an early but still authoritative account.

G. M. Young, *Victorian England: the Portrait of an Age* (Oxford, 1936), a key reappraisal, rescuing the nineteenth century from the likes of Lytton Strachey.

J. Steven Watson, *The Reign of George III, 1760–1815* (Oxford, 1960).

E. L. Woodward, *The Age of Reform, 1815–70* (Oxford, 1960).

G. S. Kitson Clark, *The Making of Victorian England* (London, 1962), like G. M. Young a high Tory, but unusually sensitive to the nature of middle-class reforming movements.

J. F. C. Harrison, *Early Victorian England, 1835–1850* (London, 1973), particularly strong on protest and radical movements.

C. Cook and Brian Keith, *British Historical Facts, 1830–1900* (London, 1975), includes economic as well as election and ministerial data.

ECONOMIC

Paul Mantoux, *The Industrial Revolution of the Eighteenth Century* (1911, London, 1961), pioneer and still perceptive study by a French historian.

J. H. Clapham, *An Economic History of Modern Britain* (Cambridge, 1933), some of Clapham's conclusions—notably over the standard of living—must be revised, but still conveys a wealth of detailed information. Best used as a supplement to Peter Mathias.

Peter Mathias, *The First Industrial Nation* (London, 1969), reasonably up-to-date synthesis.

François Crouzet, *The Victorian Economy* (London, 1982), a synthesis of recent research by the leading French authority on the British economy.

Michael Robbins, *The Railway Age* (London, 1962), thematic study of railways and society.

Charles Hadfield, *British Canals* (London, 1950), an introduction to his great series of regional histories.

L. T. C. Rolt, *Victorian Engineering* (Harmondsworth, 1970), stress on mechanical engineering.

POLITICS AND GOVERNMENT

Oliver MacDonagh, *A Pattern of Government Growth* (London, 1961), a study of passenger ship regulation as an example of administrative development.

Michael Brock, *The Great Reform Bill* (London, 1973), the 1832 Reform Act.

E. J. Hobsbawm and George Rudé, *Captain Swing* (London, 1968), the labourers' revolts of 1831.

S. E. Finer, *Edwin Chadwick* (London, 1952), study of the great Benthamite reformer.

Norman McCord, *The Anti-Corn-Law League* (London, 1975).

Asa Briggs (ed.), *Chartist Studies* (London, 1974), emphasizes geographical diversity of movement.

Beatrice and Sidney Webb, *The History of Local English Government* (London, 1908–29).

Jasper Ridley, *Palmerston* (London, 1970).

A. V. Dicey, *Law and Opinion* (London, 1906), lucid, influential but simplistic approach.

SOCIETY

J. F. C. Harrison, *Robert Owen and the Owenities* (London, 1969).

Clive Emsley, *British Society and the French Wars, 1793–1815* (London, 1979), draws on much untapped archive material.

E. P. Thompson, *The Making of the English Working Class* (London, 1963), a controversial masterpiece.

——*Whigs and Hunters* (London, 1975), law and society in the eighteenth century.

Harold Perkin, *The Origins of Modern English Society, 1780–1880* (London, 1969).

Roy Porter, *English Society in the 18th Century* (Harmondsworth, 1982).

W. R. Ward, *Religious Society in England, 1790–1950* (London, 1972).

Lawrence Stone, *The Family, Sex and Marriage, 1500–1800* (London, 1977), changes in family organization, mores, and emotions.

Brian Simon, *Studies in the History of Education, 1780–1870* (London, 1960), strong on nonconformity and educational innovation.

Owen Chadwick, *The Victorian Church* (London, 1966), definitive; despite title, deals with all the churches.

Donald Read, *The English Provinces* (London, 1964), social background to industrial revolution and Anti-Corn Law League.

John Foster, *The Class Struggle in the Industrial Revolution* (London, 1974), well-researched Marxist interpretation of industry and politics in South Shields, Northampton, and Oldham.

SCOTLAND, IRELAND, WALES

T. C. Smout, *A History of the Scottish People* (London, 1969).

E. D. Evans, *A History of Wales, 1600–1815* (Cardiff, 1976).

Gearóid O'Tuathaigh, *Ireland before the Famine, 1798–1848* (Dublin, 1972).

CULTURE

Francis D. Klingende, *Art and the Industrial Revolution* (London, 1972), Marxist interpretation of art and industry, from optimism to doubt, *c.*1750–1850.

Raymond Williams, *Culture and Society, 1780–1950* (London, 1958), study of the social critical tradition: Burke, Cobbett, Carlyle, Ruskin.

9. THE LIBERAL AGE

GENERAL SURVEYS

Asa Briggs, *The Age of Improvement* (London, 1959), a good political and social survey of the period up to 1867.

Geoffrey Best, *Mid-Victorian Britain 1851–1870* (London, 1971), a predominantly social account.

R. C. K. Ensor, *England, 1870–1914* (Oxford, 1936, often reprinted), still has material and analysis of value.

E. Halévy, *History of the English People in the Nineteenth Century*, vols. 5 *(Imperialism and the Rise of Labour, 1895–1905)* and 6 (The Rule of Democracy, 1905–1914) (rev. edn. London, 1951–2), a classic account, based on contemporary published material, which still holds its own.

ECONOMIC HISTORY

P. Mathias, *The First Industrial Nation* (London, 1969), a clear and concise account.

E. Hobsbawm, *Industry and Empire* (London, 1968), an incisive argument, stressing the socio-economic shift from industry to commerce.

D. Landes, *The Unbound Prometheus. Technological Change, 1750 to the Present* (Cambridge, 1969), the relationship of technology to industry.

SOCIAL LIFE

H. J. Dyos and M. Wolff (eds.), *The Victorian City*, 2 vols. (London, 1973), splendidly comprehensive illustrations.

G. Mingay (ed.), *The Victorian Countryside*, 2 vols. (London, 1981), the complementary work.

Robert Roberts, *The Classic Slum* (London, 1971), childhood in Salford.

Florence, Lady Bell, *At the Works* (London, 1911 edn.), vivid and acute analysis of social life in Middlesbrough.

Flora Thompson, *Lark Rise to Candleford* (Oxford, 1945, often reprinted), the Oxfordshire countryside in declne.

Owen Chadwick, *The Victorian Church*, 2 vols. (3rd edn. London, 1971), a powerful survey, rather favourable to Anglicanism.

Asa Briggs, *Victorian Cities* (London, 1963), and *Victorian People* (2nd edn. London, 1965), stimulating essays.

The Batsford series, *Victorian and Edwardian Life* in photographs (many vols. by city and county) is excellent; an important source.

V. A. C. Gatrell, B. Lenman, and G. Parker, *Crime and the Law: the Social History of Crime in Western Europe since 1500* (London, 1980).

POLITICAL LIFE

John Vincent, *The Formation of the Liberal Party, 1857–1868* (London, 1966), a brilliant if sometimes excessively paradoxical analysis.

Martin Pugh, *The Making of Modern British Politics 1867–1939* (Oxford, 1982), an intelligent synthesis of recent research.

Robert Blake, *Disraeli* (London, 1966), the standard life.

E. J. Feuchtwanger, *Gladstone* (London, 1975), the best one-volume political account.

Robert Blake, *The Conservative Party from Peel to Churchill* (London, 1970), the party's fall and rise.

Paul Smith, *Disraelian Conservatism and Social Reform* (London, 1967), sets Conservative social policy in context.

Kenneth O. Morgan, *The Age of Lloyd George* (3rd edn. London, 1978), the best introduction to Liberalism after Gladstone.

José Harris, *Unemployment and Politics. A Study in English Social Policy 1886–1914* (Oxford, 1972), a powerful critique of the early years of the welfare state.

Ross McKibbin, *The Evolution of the Labour Party, 1910–1924* (Oxford, 1974, reprinted 1983), the standard work on the party's early years.

H. A. Clegg, A. Fox, and A. F. Thompson, *A History of British Trade Unions since 1889, vol. i. 1889–1910* (Oxford, 1964), indispensable account of the complexities of politics and industrial relations.

Henry Pelling, *Popular Politics and Society in Late Victorian Britain* (London, 1968), a volume of challenging reinterpretations.

A. Rosen, *Rise Up Women!* (London, 1974), places the suffragette movement in a searching light, with unflattering consequences.

Asa Briggs (ed.), *William Morris. Selected Writings and Designs* (London, 1962), gives a useful introduction to the art and craft movement.

SCOTLAND, IRELAND, WALES

F. S. L. Lyons, *Ireland since the Famine* (London, 1971), authoritative, from an Anglo-Irish viewpoint.

Kenneth O. Morgan, *Rebirth of a Nation: Wales 1880–1980* (Oxford and Cardiff, 1981), a sympathetic account from a moderately nationalist perspective.

Christopher Harvie, *Scotland and Nationalism* (London, 1977), lively and original.

IMPERIALISM

D. K. Fieldhouse, *The Colonial Empires* (London, 1966), an excellent survey.

R. Robinson and J. Gallagher, *Africa and the Victorians* (London, 1961), a bold thesis, arguing the superiority of strategic over economic motivation.

A. P. Thornton, *The Imperial Idea and its Enemies* (London, 1959), gives an elegant and witty account of the imperial debate.

A. J. P. Taylor, *The Troublemakers* (London, 1956, reprinted 1969), a heartfelt account of a tradition which failed.

Paul Kennedy, *The Realities behind Diplomacy* (London, 1981), offers a useful survey of the relationship of diplomacy to power.

A. J. P. Taylor, *The Struggle for Mastery in Europe, 1848–1918* (Oxford, 1954, often reprinted), a powerful analysis of the consequences of Germany's bid for power.

10. THE TWENTIETH CENTURY

GENERAL

T. O. Lloyd, *Empire to Welfare State, 1906–76* (2nd edn. Oxford, 1979), a good general survey.

C. L. Mowat, *Britain between the Wars* (London, 1955), excellent on social and economic themes.

C. J. Bartlett, *A History of Post-War Britain, 1945–74 (London, 1977).*

SOCIAL AND ECONOMIC

A. H. Halsey (ed.), *Trends in British Society since 1900* (London, 1972), comprehensive and factual.

Arthur Marwick, *The Deluge* (London, 1965), covers the effects of the First World War.

William Ashworth, *An Economic History of Britain, 1870–1939* (London, 1960).

Sidney Pollard, *The Development of the British Economy, 1914–1967* (London, 1969).

J. R. C. Dow, *The Management of the British Economy, 1945–60* (Cambridge, 1964).

E. H. Phelps Brown, *The Growth of British Industrial Relations, 1906–14* (London, 1963).

Henry Pelling, *A History of British Trade Unionism* (2nd edn. London, 1971).

POLITICAL

Martin Pugh, *The Making of Modern British Politics, 1867–1939* (London, 1982), a useful survey for the student.

Samuel Beer, *Modern British Politics* (rev. edn. London, 1982), a stimulating thematic approach.

Robert Blake, *The Conservative Party from Peel to Churchill* (London, 1970).

John Ramsden, *The Age of Balfour and Baldwin, 1902–40* (London, 1978).

Trevor Wilson, *The Downfall of the Liberal Party, 1914–1935* (London, 1966).

R. I. McKibbin, *The Evolution of the Labour Party, 1910–1924* (Oxford, 1975).

Cameron Hazlehurst, *Politicians at War, July 1914 to May 1915* (London, 1971).

Robert Skidelsky, *Politicians and the Slump* (London, 1968), the second Labour government.

Henry Pelling, *Britain and the Second World War* (London, 1970).

Paul Addison, *The Road to 1945* (London, 1975).

Kenneth O. Morgan, *Labour in Power, 1945–1951* (Oxford, 1984).

BIOGRAPHIES

Alan Bullock, *The Life and Times of Ernest Bevin*, 2 vols. (London, 1960, 1967).

——*Ernest Bevin, Foreign Secretary 1945–1951* (London, 1983).

David Marquand, *Ramsay MacDonald* (London, 1977).

Keith Feiling, *The Life of Neville Chamberlain* (London, 1946).

Kenneth Harris, *Attlee* (London, 1982).

Philip Williams, *Hugh Gaitskell* (London, 1979).

Bernard Crick, *George Orwell: a Life* (London, 1980).

Michael Holroyd, *Lytton Strachey*, 2 vols. (London, 1967–8).

SCOTLAND, IRELAND, WALES

Kenneth O. Morgan, *Rebirth of a Nation: Wales 1880–1980* (Oxford and Cardiff, 1981).

Christopher Harvie, *Scotland and Nationalism* (London, 1977).

——*No Gods and Precious Few Heroes: Scotland, 1914–1980* (London, 1981).

F. S. L. Lyons, *Ireland since the Famine* (rev. edn. London, 1973), a definitive survey from the 1840s to the 1970s.

C. C. O'Brien (ed.), *The Shaping of Modern Ireland* (London, 1960).

CULTURE AND THE ARTS

W. W. Robson, *Modern English Literature* (Oxford, 1970), the best brief account.

B. Ford (ed.), *The Twentieth Century: Sphere History of Literature in the English Language*, vol. 7 (London, 1970).

John Gross, *Rise and Fall of the English Man of Letters* (London, 1969), a brilliant study.

Thomas Parry, *Hanes Llenyddiaeth Gymraeg hyd 1900* (Cardiff, 1944); English trans. H. I. Bell (Oxford, 1955), the standard survey of Welsh literature.

Percy Young, *A History of British Music* (London, 1967), the best work of its kind.

P. Kidson, P. Murray, and P. Thompson (eds.), *A History of English Architecture* (London, 1979).

Dennis Farr, *English Art, 1870–1940* (Oxford, 1978), including architecture.

CHRONOLOGY

1789	French Revolution
1790	Edmund Burke's *Reflections on the Revolution in France* published
1791	Thomas Paine's *The Rights of Man* published
1792	Coal gas used for lighting; Mary Wollstonecraft's *Vindication of the Rights of Women* published
1793	Outbreak of war with France; voluntary Board of Agriculture set up; commercial depression
1795	'Speenhamland' system of outdoor relief adopted, making up wages to equal cost of subsistence
1796	Vaccination against smallpox introduced
1798	T. R. Malthus's *Essay on Population* published; tax of ten per cent on incomes over £200 introduced
1799	Trade Unions suppressed; Napoleon appointed First Consul in France
1799–1801	Commercial boom
1801	Union with Ireland; first British Census
1802	Peace with France; Peel introduces first factory legislation
1803	War with France; General Enclosure Act simplifies process of enclosure of commonland
1805	Battle of Trafalgar: Nelson defeats the French and Spanish fleets
1809–10	Commercial boom
1811	Depression because of Orders in Council; 'Luddite' disturbances in Nottinghamshire and Yorkshire; George, Prince of Wales, made Prince Regent
1813	East India Company's monopoly abolished
1815	Battle of Waterloo: defeat of Napoleon; peace in Europe: Congress of Vienna; Corn Law passed setting price of corn at 80s. per quarter
1815–17	Commercial boom
1817	Slump; the Blanketeers' march and other disturbances
1819	Peterloo massacre: troops intervene at mass reform meeting, killing 11 and wounding 400
1820	Death of George III; accession of George IV
1821–3	Famine in Ireland
1824	Commercial boom
1825	Trade Unions legalized; Stockton and Darlington railway opens; commercial depression
1829	Catholic Emancipation, ending most denials or restrictions of Catholic civil rights, ownership of property, and holding of public office

1830	Death of George IV; accession of William IV; Liverpool and Manchester railway opens
1830–2	First major cholera epidemic; Whigs in power under Grey
1831	'Swing' riots in rural areas against the mechanization of agriculture
1832	great Reform Bill brings climax to period of political reform, enlarging the franchise and restructuring representation in Parliament
1833	Factory Act limits child labour; beginning of Oxford Movement in Anglican Church
1834	Slavery abolished in the British Empire; parish workhouses instituted; Robert Owen founds the Grand National Consolidated Trade Union: action by government against 'illegal oaths' in unionism results in failure of GNCTU and transportation of six 'Tolpuddle Martyrs'
1835	Municipal Reform Act extends local government franchise to all ratepayers
1835–6	Commercial boom: 'little' railway mania
1837	Death of William IV; accession of Queen Victoria
1838	Anti-Corn Law League established; People's Charter drafted
1839	Chartist riots
1840	Penny post instituted
1841	Tories in power: Peel ministry
1844	Bank Charter Act; Rochdale Co-operative Society founded; Royal Commission on Health of Towns
1844–5	Railway mania: massive speculation and investment leads to building of 5,000 miles of track; potato famine begins in Ireland
1846	Corn Law abolished; Whigs in power
1848	Revolutions in Europe; Public Health Act
1851	Great Exhibition
1852	Derby's first minority Conservative government
1852–5	Aberdeen's coalition government
1853	Gladstone's first budget
1854	Northcote–Trevelyan civil service report
1854–6	Crimean War, defending European interests in the Middle East against Russia
1855	Palmerston's first government
1857–8	Second Opium War opens China to European trade
1858–9	Derby's second minority Conservative government
1858	Indian Mutiny and India Act
1859	Publication of Darwin's *Origin of Species*
1859–65	Palmerston's second Liberal government
1860	Anglo-French 'Cobden' treaty and Gladstone's budget codify and extend principles of free trade
1861	Death of Albert, Prince Consort
1862	Limited Liability Act provides vital stimulus to accumulation of capital in shares
1865	Death of Palmerston (October)
1865–6	Russell's second Liberal government
1866	Russell–Gladstone moderate Reform Bill fails
1866–8	Derby's third minority Conservative government
1867	Derby–Disraeli Reform Act; Dominion of Canada Act
1868	Disraeli succeeds Derby as Prime Minister (February)
1868–74	Gladstone's first Liberal government

1869	Suez Canal opened; Irish Church disestablished
1870	Irish Land Act; Forster–Ripon English Elementary Education Act; Married Women's Property Act extends the rights of women in marriage
1872	Scottish Education Act
1873	Gladstone government resigns after defeat on Irish Universities Bill; Disraeli declines to take office
1874–80	Disraeli's second Conservative government
1875	Disraeli buys Suez Canal shares, gaining a controlling interest for Britain
1875	Agricultural depression deepens
1875–6	R. A. Cross's Conservative social reforms passed
1876	Victoria proclaimed Empress of India; massacres of Christians in Turkish Bulgaria provoke anti-Turkish campaign in Britain, led by Gladstone
1877	Confederation of British and Boer states in South Africa
1878	Congress of Berlin; Disraeli announces 'peace with honour'
1879	Trade depression; Zulu War: British defeated at Isandhlwana, win at Ulundi
1879–80	Gladstone's Midlothian campaign denounces imperialism in Afghanistan and South Africa
1880–5	Gladstone's second Liberal government
1880–1	First Anglo-Boer War
1881	Irish Land and Coercion Acts
1882	Britain occupies Egypt; Triple Alliance between Germany, Austria, and Italy
1884–5	Reform and Redistribution Acts
1885	Death of Gordon at Khartoum; Burma annexed; Salisbury's first (minority) Conservative government
1886	Royal Niger Company chartered; gold found in Transvaal; Gladstone's third Liberal government introduces first Home Rule Bill for Ireland: Liberal Party splits
1886–92	Salisbury's second (Conservative–Liberal-Unionist) government
1887	British East Africa Company chartered
1888	County Councils Act establishes representative county authorities
1889	London dock strike; British South Africa Company chartered
1892–4	Gladstone's fourth (minority) Liberal government
1893	Second Home Rule Bill rejected by the Lords; Independent Labour Party founded
1894–5	Rosebery's minority Liberal government
1895–1902	Salisbury's third Unionist ministry
1896–8	Sudan conquered
1898	German naval expansion begins
1899–1902	Second Anglo-Boer War
1899	(autumn) British disasters in South Africa
1900	Khaki election won by Salisbury; formation of Labour Representation Committee; Commonwealth of Australia Act
1901	Death of Victoria; accession of Edward VII
1902	Balfour's Education Act; Anglo-Japanese alliance
1902–5	Balfour's Unionist government
1903	Chamberlain's Tariff Reform campaign starts
1904	Anglo-French *Entente*
1905–8	Campbell-Bannerman's Liberal government

1906	Liberals win general election (January); Labour Party formed
1907	Anglo-Russian *Entente*
1908–15	Asquith's Liberal government
1908	Asquith's Old Age Pensions plan introduced
1909	Churchill's Employment Exchanges introduced; Lloyd George's budget rejected by Lords; Union of South Africa Act
1910	(January) General election: Liberal government retains office
	(May) Death of Edward VII; accession of George V
	(December) General election: Liberal government again retains office
1911	Parliament Act curtails power of the House of Lords, establishes five-yearly elections; Lloyd George's National Insurance Act; Moroccan crisis
1911–12	Railway, mining, and coal strikes
1912	Anglo-German navy talks fail
1912–14	Third Home Rule Act (for Ireland) and Welsh Church Disestablishment Act passed, but suspended
1914	(28 June) Assassination of Archduke Ferdinand at Sarajevo
	(4 August) British Empire enters the First World War
1915–16	Dardanelles expedition, ending in British withdrawal from Gallipoli
1916	Battle of the Somme; battle of Jutland; Lloyd George succeeds Asquith as Prime Minister
1917	Battle of Passchendaele
1918	End of First World War (11 November); Lloyd George coalition government returned in 'coupon election' (December)
1919	Treaty of Versailles establishes peace in Europe
1921	Miners seek support of dockers' and railwaymen's unions (the 'Triple Alliance') in major strike: on 'Black Friday' the dockers and railwaymen back down, and the alliance is broken; Lloyd George concludes treaty with Sinn Fein
1922	Fall of Lloyd George; Bonar Law heads Conservative government
1923	Baldwin becomes Conservative Prime Minister; general election
1924	(January) MacDonald leads first Labour government
	(November) Conservatives return to office under Baldwin
1925	Britain goes back on the gold standard
1926	General Strike (3–12 May)
1929	General election; MacDonald leads second Labour government
1931	Financial crisis and run on the pound; Britain abandons the gold standard; MacDonald resigns and is returned in the election to head National government
1932	Ottawa conference on imperial trade institutes protective tarriffs
1935	Conservatives win general election: Baldwin succeeds MacDonald as Prime Minister; Hoare–Laval pact on Abyssinia; Government of India Act
1936	Death of King George V; abdication of Edward VIII: George VI becomes king
1937	Neville Chamberlain succeeds Baldwin as Conservative Prime Minister
1938	Chamberlain meets Hitler at Berchtesgaden, Godesberg, and Munich
1939	British guarantee to Poland; British Empire declares war on Germany (3 September)

1940	Churchill succeeds Chamberlain as Prime Minister; withdrawal from Dunkirk; Battle of Britain
1941	*Luftwaffe* 'blitz' on many British cities; Soviet Union and United States enter the war
1942	Loss of Singapore; Montgomery's victory at El Alamein; battle of Stalingrad; Beveridge Report on social security
1943	Successful campaign in North Africa; Anglo-American armies invade Italy
1944	D-day invasion of France; Butler's Education Act
1945	End of war in Europe (8 May) and in far East (15 August); general election: massive Labour victory and Attlee becomes Prime Minister
1947	Coal and other industries nationalized; convertibility crisis; transfer of power to independent India, Pakistan, and Burma
1949	NATO founded; devaluation of the pound by Cripps
1950	General election: Labour retains power by narrow majority; outbreak of war in Korea
1951	Festival of Britain; general election: Conservatives defeat Labour, and Churchill again becomes Prime Minister
1952	Death of King George VI; Queen Elizabeth II proclaimed
1954	British troops withdraw from Egypt
1955	Eden becomes Prime Minister; general election won by Conservatives
1956	Anglo-French invasion of Suez
1957	Eden resigns; Macmillan becomes Prime Minister
1959	General election: Conservatives win with larger majority
1963	French veto Britain's application to join the European Common Market; test-ban treaty in Moscow limits nuclear testing; Douglas-Home succeeds Macmillan as Prime Minister
1964	General election: Labour under Harold Wilson win narrow majority
1966	General election: Labour win with much larger majority
1967	Devaluation of the pound
1970	General election: Conservatives under Edward Heath returned to office
1972	National miners' strike
1973	Britain enters European Common Market; Stormont government abolished in Northern Ireland
1974	National miners' strike; two general elections: Labour under Harold Wilson win both with narrow majorities
1975	Popular referendum confirms British membership of the Common Market
1976	Economic crisis: Britain obtains help from International Monetary Fund
1979	Devolution referendums in Wales and Scotland; general election: Conservatives under Mrs Thatcher returned to office; independence granted to Zimbabwe (Rhodesia)
1980	Britain becomes self-sufficient in North Sea oil
1981	Social Democratic Party founded
1982	Britain defeats Argentina in war over the Falkland Islands
1983	General election: Mrs Thatcher's Conservative government returned with massive majority; Cruise missiles installed

PRIME MINISTERS 1721–1984

Sir Robert Walpole	Apr. 1721	Viscount Palmerston	June 1859
Earl of Wilmington	Feb. 1741	Earl Russell	Oct. 1865
Henry Pelham	Aug. 1743	Earl of Derby	June 1866
Duke of Newcastle	Mar. 1754	Benjamin Disraeli	Feb. 1868
Duke of Devonshire	Nov. 1756	William Ewart Gladstone	Dec. 1868
Duke of Newcastle	July 1757	Benjamin Disraeli	Feb. 1874
Earl of Bute	May 1762	William Ewart Gladstone	Apr. 1880
George Grenville	Apr. 1763	Marquess of Salisbury	June 1885
Marquess of Rockingham	July 1765	William Ewart Gladstone	Feb. 1886
Earl of Chatham	July 1766	Marquess of Salisbury	July 1886
Duke of Grafton	Oct. 1768	William Ewart Gladstone	Aug. 1892
Lord North	Jan. 1770	Earl of Rosebery	Mar. 1894
Marquess of Rockingham	Mar. 1782	Marquess of Salisbury	June 1895
Earl of Shelburne	July 1782	Arthur James Balfour	July 1902
Duke of Portland	Apr. 1783	Sir Henry Campbell-	
William Pitt	Dec. 1783	Bannerman	Dec. 1905
Henry Addington	Mar. 1801	Herbert Henry Asquith	Apr. 1908
William Pitt	May 1804	David Lloyd George	Dec. 1916
William Wyndham		Andrew Bonar Law	Oct. 1922
Grenville	Feb. 1806	Stanley Baldwin	May 1923
Duke of Portland	Mar. 1807	James Ramsay MacDonald	Jan. 1924
Spencer Perceval	Oct. 1809	Stanley Baldwin	Nov. 1924
Earl of Liverpool	June 1812	James Ramsay MacDonald	June 1929
George Canning	Apr. 1827	Stanley Baldwin	June 1935
Viscount Goderich	Aug. 1827	Neville Chamberlain	May 1937
Duke of Wellington	Jan. 1828	Winston Churchill	May 1940
Earl Grey	Nov. 1830	Clement Attlee	July 1945
Viscount Melbourne	July 1834	Winston Churchill	Oct. 1951
Duke of Wellington	Nov. 1834	Sir Anthony Eden	Apr. 1955
Sir Robert Peel	Dec. 1834	Harold Macmillan	Jan. 1957
Viscount Melbourne	Apr. 1835	Sir Alec Douglas-Home	Oct. 1963
Sir Robert Peel	Aug. 1841	Harold Wilson	Oct. 1964
Lord John Russell	June 1846	Edward Heath	June 1970
Earl of Derby	Feb. 1852	Harold Wilson	Feb. 1974
Earl of Aberdeen	Dec. 1852	James Callaghan	Apr. 1976
Viscount Palmerston	Feb. 1855	Margaret Thatcher	May 1979
Earl of Derby	Feb. 1858		

STUARTS AND HANOVERIANS 1603–1837

DESCENDANTS OF QUEEN VICTORIA

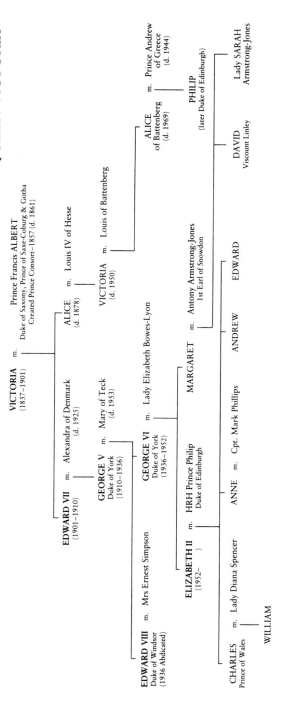

ACKNOWLEDGEMENTS

THE illustration on page 81 is reproduced by gracious permission of Her Majesty the Queen.

Photographs and illustrations were supplied by, or reproduced by kind permission of, the following: Abbot Hall Art Gallery, Kendal 5; Aberdeen University Library, G. W. Wilson Collection 57, 64(foot); Aerofilms 144; BBC Hulton Picture Library 16, 30, 64(top), 69, 73, 75, 78, 87, 96, 98, 111, 117, 122, 133, 138, 141, 150; Beamish North of England Open Air Museum 10; Birmingham Public Libraries, Sir Benjamin Stone Collection 61; Blackpool Central Library 71; British Library 45; Cadbury Ltd. 1; Camera Press 187; Mary Evans Picture Library 52; Humanities Research Centre, Texas, Gernsheim Collection 90; Imperial War Museum, London 119, 124, 157; Huw Jones 178; John Lewis Partnership 82; Museum of English Rural Life, Reading 66; National Film Archive Still Library 172; National Gallery of Scotland 9; National Maritime Museum, London 18; National Portrait Gallery, London 3; New Lanark Conservation 13; Popperfoto 86, 155, 164, 183; Public Record Office 37; Ann Ronan Picture Library 47; *The Standard* 130; Strathclyde Regional Archive 107; Tate Gallery 161; Trades Union Congress Library 136; Victoria & Albert Museum 41, 84.

INDEX

Persons are indexed under the name or title used in the text, with cross-references where necessary to alternative names. Page numbers in *italics* refer to illustrations or maps.

railways, 37–40, *37, 38, 41, 57*, 62
Redmond, John (1856–1918), 127
Reform Club, 41
religion,
  Christianity, 134–5; and working classes,
  72–4; *see also* Christian Church; Church
  of England, etc.
Rennie, John (1761–1821), 13
retail trade, *82*
Rhodes, Cecil John (1853–1902), 94, 98
Rhondda, David Alfred Thomas, Viscount
  (1856–1918), 121
riots, 15, 83; *see also* 'Captain Swing';
  Gordon riots
Roberts, Lord (Sir Frederick Sleigh)
  (1832–1914), 113
Robertson, William (1705–83), 6
Robey, George (1869–1954), 140
Rochdale Pioneer store, 31
Roman Catholicism, 51, 73–4; *also* 134
  emancipation, 26, 27
Rosebery, Archibald Philip Primrose, 5th
  earl of (1847–1929), 92
Rosenberg, Isaac (1890–1918), 119
Rowntree, Seebohm (1871–1954), 106, *107*,
  121
Royal Academy, 149
Royal Air Force, 152, 156
Rugby School, 33–4
Ruskin, John (1819–1900), 46, 101
Russell, Bertrand, Earl (1872–1970), 160
Russell, Lord John, Earl (1792–1878), 27, 40,
  56, 57, 58
Russia, 44, 95, 153, 159, 166
  Bolshevik revolution, 116, 126
Rutherford, Margaret (1892–1972), *172*

Sainsbury's stores, 82
Saint-Simon, Henri de (1760–1825), 44
Salford (Lancs.), 61
Salisbury, James, 4th marquess of
  (1861–1947), 122
Salisbury, Robert, 3rd marquess of
  (1830–1903), 57, 71, 76, 80, 81, 86, 88, 91,
  92, 104–5, 106
Salvation Army, 73
Sandringham (Norfolk), *86*
Sassoon, Siegfried (1886–1967), 119
Scarborough (Yorks.), 71
Scarman, Leslie George, Baron (b. 1911),
  187
science and technology, 186; *see also*
  industry
Scotland, 4, 6, 7, 15, 19–20, 25, 27, 28, 30, *30*,
  48
  agriculture, 63–5, 64
  education, 33, 66
  Nationalists, 92, 132, 177–8, 182
  religion, 17, 36, 91–2
  see also Edinburgh, Glasgow
Scott, Sir Walter (1771–1832), 2, 25
seaside resorts, 71–2, *71*
SEATO, 175
Second World War, 154–67

Shaftesbury, Anthony Ashley Cooper, 7th
  earl of (1801–85), 32
Sharp, Cecil (1859–1924), 65
Shaw, George Bernard (1856–1950), 100,
  102, 133, 144
Shaw, Richard Norman (1831–1912), 101,
  149
Shelley, Percy Bysshe (1792–1822), 24, 36
Shinwell, Emanuel (b. 1884), 163
Sidmouth, Henry Addington, Viscount
  (1757–1855), 25
Simon, Sir John (1816–1904), 33
Simon, Sir John, Viscount (1873–1954), 124,
  153
Simpson, Mrs Wallis, duchess of Windsor
  (b. 1896), 145
Singapore, 21, 149, 159
Sinn Fein, 128, 129, 179; *see also* Fenianism
Skye, Isle of, *64*, 92
slavery, 7, 27, 93
Slough (Bucks.), 146
Smeaton, John (1724–92), 13
Smiles, Samuel (1812–1904), 39, 54
Smith, Adam (1723–90), 6, 7, 15, 20, 21, 33
Smuts, Field Marshal Jan Christian
  (1870–1950), 126
Social Democratic Federation, 102
Social Democratic Party, 186, 188
socialism, 101–2
Somme, battle of the (1916), 118, *119, 124*
South Africa, 21, 97–9, 158
South America, 21, 26
Southend (Essex), 71
Southern Rhodesia, 185
Soviet Union, *see* Russia
Spain, 151
  Civil War, 152
  see also South America
Speenhamland system, 21
Spencer, Herbert (1820–1903), 54
Spencer, Stanley (1891–1959), 149
Spender, Stephen (b. 1909), 148
Staithes (Yorks.), *52*
Stanley, Henry Morton (1841–1904), 93
Stanmore (Middx.), ribbon development,
  144
steel industry, 146, 168, 181
Stephenson, George (1781–1848), 3, *10*, 38,
  39
Stephenson, Robert (1803–59), *37*, 39
Strachey, Lytton (1880–1932), 133, 134
Sudan, 95, 97
Sudetenland, *150*, 152
Suez Canal, 97, 158, 173
Sutcliffe, Herbert (b. 1894), *141*
Sutherland, Graham (1903–80), 163
Swift, Jonathan (1667–1745), 7

Taff Vale case (1900–1), 104, 110
Tait, Archibald Campbell, Archbishop of
  Canterbury (1811–82), 32
Tariff Reform, *103*, 105, 108
Tawney, Richard Henry (1880–1962), 140,
  174